THE NATIONAL TRUST GUIDE TO

LATE GEORGIAN AND VICTORIAN BRITAIN

THE NATIONAL TRUST GUIDE TO

LATE GEORGIAN AND VICTORIAN BRITAIN

From the Industrial Revolution to World War I

JOHN WALTON

GEORGE PHILIP
THE NATIONAL TRUST

British Library Cataloguing in Publication Data

Walton, John, *1948–*
    The National Trust guide to late Georgian and
    Victorian Britain: from the Industrial
    Revolution to World War 1
    1. Great Britain, 1714–
    I. Title
    941.07

ISBN 0-540-01185-1

© John K. Walton 1989
Published by George Philip Limited, 59 Grosvenor Street,
London W1X 9DA, in association with The National
Trust, 36 Queen Anne's Gate, London SW1H 9AS

Printed in Great Britain by BAS Printers Limited,
Over Wallop, Hampshire

END-PAPERS *Halifax's Piece Hall, built as a cloth
market in 1775.*

HALF-TITLE *A typical late Victorian trade-union
membership certificate.*

TITLE-PAGE *William Williams' view of Coalbrookdale
in 1777: a distant vision of smoke and flame in an
otherwise verdant landscape.*

Illustration Sources and Acknowledgements
E T Archive Ltd pp. 8–9 (Museum of English Rural Life,
Reading), 73 (Private Collection), 76–7 (Museum of
English Rural Life, Reading), 91 (Museum of English
Rural Life, Reading, Mrs Burford), 96 (The Beauford
Centre), 100–1, 141, 149 (The National Railway Museum,
York), 150–1 (The National Railway Museum, York), 195
(Museum of English Rural Life, Reading), 228–9 (The
Victoria & Albert Museum); The Bowes Museum, Barnard
Castle, Co. Durham p. 75; Howard Colvin p. 41; Clive
Coote pp. 132–3; Mary Evans Picture Library pp. 167,
193, 220, 224–5; Fotomas Index pp. 1, 198; Ray Gardner
p. 144; George H. Hall pp. 71, 94; Hulton Picture
Company pp. 126, 134–5; A. F. Kersting pp. 18–19, 28–9,
30–1, 32–3, 34–5, 37, 43, 48–9, 54–5, 56, 57, 59, 112–13,
137, 142–3, 202–3, 208, 238, 239; Leeds City Council pp.
180–1; Manchester Public Libraries, Central Library p.
114; The Mansell Collection pp. 15, 36, 93, 105, 106–7,
110, 118–19, 120–1, 123, 128–9, 138–9, 158–9, 162–3,
188–9, 191, 196, 200, 230, 250; Musée des Beaux Arts
Grenoble p. 242–3; The National Museum of Wales pp.
11, 44; The National Trust pp. 13, 20, 24–5, 27, 39, 52, 61,
62, 65, 67, 68, 69, 81, 82, 83, 84, 85, 86, 87, 88, 97, 109,
116, 145, 169, 171, 173, 174, 175, 176, 183, 184–5, 186,
206, 214, 218, 222, 234–5, 241, 249, 253; Royal
Commission on the Historical Monuments of England pp.
154–5, 207, 210–11, 215, 216–17; The Science Museum pp.
147, 170 (below: David Souden); Shrewsbury Borough
Museum Service pp. 2–3; Sussex Archaeological Society p.
178; The Tate Gallery p. 46; Ulster Museum pp. 89, 95,
98; Derek G. Widdicombe endpapers, pp. 102, 124
(photog. Colin Westwood), 165, 170 (above), 172, 247
(photog. Noel Habgood).

Contents

For Jenny, with love

Acknowledgements

I am very happy to thank the many friends and colleagues who have helped in the making of this book. In the absence of footnotes, some will remain invisible; but I want to stress that I have drawn heavily on the work of others, and that this book would not have been possible without the great expansion of the study of social history which has taken place in the last twenty years or so. But there are specific debts which I must acknowledge. My colleagues David Arnold, John Mackenzie and Mike Winstanley provided references, loaned books and helped to rescue me from errors and omissions. Bill Fuge was a mine of information on Irish country houses and many other things, as well as being a congenial comrade in the pursuit of second-hand books. Jeanette Brock and Pat Gibb helped me to come to terms with Glasgow, although Pat's efforts to teach me the local language appear to have come to nothing. Alistair Mutch's comments made a considerable difference to Chapter 4, and Carole Taylor made sure that I gave Ellen Terry her due. Bruce Hanson and Bridie Diamond discussed John Ruskin's importance with me to good effect. Alan Crosby came up with a key reference when I needed it most. Lydia Greeves, meanwhile, has been a model editor, and her work has much improved the text. Mary E. Turner made useful comments on Chapter 7, and Audrey Cox most kindly acted as 'book-taster' for the whole typescript. I owe her a great deal. Jenny Smith also read everything, preserved me from errors and infelicities, and generally kept me up to the mark. The dedication says the rest. As always, the remaining mistakes and misinterpretations are mine and mine alone.

John Walton
Preston, 24 October 1988

CHAPTER ONE

Introduction: Britain 1750-1914

Much of the Britain of the mid eighteenth century would look, sound, smell, even feel and taste disturbingly different to an observer from the Britain of the late twentieth century. The distance, after all, is spanned by the busiest quarter-millennium in human history. And even where landscape and housing might at first sight appear disarmingly familiar, the briefest conversation with an inhabitant would reveal alarming disparities in beliefs and attitudes: not only in conceptions of how things worked, or of the place of God or magic in the Universe, but in notions of what is 'common sense' or even what is thinkable. We are dealing with a society in which (for example) literacy was very patchy and insecure below the level of the farmer and the small shopkeeper (and kept beyond the grasp of the vast majority of women); in which the fastest land transport went at the speed of a galloping horse (on the best roads, and only for the wealthy); in which pain of all kinds, from toothache to childbirth, went effectively unrelieved, and the average life expectancy for a new-born infant was 36 or 37 years, held down by Third World levels of infant mortality and the unchecked ravages of a formidable battery of infectious diseases. London was a city of world importance, but the second largest town in Britain was either Bristol or Edinburgh, each of which had fifty thousand or so inhabitants, and the vast majority of people lived in scattered hamlets, villages or tiny market towns.

The Britain of 1914 feels much closer to our own experience; and the older we are, the closer it feels. The great conurbations were firmly established; the infant internal-combustion engine was beginning to complement (but not yet to challenge) the dominance of the steam railway, the electric tram and that still vital (and odorous) source of locomotion, the horse; mass literacy had helped to spawn mass communication, with a flood of newspapers and cheap literature aimed at a vastly swollen working-class market; the cinema had confirmed its popularity as a source of education and (much more importantly) escapist entertainment; the conquest of smallpox was effectively complete, that of many other scourges was well advanced, and a dramatic decline in infant mortality was well under way; and significant

numbers of women were working outside the home, in offices, shops and factories as well as in domestic service. A less ambitious time-traveller, stopping off in the Edwardian years rather than risking the culture-lag of a journey to the eighteenth century, would find conversations easier to conduct. Misunderstandings would abound, but total mutual incomprehension would be less prevalent.

But we must not oversimplify these contrasts. In some ways, Edwardian Britain is just as foreign a country to us as the Britain of the mid eighteenth century; and both Britains contained within themselves an enormous variety of regional and local experiences, the diversity of which was only partially undermined by the innovations in transport, migration, communications and literacy. Nor should we write off the Britain of 1750 as economically and culturally remote, an incomprehensibly distant Erewhon on the far side of the steam-capped mountains of the Industrial Revolution, a world we have lost and cannot find again. This was already a changing and developing society, in which competitive individualism was struggling to break the bonds of the customary and the collective, and in which we can already find seemingly familiar social tensions and preoccupations. Its people, when they speak to us across the centuries, are recognisable as well as being different.

The Britain of 1750 was much more agricultural, much more wooded, much more thinly populated and much quieter than that of 1914. It contained fewer than 9 million inhabitants. By 1911, however, the population had risen more than fivefold, to just over 45 million; and the sheer scale of this multiplication of people, which was completely without precedent, was at the root of the deepest and most important changes in the ways people lived. These extra people had to be housed, fed, employed and amused. They also had to be governed. The ways in which governments and families came to terms with the increasingly crowded state of these islands will form some of the central themes of this book.

This population growth was not evenly spread. It was concentrated disproportionately into certain industrial and commercial regions: the area which became Greater London; the emerging conurbations of south Lancashire, the West Midlands and the West Riding of Yorkshire; the Glasgow–Edinburgh corridor and the adjacent industrial areas of central Scotland; and smaller industrial districts like Tyneside, Wearside and

PREVIOUS PAGES *Getting in the barley harvest at the turn of the century, using a horse-drawn reaping machine. There is plenty of back-breaking work for those binding and stacking the sheaves, including the woman on the right; but there is still time for a smoke in the sunshine.*

Paul Sandby's view of a rural coal-mine in about 1786. The winding is still being done by horse-gin rather than steam-engine.

Teesside, the South Wales valleys, the East Midland mining and hosiery region and the Belfast district. It was here that the great staple industries of Britain's industrial pre-eminence became, it seemed, immutably established: cotton and wool textiles, engineering, iron, steel and chemicals, coal-mining, hardware and shipbuilding. Here were created whole new landscapes, whose essential ingredients were brick, soot, smoke and flame, and whose skylines were accented by cranes and chimneys as well as church spires and civic campaniles.

These transformations were more a product of the second half of the nineteenth century than of earlier years, despite the precocious rise of the Shropshire coalfield or the factory towns of Manchester and its hinterland. Until the 1820s and 1830s it was rural rather than urban population growth and economic change that made the most noticeable impact on the landscape. The countryside in southern and eastern England saw considerable population growth in this period, founded on earlier and more universal marriage, the decline of living-in farm service and the survival of increasing numbers of children. Uncontrolled, 'open' agricultural villages swelled: their inhabitants provided cheap and seasonal labour for the substantial farmers who were the main gainers from rising demand for farm produce, from the continuing enclosure of open fields and commons and from improvements in crop rotations and selective animal breeding. Large landowners also did well, especially where their

11

agricultural rents could be augmented from urban development or mining royalties. Handsome Georgian country houses proliferated, with their pediments, columns and symmetrical façades claiming kinship with earlier modes of civilisation. The substantial brick farmhouses of the prospering lowland English midlands were no less culturally self-confident.

But there were other patterns of rural change. In parts of the Scottish Highlands populations doubled between 1755 and 1821, largely owing to the subdivision of land holdings which potato cultivation made possible. Over much of Scotland, textile manufacture and a wide range of other activities developed to augment family incomes, and enclosure and the foundation of new nucleated villages proceeded apace from the late eighteenth century. Similar changes were occurring in many areas of Northern Ireland.

In much of midland and northern England the growth of domestic manufacture, especially hand-loom weaving, helped to eke out the incomes of smallholders and cottagers, and often became the mainstay of family economies in its own right. It also encouraged earlier marriage and larger families, as independent livings could be made more readily and child labour was at a premium. In some places, such as the Derbyshire Peak and the Furness Fells around Coniston, mining or quarrying could be combined with small-scale pastoral agriculture.

So much of upland Britain saw the development of a landscape of small farms and cottages, with intensive low-technology agriculture and widespread piecemeal enclosure of moorland and waste, and with a precarious farming economy supported by mining or manufacturing. This was more characteristic of early industrialisation than the monster foundry or multi-storey factory, although it was less arresting and attractive to contemporary painters and social commentators.

But the growth of towns and large-scale industry was accelerating rapidly by the second quarter of the nineteenth century. In 1750, about one in six of the population of England and Wales lived in towns of more than ten thousand people. By 1851 the figure was more than two in five. In round numbers, just over a million people lived in towns of this size in 1750, and nearly eight million in 1851. London was uniquely enormous, with 675,000 inhabitants as early as 1750, and 2.3 million in 1851. But it was not an industrial town, in any sense associated with factories and furnaces. It depended heavily on administration and trans-port, and on servicing the high living of its wealthy citizens, and of the gentry and aristocrats who came for the London season, to see, be seen and enjoy themselves. London had its manufactures, but they were produced by sweated labour in garrets and workshops, without the benefit of steam-engines or sophisticated machinery. Henry Mayhew's famously vivid portraits of needleworkers, toy-makers and cabinet-makers bring this world to life, and cast light on the related worlds of casual dock labour, street trading, vice and desperate poverty; but it is a far cry from the alternative universe of the factory.

In the English provinces, ports and dockyard towns grew fastest for most of the eighteenth century: the specialised manufacturing centres only took up the running towards the turn of the century. But by the 1820s the cotton factory towns around Manchester were growing apace, as steam power set a premium on urban sites where coal and labour were in easy supply. The early factories, in the sense of large units of production which used continuously-operated, sophisticated machinery, the division of labour and imposed work-discipline, had been water-powered and mainly rural in their locations, as at Styal (NT) or New Lanark in Scotland. The factory *town*, as opposed to the factory village, was new and distinctive, the basis for much alarmed contemporary comment. But factories came slowly even to the most dynamic of the West Riding textile towns, and industrial growth in Birmingham, the Black Country and the East Midlands depended more on workshops and an urban version of the domestic system of production. There were new towns of other kinds: resorts like Bath and Brighton, or inland transport centres like Stourport on the Severn. Some of the older county towns became havens of polite society, and theatres, assembly rooms and Georgian squares spread even in places whose population stagnated. And by the later eighteenth century every provincial town of any size was emulating London by generating its own suburbia of ribbon development and rural retreats on the urban fringe.

These developments were less pronounced in most of Scotland and Northern Ireland. Glasgow with its cotton factories and other industries, and Edinburgh with its professional men and pillars of

---

William Bell Scott's mural painting, Iron and Coal, *at Wallington Hall, Northumberland: a celebration of mid Victorian industrial progress on Tyneside.*

Whatsoever·thy·hand·findeth·to·do·do·it·with·thy·Might·

In the NINETEENTH
CENTURY, the Northumbrians
show the World what can be
done with Iron and Coal.

polite society, set a pace which left even Aberdeen and Paisley far behind. In Northern Ireland Belfast's population had reached 37,000 by 1821 (when Liverpool's was about four times as numerous), and it accounted for perhaps one-fortieth of the people of the six counties. The other towns were insignificant by the English standards of the time.

The century after 1750 saw a widening divergence in the experiences of the British regions. At one extreme in England and Wales, between 1801 and 1851 the population of Lancashire and Monmouthshire more than trebled under the stimulus of the new industries; at the other extreme, Herefordshire, Merionethshire and Radnor grew by less than one-third. In Scotland, Perth and Argyll increased by only 10 per cent from small beginnings, while Lanark, in the central industrial belt, outpaced the most dynamic English counties. The number of people per square mile in 1851 ranged from well over six thousand in metropolitan Middlesex to fewer than a hundred in Westmorland and three Welsh counties; from nearly seven hundred in Renfrew to fourteen in Sutherland. All this was remarkable enough; but much more was to follow.

Between 1851 and 1911 the population of England and Wales doubled again, to 36 million, from its already unprecedented mid-century size. The urban population more than trebled, and on one definition Greater London accounted for more than seven million in 1911: more than the total population of England, Wales and Scotland in 1750. London's suburbs devoured the Home Counties' countryside with an ever more voracious appetite, and they were prominent among the fastest-growing urban areas of this expansive period. The great provincial cities became recognisably the centres of conurbations, as their own populations swelled beyond the half million and on towards the magic million.

More and more of the older industries moved into factories and towns: cotton weaving in Lancashire around mid century, hosiery and footwear in the Midlands rather later, Black Country metalworking later still. Some languishing urban economies had a new lease of life: Coventry's ribbons gave way to bicycles and then to motor cars. New technologies, some literally inconceivable in 1750 or 1800, brought new towns into being. Steam railways opened out natural resources, bringing coal, iron and new techniques together to promote explosive urban growth at Barrow or Middlesbrough, and generating new

towns to service their own needs at Crewe or Swindon. They also helped to stimulate the rise of popular holiday resorts. The building of ocean-going steamers of increasing size and complexity provided a very different basis for the growth of coastal towns, as did the rise of the fishing industry on a novel scale.

The inhabitants of these expanding towns gained access to new foods, technologies and pleasures, such as Danish bacon, Russian eggs, cheap jam and biscuits, fish and chips; piped water, gas lighting, and subsequently electricity; public parks and libraries, music-halls, cheap letters and newspapers, sheet music and pianos, and eventually the cinema. Some of these novelties were double-edged: they carried costs as well as benefits. Some reached further down the social scale than others, and all towns included a substantial number of families who lived on the breadline in slum housing, and whose enjoyment of these improvements was at best occasional. The regular trade depressions brought periodic setbacks to the living standards of almost every urban family. But the transformation of English urban life and culture between 1850 and 1914 makes the developments of the previous century pale into insignificance.

Meanwhile the countryside of England and Wales was losing people with gathering momentum. There was a sustained fall in the number of farm-workers, who by 1901 had declined to little more than half the peak figure of 1851. The population of farmers fell more gradually, with a 10 per cent loss over the same period; and some agricultural craftsmen, such as blacksmiths, became more numerous for much of the period. Farm-workers who remained on the land saw their wages rise considerably, even in the impoverished south and east, although much severe rural poverty remained when children were young, and in old age. There were major changes in farming practices. The mid Victorian years, the 1850s, 1860s and 1870s, saw heavy investment by landowners in drainage and new farm buildings, although the spread of machinery was slow and patchy. They also saw increasing specialisation by areas in what they did best, and a growing interest in satisfying urban markets.

From the late 1870s foreign competition and bad harvests hit cereal farmers with particular severity, and there was widespread conversion of arable to pasture, especially in the south and east. The high levels of mid Victorian investment proved unremunerative under the new conditions, and agricul-

The Titanic, *pride of Belfast's Harland and Wolff shipyard, begins her ill-fated maiden voyage from Southampton in 1912.*

tural land lost much of its investment value, damaging the finances of landed families. But land ownership continued to prise open doors which were otherwise closed to the newly wealthy and socially ambitious. Lower down the scale, romantic visions of the simple life drew late Victorian professionals to country cottages, but the tide of human aspiration and opportunity was flowing overwhelmingly off the land and into the towns.

This theme was even more pronounced in Scotland and Northern Ireland. Much Scottish Lowland agriculture continued to flourish, but the collapse of the potato crop and other aspects of the Highlands and Islands economy in the 1830s and 1840s led to a new round of clearances, evictions and emigration, exacerbating trends which had begun in the late eighteenth century. Landlords

went over from cattle to sheep ranching and later, often, to deerstalking and grouse moors. Meanwhile the urban belt of central Scotland continued to soak up rural migrants, as Glasgow's population reached 761,000 in 1901 and its citizens rejoiced in its status as 'second city of the Empire', although it combined industrial and commercial prosperity with appalling tenement slums.

Belfast's population increased more than tenfold to 387,000 between 1821 and 1911. Its shipyards built the *Titanic* and many less famous but less unfortunate marine giants, and its linen industry prospered. But no other town in Northern Ireland displayed anything like this dynamism, and rural society was irreversibly affected by the potato famine of the mid 1840s. The six counties were hit less hard than most of Ireland, but after the disaster itself the rural population continued to decline through emigration, fewer and later marriages, and declining marital fertility. Even in the more industrial eastern counties of Ulster the 1911 population was only two-thirds that of the pre-famine peak, while in Fermanagh the figure was only two-fifths. Here as elsewhere in Britain, most of the rural domestic manufactures which had been so important in the 1830s had gone into sustained and terminal decline. The vital energies of the new society were channelled into the cities.

Industrialisation thus concentrated people, change and growth into some areas, while others became quiet backwaters. The widening economic contrasts, especially after about 1840, were paradoxically accompanied by improving communications and an associated trend towards cultural homogeneity. Between the 1830s and the 1890s the railways reached into the remotest corners of Britain: in Northern Ireland as well as England and Wales, very few people lived more than 5 miles from a station by 1900, and only the most depopulated areas of Scotland were out of reach of the determined train traveller. Migration was often seasonal, and rarely a one-way process: migrants wrote home, and sometimes returned, with new ideas and tales of the outside world. Welsh, Irish and Scots Gaelic declined as everyday languages, and schooling introduced children to a standard, approved range of cultural orthodoxies. Local customs and traditional leisure pursuits, still widely flourishing in the 1830s, gradually died out where they were not relegated to the children or self-consciously perpetuated at the instigation of folklore enthusiasts or promoters of tourism. Vernacular housing styles were overridden by an avalanche of cheap stock brick, Welsh slate and builders' pattern books. The backwaters themselves were being polluted by the spreading ripples of new urban ways of life.

Emotive metaphors like this, whether justified or not, had a special appeal to the growing band of city dwellers who sought to save, sustain and retreat to an idealised version of an older English countryside which somehow embodied all the lost virtues of true Englishness. The Irish, Scots and Welsh sustained their own varieties of this vision, each with its own fiction, poetry and visual and musical strands. The results were mixed, just as the reality was itself confused, the countryside having never been the innocent Arcadia that some of its proponents envisaged. The trends towards standardisation, accompanied by the erosion of older attitudes and values, proceeded piecemeal and with different results, compromises and syntheses in different places. Many deep-rooted regional characteristics persisted, but new local and other collective identities emerged alongside them.

So far I have talked mainly about population, industries, towns and landscapes, introducing themes which will be developed in the main body of the book. One or two further sets of issues will also be discussed at greater length. The changes I have outlined, gathering momentum as they did from the 1830s and 1840s onwards, were associated with the development of an increasingly complex social structure. Mid eighteenth-century British society was already changing, but at the core of its social pecking order was relationship to the land: landowners with various sizes of estate, from aristocrats with broad acres and palaces to yeomen and husbandmen who owned their family farms and aspired to little more than self-sufficiency; tenant farmers and rural middlemen of various kinds, some quite prosperous, but subordinate in their status; and labourers and cottagers, some more skilled or secure than others. Urban merchants, manufacturers and professional men were growing in numbers and prosperity, and some were acquiring landed estates; but they were only just beginning to complicate the established order of traditional society.

By 1914 the picture was very different. The landed aristocracy, resilient and adaptable, remained at the top of the social pyramid; but the newer wealth of bankers, shipowners and great industrialists had also to be reckoned with. Below them stretched the complex hierarchy of the middle classes, from the secure and substantial professionals and manufacturers to the clerks and shopkeepers who sustained the new bureaucracies and supplied the new needs of teeming urban populations. Overlapping with the clerks in social position, with mutual suspicion, were the aristocrats of labour, the skilled, supervisory or otherwise privileged élites of manual labour. Below them were further gradations, through the less-skilled in regular and secure work, to the casual labourers living from hand to mouth, and the so-called 'residuum' or 'dangerous classes', the 'underworld' so deeply feared by self-consciously respectable Victorians and Edwardians.

The great shibboleth of 'respectability' cut across all these distinctions, although it was very much in the eye of the beholder; and within each family women continued to occupy subordinate positions, despite Victorian improvements in their rights and legal position. Significantly, domestic service continued to be the main outlet for the paid labour of working-class women, and unpaid philanthropy for their middle- and upper-class sisters, despite the growth of new opportunities in school-teaching, nursing and clerical work from the late nineteenth century. Perhaps it is also significant that the home was the last sector of the industrialising economy to feel the full weight of labour-saving technology; and this process only began in earnest in the early twentieth century.

The changes of this period add up to Britain's emergence as the first industrial nation, occupying a unique place on the stage of world history. The reasons for this are beyond the scope of this book; but the growing importance of world trade and world markets to farmers, industrialists and workers in the remotest corners of Britain is an inescapable backcloth to the story. The widening and deepening British presence in North America, India, Australasia and Africa, to say nothing of the Near East and parts of Asia, and the English merchant communities in Latin America, helped to stimulate the markets which fuelled and sustained the astonishing growth and transformation of key British industries. Britain's primary role in the emergence of this world economy was reinforced by a sustained export of people: younger sons of gentry to Australia or South Africa, Scots to Canada and the Antipodes, cotton workers to the eastern United States, agricultural workers to the temperate zones of every continent. In return, Britain acquired its own populations of Blacks, Chinese, European Jews, Italians and many others. A sense of imperial power and destiny was reinforced by the tales of returning soldiers and seamen, and from late Victorian times, at least, by schoolbooks and popular literature. Much of Britain's hidden wealth was acquired through the profitable exploitation of distant resources; and the competition for these fuelled the international rivalries which reached a temporary culmination in the First World War. To develop these themes fully would require another, and a different, book. This one deals with the impact of these changes on the British people, rather than the reasons for them or the impact of the British on the rest of the world. I begin by looking at those who held power in this dynamic and innovative society, and the ways in which they held on to it through changes which might well have threatened to unseat them.

CHAPTER TWO

Prestige and Property

Throughout the upheavals and transformations of this period, rural Britain continued to be governed by its great landowning families. They dominated the making of laws in Parliament; they kept the social and political leadership of all but the most industrial of the counties; and in those villages where the land was in their hands and their country houses loomed large in the landscape, their control could be almost all-pervading. Admittedly, there were many 'open' villages with divided property and diverse employment where their writ did not run; but their rural power was still overwhelming. The larger towns broke free of the aristocratic embrace, as merchants and industrialists took on the leading roles in their municipal government; and in some industrial villages, and even towns, a patriarchal employer or even a company might play the squire. Everywhere, indeed, the dominance of the older landed families came under challenge in some respect, at some point in the nineteenth century. But only on the eve of the First World War did Lloyd George's new taxation, and his land reform proposals, begin to pose a real threat to the landed élite, although the finances of many landed families were becoming shaky from the late 1870s onwards. Aspiring new wealth still needed a

PREVIOUS PAGES *Petworth, West Sussex: the imposing and sublimely self-confident centre of an aristocratic empire.*

BELOW *An idealised portrait of Benjamin Disraeli in 1844, when he was an aspiring young politician 'on the make', and a thorn in the side of the Prime Minister, Sir Robert Peel. The purchase of Hughenden and its estate gave him the weight and respectability he needed to 'climb the greasy pole' to high office.*

country seat, even only a small and ornamental one, to gain full acceptance in high society. Thus Disraeli had to borrow money from his aristocratic patrons in 1847 to finance the purchase of Hughenden Manor (NT), and enable him to become MP for Buckinghamshire rather than a corrupt small-town constituency: this was a necessary preliminary to pursuing the Conservative leadership. Also significant was the sustained debate over the propriety of creating peerages without a substantial landed base.

Contemporaries were impressed by the resilience and adaptability of Britain's established governing class. What surprised them, especially when they came from other cultures, was not just its survival, but its ability to blossom and flourish in a changing and superficially inimical environment. Hippolyte Taine, a French professor who paid several extended visits to England during the 1860s, was particularly impressed; and his views are worth quoting at length because they are still widely held. He tells us that the English aristocracy and gentry

> kept in touch with the people, opened their ranks to talent, recruited to their number the pick of the rising commoners; and they have remained the ruling class, or at least the most influential class in both parish and State. To that end they have adapted themselves to their time and their new role. They have made themselves into administrators, patrons, promoters of reform and good managers of the commonwealth; they have become well-informed and well-educated men, men who apply themselves to work and are capable and who, as citizens, are the most enlightened, the most independent and the most useful of the whole nation.

These opinions are coloured by Taine's jaundiced contrasting ideas about the French nobility, and by the kindly way in which he was treated by his hosts. They also reflected comparatively recent changes in the attitudes and behaviour of landed society. But by the 1860s he was far from alone in thinking that England's old ruling class retained power and influence because it deserved to: its members had moved with the times and taken a sustained, benevolent interest in the needs of their tenants and dependants, and of the nation as a whole. They had fulfilled the duties which, in England, were necessary concomitants of the rights of property.

These opinions were, and are, not universally held. There was much criticism of landed society for lack of enterprise, corruption, nepotism and obstruction of new wealth and new talent. Aristocrats and gentry have been accused of

putting their attachment to leisure, display, field sports, high culture and the countryside ahead of any commitment to efficient management and the maximisation of profit; and they have been blamed for spreading such attitudes to the more dynamic sectors of society, corrupting industrialists by their seductive example. From a different perspective, landed society has been attacked for grinding the faces of the rural poor, and for taking an unfair share of the profits of hard-working farmers, while hiding behind a façade of benevolent paternalism. We cannot ignore these criticisms.

The aristocracy and gentry embraced a rich variety of people, experiences, wealth, influence, attitudes and life-styles. In 1873, for the first time since Domesday Book in 1086, an official survey of landownership and rental values was made. It was done at the behest of the Earl of Derby, a leading Conservative politician, in the hope of disproving the widely-held belief that the whole country was owned by only 30,000 individuals; but its embarrassing finding was that four-fifths of the land in the United Kingdom was owned by fewer than 7000 people. The survey dealt only in landed property, and it excluded London; but with all its limitations, it offers an anatomy of Britain's landed ruling class at the height of its mid Victorian prosperity.

At the top, just below the royal family, were the great titled families with their extensive estates, their inherited opportunities for political influence on the national stage, their armies of retainers and their multiplicity of country houses. Trollope's famous Duke of Omnium, in the *Palliser* novels, had his counterparts in real life, and at times, in places, it must have seemed as if they really did own everything. In 1873 the Duke of Devonshire owned nearly 200,000 acres in fourteen counties of England and Ireland, which brought in over £180,000 per year (which should be multiplied by at least a hundred for a rough indication of its purchasing power in the late 1980s). He owned the land on which the up-market resorts of Eastbourne and Buxton were developing, and he played a dominant part in the finances of the mushrooming iron and steel town of Barrow-in-Furness, and the immensely prosperous Furness Railway which fed its growth. As well as Chatsworth and Hardwick (NT) in his Derbyshire heartland, he had five other mansions in Yorkshire, north Lancashire, Sussex, Suffolk and Ireland, and three majestic London town houses.

This was the result of the 7th Duke's pulling together the estates of several branches of the family at his accession in 1858; but his circumstances were not without parallel. Most famously of all, the 2nd Duke of Sutherland owned well over 1,000,000 acres in the county of that name, leaving very little for anyone else, and his wife held more than half of neighbouring Ross-shire. The income from these vast but barren estates was matched pound for pound by his much smaller (though still extensive) West Midlands industrial holdings: a reminder that land was much more valuable, in money and influence over tenants and dependants, in some parts of Britain than in others. The Dukes of Hamilton, with land in six counties and the status of Hereditary Keeper of Holyrood House, and the Duke of Norfolk, who lived at Arundel Castle in Sussex but owned a large proportion of industrial Sheffield, were operating in the same league. If London holdings had been taken into account, however, the Duke of Westminster would have emerged as Queen Victoria's wealthiest subject at the time of this survey.

Securely perched on the ledges below this handful of grandees was a rather larger number of major aristocrats, whose holdings might add up to 50 or 100 square miles, with rent-rolls up to £100,000. The Marquess of Londonderry, with his lucrative coal-bearing estates in County Durham and his broad acres around Mount Stewart (NT) in County Down, was prominent among these. The Earl of Stamford and Warrington, whose estates spanned eight counties, and Lord Leconfield, whose main seat at Petworth (NT) in Sussex was the opulent base camp of a far-flung empire which extended to Cumberland mines and mountaintops and to the Atlantic coast of Ireland, are further examples among many possible ones. A few families in this category were firmly established in a single county, such as the Marquess of Ailsa in Ayrshire and the Earls of Aberdeen at Haddo House (NTS) in Aberdeenshire; but most of these magnates, like the greatest dukes but on a slightly less magnificent scale, had more than one seat and more than one territory associated with their names.

Below these still very elevated social strata, and shading imperceptibly into them, were those great landowners whose wealth was less imposing and whose territorial influence was more local, but who were prominent among the leading members of county society. Most were titled, and many had deep roots in their localities. All had command of the 10,000 acres or more which contemporaries and historians have adopted as the magic figure which divides the 'great' landowners from the rest. This is, perhaps, the lowest level of the aristocracy: although acreage and income were not everything, and tradition and associations counted for a great deal, an aristocratic life-style usually demanded a five-figure acreage. Into this category fall the Earls of Mount Edgcumbe in Devon, Sir John Harpur Crewe of Calke Abbey (NT) in Derbyshire and the Earls of Belmore at Castle Coole (NT), Enniskillen. There were some untitled families, like the Leghs of Lyme Park (NT) in Cheshire: a reminder that there was never an exact relationship between title, wealth and acreage, and that the social pecking order of the aristocracy and gentry was a complex business.

This point is underlined when we look at the next layer of the social pyramid, the families whom historians know as the 'greater gentry', with their compact estates of between 3000 and 10,000 acres, their considerable local economic and social standing, and (in many cases) their traditional association with a particular house and tract of countryside: for their ranks included many baronets, and lords of varying status, as well as 'plain' gentlemen. Thus in 1873 we have W. L. Wiggett-Chute of The Vyne (NT), Basingstoke, whose family had been in occupation for more than two centuries, and Sir Alexander Chichester, Bt., whose family had held Arlington Court (NT), near Barnstaple, since the fourteenth century. Roots as deep as these were unusual, and at this level of landed society new families were always trying to become established. But it was the securely-established (or so it seemed) county gentry, with their proud pedigrees, long rent-rolls and substantial mansions, who had historically formed the core of the governing class of rural England.

Below this level came the squires, whose estates often stood dangerously close to the minimum of 1000 acres and £1000 per year in rents which was deemed necessary to support a landed gentleman in suitable style. The squire might dominate his village, serve as a Justice of the Peace for the county and have political influence over his tenants, but outside his own locality he carried little weight. Despite the size of their house and the magnificence of its furniture, the Yorkes of Erddig (NT), near Wrexham, seem to have fallen into this category.

But the Yorkes and their like were accepted members of the landed élite. Most of the lesser gentry were much less secure. They had fewer resources, whether economic, social or cultural. Many were unable to keep up appearances without large-scale borrowing on the security of their estates. A Welsh gentleman's waspish comments about his neighbours in 1853 bring out more general symptoms of pride, parochialism and financial insecurity:

Each Welsh gentleman is a petty prince possessing a little mind and not able to see further than his own nose with at the same time an unbounded opinion of his own consequence and a vast amount of jealousy of his neighbours and but in general a very small amount of ready cash.

This jaundiced view draws attention to the uneasy social position of the lesser gentry and those who aspired to that status. Many shared their parishes and villages with others of similar standing, and lacked the clear-cut social position of the squire. At the bottom, it was hard to say where the gentry began or ended. Edward Short remembers from his boyhood at Warcop in Cumbria in the early twentieth century that the Chamleys

were not really gentry, though they thought they were and we accorded them the status. They were in fact descended from a Kendal miller who had nine children the youngest of whom came to Warcop to farm the rather bleak Moor House farm. . . But two or three generations transformed a farming family into at any rate a passable imitation of gentry.

So thought the son of a local shopkeeper: Mrs Wild, the Lady of the Manor, may have had different ideas. Elsewhere in Cumbria, on the other hand, the Brownes of Troutbeck (NT) owned 735 acres in 1846, when they were long established as a local office-holding family of standing, but preferred to keep their customary identification with the yeomanry, and did not look for the social promotion which so many less-qualified families avidly sought. Here as elsewhere, it was impossible to draw a clear line between gentry and lesser landowning yeomanry or substantial farmers. The position was complicated by the continuous movement of younger sons from the gentry into commerce and the professions, and the return traffic of successful and socially aspiring businessmen on to the land.

The idea of the 'gentleman' was never very clearly defined in this period. There was no need to display a coat of arms or a blue-blooded pedigree (though these things helped). What counted was the ability to live a comfortable and cultivated life without having to engage in manual labour, and the possession of a sufficient veneer of education and good manners to allow for acceptance in polite society. Acceptance came more readily to those who recognised that wealth carried responsibilities

as well as rights, and treated their tenants and dependants with fairness and consideration, contributed appropriately to charities and acted as unpaid administrators in whatever sphere of government seemed to match their station.

Already by 1750 many urban professionals and receivers of unearned income were aspiring to gentility without the support of a substantial landed estate; and during the nineteenth century the term 'gentleman' came to be used with increasing lack of discrimination, to embrace a widening range of occupations and to include all retired tradesmen who were capable of keeping up appearances. Thus Blackpool Corporation in the late nineteenth century included under the label 'gentleman' several retired grocers, publicans, boarding-house keepers and assorted tradesmen, while Westmorland County Council in Edwardian times contained a 'gentleman' who was described more revealingly in a trade directory as 'nailmaker and bird stuffer'. Long before 1914 the word 'gentleman', in isolation, had become detached from any necessary implication of the ownership of landed property.

This elasticity in the use of the label 'gentleman' tells us quite a lot about the changing nature of British society in this period; but it makes it very difficult to answer important questions about what proportion of the population were members of the gentry, and whether that proportion changed over time. The higher up the social scale we go, however, the easier it is to be precise. The hereditary, territorial aristocracy are well documented. Thus the number of English peers (from dukes at the top to barons at the bottom) grew from 181 in 1760 to 524 in 1900. Scottish and Irish peers without English titles numbered 200 in 1760, 237 in 1800, but only 129 in 1890. Even the English peerage expanded far less rapidly than the overall rate of population growth. Significantly, too, it was the barons or 'plain' lords who accounted for the vast majority of the new creations, while at the very top, the number of dukes remained remarkably constant at about twenty throughout the period. Baronets, the lowest level of the hereditary titled aristocracy, were more numerous, but successive monarchs and governments were far from profligate in promoting them: there were 638 in 1760 and 954 in 1900. Even in the mid eighteenth

OVERLEAF *The Brownes of Townend, Troutbeck, in south Cumbria, could have aspired to the rank of gentlemen, but preferred to remain on the topmost rung of the yeomanry.*

century, the titled, hereditary nobility were far thinner on the ground in Britain than in any other European monarchy; and the disparity widened throughout the next century and a half. It was becoming easier to claim the label 'gentleman' in Britain; but it was, if anything, becoming more and more difficult to acquire a hereditary title, and to become a duke was almost impossible except by inheritance.

Landownership is more revealing than title if we try to assess the numbers and influence of the very rich and powerful. In this respect the 1873 *New Domesday Book* is quite a reliable guide for the whole period: there do not seem to have been major changes in the pattern of landownership in Britain between 1750 and 1914, although important developments were to follow hard on the heels of the First World War. In 1873 ten people owned more than 60,000 acres apiece in England, 49 had more than 30,000 acres, and 1688 had 3000 acres or more. This élite owned more than two-fifths of the cultivated area of England. A further one-seventh was owned in blocks of between 1000 and 3000 acres by 2529 substantial squires. These four thousand or so families formed the core of the English aristocracy and gentry, although perhaps twice as many again might advance some sort of plausible claim to landed gentry status. This is an impressive concentration of landed property. The pattern in Wales was very similar, and the peers and greater gentry owned just over half the acreage of the six counties which became Northern Ireland. In Scotland the concentration of ownership was even more pronounced: the peers and greater gentry between them owned three-quarters of the land, and every third acre was in the hands of a titled aristocrat.

This evidence is a little misleading, because the great estates tended to be concentrated in the least fertile and most thinly-populated areas. The Highlands and Islands, along with Aberdeenshire, included the most aristocratic areas of Scotland, although smaller landowners predominated in Shetland and parts of Orkney. But vast empty acres in Argyll and Sutherland generated disproportionately small revenues, in contrast with the improvable lowlands of Aberdeenshire. In the industrialising Lowlands and on the Borders smaller estates were much more in evidence, and the value per acre was much higher. In England and Wales the pattern was more complex. The aristocracy and gentry (including squires) owned more than five-sixths of Northumberland and nearly four-fifths of Caernarvonshire, in north-west Wales, and of little Rutland. At the other extreme, they held just over one-fifth of metropolitan Middlesex, with its urban housing and market gardens, and one-third of Cambridgeshire, with its fenland freeholders. Great estates of 10,000 acres or more were thin on the ground in the Home Counties, but also on the Welsh border. Certain areas, like the so-called 'Dukeries' district of Nottinghamshire, became aristocratic strongholds, but it is difficult to discern an overall logic to the geographical spread of large-scale landownership outside Scotland. But it is important to note that the aristocracy and gentry were far from being evenly distributed through Britain, and that their influence varied county by county and village by village.

Not all aristocrats owned broad acres. The 1873 return found two peers with only a solitary acre apiece. Such evidence is a reminder that there was a lot of movement into and out of the ranks of the large landowners and gentry. Younger sons of substantial landowning families often had to make their own way in the world, and many disappeared from the élite. Many families simply failed to produce heirs and died out, especially in the eighteenth century; and some were overwhelmed by extravagance or financial misfortune. But what sort of people replaced those who dropped out? And how readily were they accepted by the established families?

Most upward movement into landed society stopped at the level of the lesser gentry or, at best, the squirearchy. Many purchasers of country houses and small estates failed to make the transition to long-term acceptance into county society. Some never sought it, wanting only a pleasant and imposing country retreat in which to entertain and impress relatives and business associates. This was especially prevalent in the countryside around London and in the industrialising districts. Thus one in five of the owners of large country houses in mid eighteenth-century Hertfordshire were newcomers, rising to one-third or more in the nineteenth century. One-third of these purchasers sold in their own lifetimes, and only perhaps two in five founded new county families. In Northamptonshire and Northumberland the proportion of newcomers was always much smaller than in Hertfordshire, whose proximity to London attracted unusual numbers of merchants and bankers, politicians and lawyers into its pleasant and convenient rural acres.

Many newly-risen gentry thus proved to be mere transients. And some occupants of great houses were mere tenants of absentee owners, lacking in economic weight and uncertain of their local prestige. Thus Mr Ogilby, tenant of Ketteringham Hall in Norfolk in the 1830s, could be publicly rebuked from the pulpit by an earnest new Evangelical vicar for his allegedly irreligious life-style, with no way of asserting himself in return: an experience which was common enough for established landlords in Scotland, but amounted to a signal humiliation in an English village. But what deserves most emphasis is the survival of large numbers of old-established families who gave a core of stability and continuity even to the most volatile of counties. At any point between 1750 and 1880 about half of the big country-house families in Northamptonshire and Northumberland had been resident for six generations or more, although the Hertfordshire figure was much lower. Moreover, it was the biggest estates, the ones which were most likely to carry prestige and social standing at a high level, which were most likely to stay in the same family for long periods.

There was a bedrock of continuity in landed society, but, except at the very highest levels, it was never a closed caste. Those who pursued acceptance had to play by the established rules, and full endorsement of the family's status might not come until the second or third generation. The predominant background of new families changed over time. In the later eighteenth century, a prosperous time for agriculture, many families from the yeomanry and the margins of the gentry were able to extend and consolidate their estates, and secure acceptance among the county élites. Overseas merchants also came increasingly to the fore as estate purchasers at this time, around prospering provincial trading centres such as Liverpool, Leeds and Glasgow as well as in the London area. Some merely speculated in land, and others sought only the prestige and enjoyment of a convenient country address; but others took root. East India Company merchants were especially likely to move into landed society at a high level. Perhaps the most famous 'nabob' of all, Robert Clive, spent over £200,000 on land in Shropshire during the 1760s and 1770s, and accumulated collections which eventually found a home at Powis Castle (NT) in Wales. Being a connoisseur and collector was a good short cut to aristocratic acceptability. The wealth of India was widely distributed around the English countryside, and at Sezincote, in Gloucestershire, the Cockerell family chose to build their house in a carefully calculated mixture of Hindu and Muslim architecture, in the

The officers of the East India Company brought back an astonishing variety of treasures from their turns of duty, such as this ivory playing card from India, now in the Clive Museum at Powis Castle.

style of the Moghul Akbar, with appropriate temples and other garden furnishings.

Bankers and brewers were also moving into the landed élite at this time, some of them lastingly and at high levels. The most spectacular expression of this trend, the house and landscape gardens of the Hoares at Stourhead (NT) in Wiltshire, was already well advanced by 1750, but there was more embellishment to come, as the Hoares continued to prosper from their loans to the aristocracy. Or there was the London brewing family, the Whitbreads, who colonised an extensive tract of Bedfordshire, eventually acquiring Southill Park from the Byngs, Viscounts Torrington, and crashing into the county élite almost with a single bound.

Financiers continued to provide highly visible transfusions of acceptable new blood into the greater gentry in the nineteenth century. Thus the Barings became major, titled landowners in Hampshire; the Rothschilds made a multiple assault on Buckinghamshire, at Ascott (NT), Mentmore, Halton, Aston Clinton and Waddesdon (NT), as well as nearby Tring, converting

The orangery at Sezincote, Gloucestershire: a unique example of the adoption of Indian architectural styles for an English country house. Only the Brighton Pavilion is remotely comparable; and that amazing confection draws on a much wider spread of influences.

The landscaped gardens at Stourhead, Wiltshire, with three of the points of interest provided by the Hoares for the amusement of themselves and their guests: the five-arched bridge, the Pantheon and the rustic cottage. The rhododendrons are relatively recent intruders.

PREVIOUS PAGES
Leopold de Rothschild's rambling black-and-white mansion at Ascott, Buckinghamshire. The remains of the original seventeenth-century house are in the middle, with Leopold's late Victorian extension to the right, and a further addition of 1938 on the left. In recent years a terrace has been constructed in front of the house.

RIGHT *The Baron Ferdinand de Rothschild preferred to build a French château in Bath stone on the hilltop site he acquired at Waddesdon, Buckinghamshire. He employed a French architect, used French Percheron horses in the construction process, and filled the completed building with French woodwork and furnishings. The Baron is said to have remarked, 'Chambord has 450 rooms. Waddesdon is a pygmy beside it.' But Buckinghamshire was duly impressed all the same, and the Italian fountain completes the picture of cosmopolitan affluence.*

some of their vast international financial resources into local social and political influence and finding appropriate homes for their art collections; and Samuel Jones Loyd spent £1,670,000 of his immense fortune on land between 1823 and his death in 1883, earning himself the title of Lord Overstone.

These great banking families were among the biggest spenders in the nineteenth-century land market. The manufacturing dynasties of the Industrial Revolution had less money to play with; but some of the biggest names did try to move into landed society on the grand scale. Sir John Guest of the famous Dowlais Ironworks bought his way into Poole politics as well as Dorset county society by his purchase of the Canford estate from Lord De Mauley in 1845. The descendants of Sir Richard Arkwright, famous as the inventor of the water

Sir William Armstrong: inventor, industrialist, experimental scientist, fisherman, landscape gardener and builder of Cragside on the hillside above his childhood haunts on the River Coquet in Northumberland.

frame in cotton spinning, put down landed roots in several counties, although their impact in each place was limited by the division of resources between several sons, rather than following the aristocratic practice of favouring the first-born. Or again there were the Heathcoats, lace manufacturers, the dominant employers at Tiverton in the early nineteenth century, who became transmogrified into the Heathcoat-Amorys of Knightshayes Court (NT), with over 5000 Devonshire acres in the early 1870s.

These examples are conspicuous but exceptional. What stands out is the limited extent to which industrial wealth was converted into really substantial rural landownership. Only after 1880, as agricultural depression pushed down land prices over much of Britain, did large numbers of newly-risen industrialists start building big new country seats. But most followed a similar route to Sir William Armstrong, who became Baron Armstrong of Cragside (NT). Armstrong had prospered as a practical scientist and business magnate on Tyneside; and the house from which he took his title, in Northumberland's Coquet Valley, was designed for pleasure and the entertainment of important guests rather than as the centre of an agricultural estate with a dependent tenantry. The 1729 acres of grounds were used for a magnificent experiment in landscape gardening: indeed, they could have been used for little else. The Armstrong family did take on appropriate roles as social leaders in nearby Rothbury, but they fell far short of establishing a local squirearchy on the traditional model. Cragside was a Victorian prodigy house without a supporting estate, although Armstrong did eventually acquire well over 10,000 acres elsewhere in Northumberland.

There were significant parallels around the turn of the century. Castle Drogo (NT), in Devon, designed by Lutyens for Julius Drewe, who had made a rapid fortune out of Home and Colonial Stores, is an extravagant and romantic case in point. These ventures were unusual in their scale, but most industrialists who moved into opulent country houses had similar priorities: to enjoy, to indulge fantasies, to make an impression. Many were happy to accept the social recognition and

RIGHT Castle Drogo, Devonshire, Sir Edwin Lutyens, famous for his work in the building of New Delhi, designed this monumental house for Julius Drewe, the founder of Home and Colonial Stores. Building began in 1910, and the house took twenty years to complete.

public responsibility that went with nomination as a Justice of the Peace for the county, which was a cut above holding the same office in a town, as it meant mingling regularly with the aristocracy and gentry on their traditional terrain. Industrial and commercial wealth, legitimated by small estates and country residences, began to invade the Lancashire bench of justices as early as the 1830s and 1840s, although the change came later and more slowly elsewhere, even in other industrialising counties. But membership of the *county* élite in this fashion was not membership of the *landed* élite in its fullest sense; and few industrial or commercial magnates aspired to that.

So most industrialists who moved in landed society did so without transferring a major part of their resources into land, or becoming the landlords of broad acres, or founding a landed dynasty. Even the ennobled industrialists who were proliferating towards the turn of the century, such as Lord Ashton, 'Lord Linoleum', the near-dictator of Lancaster, followed this pattern. Thirty-nine cotton magnates of the 1830s and 1840s (or their immediate descendants) owned 1000 acres or more by the early 1870s, when on one calculation over 20 per cent of Lancashire's landed élite had obtained their wealth through industry over the past century or so. But almost all were on the bottom rungs of the landed ladder, and other counties which industrialised later, less dramatically, or hardly at all, saw far less industrialist activity in their land markets and county social institutions.

Law and government service had provided many recruits to landed society in the early eighteenth century, but this pattern was not sustained, although there was a revival of interest in landed estates by successful lawyers in the Edwardian years. The limited movement of lawyers into land is hard to explain, for rewards in the profession were very unevenly distributed, and successful barristers, especially, could make a great deal of money. But government office, at all levels, offered fewer and fewer opportunities for corruption and embezzlement during the later eighteenth century and afterwards, owing to the growth of more efficient, salaried bureaucracies and changes in expected standards of public morality.

So throughout the period there was a steady flow of new recruits into the lesser gentry and squirearchy. Social acceptability at these levels was becoming more a matter of education, manners, cultural attainment and life-style than of pedigree and land, although as one moved up into the aristocracy the traditional criteria were of greater significance. The economic centrality of land was being eroded. Financially it was becoming less lucrative compared with other investments, especially after the Napoleonic Wars and above all in the late Victorian agricultural depression. The rise of government bonds and other secure investments meant that land was no longer a uniquely safe outlet for otherwise insecure fortunes.

Moreover, changing political aspirations and practices greatly reduced the electoral influence a large landlord could wield. The range of socially acceptable ways of bringing pressure to bear on tenants to vote the 'right' way, the so-called 'legitimate influence' of the landlord, was narrowing even before the introduction of the secret ballot in 1872 and the extension of the vote to every qualified male householder in the counties in 1884, which set the seal on the decline of the great estate as political fiefdom. The waning economic and political potency of broad acres, as such, helps to explain the preference of rising industrialists and merchants for impressive country houses but relatively small estates. The pleasures of country life were becoming more accessible in the railway age, too, and the opulent denizens of town houses or villas on the urban fringe could hunt, hire shooting rights or hope for invitations to country-house parties: for all these developments went hand in hand with the growing ease of access to county society for people with wealth and address but little land or lineage.

Social mixing might be one thing, however: full acceptance was often quite another. Thus the cotton-spinner and merchant Samuel Greg entertained nearby gentry families at Quarry Bank House, Styal (Cheshire), where his famous mill was situated, at the turn of the eighteenth and nineteenth centuries. Greg and his wife came of well-established, opulent, cultured Liverpool and Belfast mercantile stock, and Greg's Manchester trading and religious connections put him in the front rank of the town's élite. His visitors, however, could reveal their patronising snobbery among themselves, even as they expressed their admiration for '. . . the cultivation of mind and refinement of manners which Mrs Greg preserved in the midst of money-making and the somewhat unpolished community of merchants and manufacturers. Mr Greg too was most gentlemanly and hospitable. . . .' There would, of course, have been no need to say this sort of thing about *real* equals; and the Gregs were not even aspiring to move out of their mercantile station in life. Those who

*Samuel Greg, cotton merchant and manufacturer of Styal,
Cheshire, presents himself and his family for their portrait
with suitable sobriety and decorum. Mr Greg's clothing and
demeanour, and the prominently-displayed quill pen and
business document, show his position as a prosperous but
unassuming merchant, who knows his place in the social order.*

pushed a little harder must have had to bear the
occasional snub, or at least to have endured subtle
varieties of social discomfiture.

Too much social striving from inadequate
origins invited scorn or the cold shoulder; but
established members of the gentry were not
immune from calumny if they failed to meet the
expected standards of their peers. The rustic,
boorish backwoods squire, lacking in the social
graces and refined accents of the assembly or
ballroom, was a stock literary and theatrical
caricature, especially during the century after the
Restoration; but the pressures to conform to the

standards set at the London season and its
provincial counterparts ensured that by the later
eighteenth century the new model of urbanity and
cultivation had practically swept all before it. A few
survivors, like Sir Tatton Sykes of Sledmere,
straggled on into the mid Victorian years; but by
that time their rejection of refinement looked
anachronistic to the point of eccentricity.

Perhaps the worst failing in a landed gentleman,
however, was a more general rejection of his duty to
live up to his status. Miserly, reclusive behaviour, a
niggardly attitude towards social inferiors, a failure
to participate in the duties of local government and
to take the lead in supporting deserving causes, and
a lack of ostentatious spending and display of the
sort deemed necessary to sustain the 'port' of a
gentleman: these were, to most contemporaries,
the least forgivable shortcomings. Even the
reclusive and pathologically shy Sir Henry Harpur
of Calke was forced by the insistence of these social
demands to serve as Sheriff of Derbyshire in 1794,
and even to command the First Troop of the

volunteer Derbyshire Yeomanry Cavalry during the succeeding period of war and social unrest. It was more excusable to be a spendthrift, and even a rake, than to ignore these imperatives. The obituary of one Essex gentleman, published in the *Ipswich Journal* in 1788, was unusually outspoken, but tells us interesting things about contemporary attitudes:

His morals were rather of the relaxed kind, but as his gratifications were always manly, and even benevolent, they may certainly be excused in these licencious (*sic*) times. His great wealth was acquired more by management than dishonour; and employed in promoting conviviality, and supporting indigence.

Half a century later, and for a long time afterwards, the ascendancy of Evangelicalism and Victorian sexual respectability would have inhibited the public expression of such sentiments; but there remained an admiring audience for aristocratic peccadilloes. Outside the sterner religious circles gossip about gambling, extravagance or sexual misdemeanours was far less damaging than tales of meanness or evasion of responsibility.

For those who aspired to acceptance into the landed élite, there were ways of easing the path to complete assimilation. Religion remained important, nominally at least, even though the barriers to full civil and educational rights for non-members of the Church of England crumbled successively during the nineteenth century. Attendance at the services of the established church, and repudiation of existing connections with Nonconformity, demonstrated the compatibility of a rising family's attitudes with the expectations and values of landed society. Many merchants and industrialists were Anglicans anyway, but there was a steady trickle of conversions among the socially ambitious.

Marriage into a landed family was an obvious route to social acceptance. But for such a family to be willing to contemplate an alliance with new wealth, the aspiring partner already had to be suitably wealthy and personable. As Henry Stebbing advised in 1755, the poor normally married among the poor, 'the middle rank among the middle rank, and the rich and noble among the rich and noble. . . . The lower class of men have it not in their *power* to marry above their rank, or very rarely. The rich and great have as rarely so little *pride* as to permit them to marry below theirs.' Even the growing dominance of the ideal of romantic love as the proper basis for a marriage, which was rapidly making the dynastic or mercenary arranged marriage generally unacceptable among the aristocracy in the later eighteenth century, did not in practice widen the range of socially acceptable partners. Romantic attachment was severely discouraged if it crossed the boundaries of acceptable wealth and status. So at least three-quarters of the wives of titled aristocrats came from the aristocracy and gentry, while only 3 per cent of aristocratic men married the daughters of wealthy merchants.

Marriage to an aristocrat's daughter was out of reach for all but the wealthiest and best-connected of the new entrants to landed society. The banker Henry Hoare, the founder of the Stourhead estate, had to accept an unfavourable financial settlement when he married the daughter of a minor peer; and this trading of wealth against status remained an expected feature of such marriages. There may have been some relaxation of these attitudes in the later nineteenth century, when American heiresses became increasingly acceptable to hard-pressed aristocrats and there was a spate of marriages between peers and actresses. But, important though it was that intermarriage between the aristocracy and the business world was possible and sometimes acceptable, it was unusual; and it was not so much a route into landed society for outsiders, as a confirmation that they had indeed made a successful transition.

The intermingling of landed and other kinds of wealth took place more easily and frequently a little lower down the scale. The squires and lesser gentry were much more open to new blood, and often much more in need of new money. It was at this level that manufacturers, professionals and most merchants found opportunities for socially advantageous marriages; and these relationships were eased because the gentry had their own family connections with business and the professions, as younger sons were sent out to make their own way in the world while the eldest succeeded to the estate. Around 1800 we find that the Dickinsons of Lamplugh (Cumberland) counted among their close relatives an attorney, a liquor merchant, and even a grocer and a mariner. Further north, most of the Glasgow colonial merchants of the later eighteenth century, the so-called 'Tobacco Lords', came from the landed gentry, and when they bought their way back into land they were readily accepted into county society, even though almost all of them continued to carry on their businesses. This was an unusually close relationship between land and commerce, and relatives 'in trade' might sometimes be treated with reserve or even disdain; but the existence of these connections is important.

They help to explain the limited social distance between the gentry and the business class which made it relatively easy to convert wealth into high status and access to power *via* a landed estate and an appropriate way of life.

The aristocracy were consistently more socially exclusive when choosing careers for younger sons, showing a strong bias towards the fashionable regiments, the church, the law and the civil service. But even the haughtiest and most aloof of the grandees were willing to augment their landed incomes through the profits of trade and industry. Not only were their estates farmed commercially: they were also prominent among the investors in mining, transport improvements and urban development. Such activities brought many of the leaders of landed society into the rivalries and decision-making processes of the Industrial Revolution; and they took on these crucially important, lucrative and sometimes risky roles with hardly a qualm.

There was intense activity in agriculture. Investment in enclosure, drainage of wetlands and heavy soils, the promotion of new crops and new breeds, the patronage of agricultural shows: all had active encouragement from members of the aristocracy and gentry. Thus the 1st Earl of Sheffield served as President of the Board of Agriculture, a national body which promoted agricultural improvement, from 1803 onwards; and from its formation in 1793 this organisation was consistently dominated by aristocrats. The 3rd Earl of Egremont established a cattle show at Petworth in the 1790s, and was heavily involved in the foundation of the Sussex Agricultural Society in 1798. In the mid nineteenth century a second Calke recluse, Sir John Harpur Crewe, derived much of his enjoyment and most of his contact with the outside world from breeding and showing longhorn cattle and Portland sheep.

But really effective innovators were a small minority. Many were merely playing at fashionable forms of farming, like the Scottish improvers who

Sir John Harpur Crewe's longhorn cattle and Portland sheep graze in the grounds of Calke Abbey, Derbyshire.

sought to introduce the new Norfolk methods without adjusting for differences in soil and climate. Much of the direct aristocratic involvement was concentrated into the later eighteenth century, and in the long run most of the really effective initiatives came from the farmers rather than the landlords. Perhaps the most important contribution of the great estates was to provide capital and exert pressure for enclosure in the second half of the eighteenth century and for land drainage in the middle decades of the nineteenth, with a view to boosting their rent-rolls to finance an increasingly expensive life-style.

But large landowners in general were more interested in embellishing their houses and parks than in the hard graft of managing improvements on their tenants' farms; and the driving force here was increasingly likely to be a professional land agent. Where innovations were actively pursued, too, they could be controversial, especially where they involved rearranged farms and evicted tenants. The landlords' willingness to encourage agricultural innovation was a necessary element in the transformation of British farming; but the vast majority of them responded passively to the opportunities afforded by new markets and methods, rather than initiating change on their own account. These responses were important, but the main reasons for the changes lay elsewhere.

Many aristocrats and gentry were happy to benefit financially from the immense expansion in mining and quarrying during the period. Gold and silver apart, minerals under the soil had long been agreed to be the property of the landowner as opposed to the Crown, and by 1750 there was already a well-established tradition of aristocratic involvement in mining. The rapid development of the coal, iron, slate and (until mid Victorian times) the copper, tin and lead industries subsequently brought great increases in the scale of existing businesses, and enabled many more landowning families to reap the profits, and sometimes to share in the risks. Coal-mining was the most widespread: the roll-call of landed families with a stake in what one Marquess of Londonderry called 'our Black Diamond trade' would be inordinately long. Coal receipts augmented landed revenues, often on a very substantial scale, over much of Lancashire, West Cumberland, the Midlands and South Wales, and in Ayrshire, Fife and the central Scottish Lowlands. Above all, it dominated the economy of the Marquess's own patch, the north-eastern corner of England around Durham, Sunderland and Newcastle. The 1st Earl of Durham was once

referred to as 'His Carbonic Majesty', and the 2nd Earl was so eager to make the most of his coal that he allowed the foundations of the family seat at Lambton Castle to be undermined by the workings, and had to spend more than £20,000 on stabilising them in 1854.

But even here it was rare for mineral income to outweigh more traditional landed revenue in the total economy of an estate. There was a growing, and general, tendency for landowners' mining incomes to derive from royalties rather than profits: they leased the coal under their estates to businessmen who undertook the day-to-day running of the mines and took most of the financial risks. By the mid Victorian years it was unusual for a large landowner to be directly involved in managing his own collieries; by the 1890s it was quite exceptional. Most of the expertise and hard graft, as in agriculture, came from agents and other paid advisors. Some aristocratic coal-owners, such as Lord Granville in Staffordshire until the 1890s, also owned ironworks, and in 1865 the Earl of Crawford and Balcarres revelled in his position to the extent that he was happy to be listed in local trade directories as a 'coal merchant'. The Pennants of Penrhyn Castle (NT) in North Wales were among the minority who continued to take an active part in managing their minerals in the twentieth century, as they continued to preside over their immensely lucrative slate quarries. Important though the big landowners' contributions to mining investment might be, theirs was seldom, and in the nineteenth century decreasingly, an active or innovatory role.

The high transport costs of coal and other minerals led large landowners into promoting and investing in road improvements, canals, docks and railways, although here again much of the initiative and advice came from agents and other specialists. Most famous of all was the 3rd Duke of Bridgewater's canal system, which linked his Worsley collieries with Manchester in 1761 and was later extended to provide direct access to Liverpool. The engineering was the brainchild of the Duke's agent, John Gilbert, and of the self-taught genius James Brindley; but the financial

Penrhyn Castle, the magnificent but forbidding neo-Norman baronial home of the Pennants in North Wales; and (OVERLEAF) Alfred Sumners' view of the intricately-terraced slate quarries whose proud and highly-skilled workers generated a large proportion of the family's income.

The slate quarry at Penrhyn, profits from which helped to finance the Pennants' neo-Norman castle above Bangor (SEE PREVIOUS PAGE).

risks, the determination and the pertinacity were the Duke's. There was no equivalent aristocratic ushering in of the railway age, although the Duke's successor, the 2nd Marquess of Stafford, was an unlikely rescuer of the Liverpool and Manchester Railway project when it ran into trouble in 1825. Less dramatically, large landowners were generally eager to encourage canals and railways serving their estates as soon as the technologies had proved themselves. Thus the Wansbeck Valley Railway, in remotest Northumberland, was effectively made possible by the £30,000 investment of Sir Walter Trevelyan, whose Wallington estate (NT) was nearby.

Landowners might also spend heavily on docks and harbour improvements, especially when they sought to sell coal in distant and competitive markets, or held land which was strategically placed to meet the needs of coalowners. The Lowthers at Whitehaven and their West Cumberland neighbours in the eighteenth century, the 3rd Marquess of Londonderry at Seaham (County Durham) in the 1820s, and most spectacularly of all, the Bute estate at the 'coal metropolis' of Cardiff during the middle quarters of the nineteenth century, are all cases in point.

These initiatives, and others like them, led their promoters into the planning and development of towns. The cultivation of streets, houses and commercial buildings on large landed estates became increasingly widespread and lucrative in the nineteenth century, as legal devices were developed to enable long building leases to be issued. This meant some control could be exercised over the nature and standard of development, while an income from ground-rents could be assured and immense profits could be hoped for when the time came for the leases to be renewed. Ninety-nine years was a common period: a long time in an individual's perspective, but a short interlude in the life of a major landed estate.

In the railway age, especially, landowners founded seaside resorts as well as ports on their estates, whether on a grand scale like the Mostyns at Llandudno or in a more modest way like the Eltons at Clevedon (NT) near Bristol. Some of this activity involved taking advantage of land which happened to lie on the edge of an expanding settlement, rather than attracting development to a virgin site; and this more passive, at best opportunistic approach was also characteristic of much aristocratic involvement in urban development inland. Other things being equal, however, aristocratic landowners and their agents preferred to develop substantial, spaciously-planned middle-class houses on their urban estates. Where these were well sited, preferably uphill and upwind of the town and its industries, 'miniature west ends' appeared, as on the Calthorpe estate at Edgbaston (Birmingham). Most of all, a few favoured aristocrats profited enormously from the rise of the West End of London itself: the Georgian development of Bloomsbury and the spread of expensive terraces westwards in the nineteenth century swelled the coffers of the Dukes of Bedford and Portland, the Cadogan estate and especially the Grosvenors, who became Dukes of Westminster, an unusually appropriate title.

Aristocratic estates were well suited to supplying this kind of controlled, up-market development: they were usually extensive in area, and their owners and managers were more likely to build for the future than to take a quick profit and run. Planning to a high standard was both possible and likely to be profitable. But this did not always happen: where the lie of the land was unfavourable, or there was not enough up-market demand, or there were immediate financial pressures on the estate, aristocrats could allow dismal working-class streets and smoky factories to crowd and pollute their fields. Such was the case on much of the Duke of Norfolk's Sheffield estate, and in many other industrial towns.

Where large landowners in England provided high-quality housing for the working class, it was invariably on estate villages in the countryside. In Scotland and Ireland rural landowners were more ambitious, promoting market towns, industrial villages and especially fishing settlements where hitherto even the smallest concentrations of housing had been most unusual, with a view to increasing the prosperity, and the rental value, of their estates. During the century after 1730 the Scottish countryside, especially in the Lowlands, became liberally sprinkled with neat stone-built nucleated villages; and some old towns, like Cromarty, were extensively rebuilt at the landlord's behest. In Northern Ireland, too, new villages and small market towns were laid out, and landlords encouraged the linen industry. They were also eager promoters of road and bridge improvements.

The aristocracy and gentry were thus heavily involved in many aspects of the transformation of the British economy in this period; or at least, many individuals among them were. Two landed families even leased lighthouses from the Crown in the early nineteenth century, and made enormous profits by collecting tolls at nearby ports from the ships that passed them. But this was essentially parasitic; and we must not make too much of the aristocratic contribution to the growth of industry, transport and towns. Only those landlords whose estates were well-placed or well-endowed were able to profit from mineral exploitation or town growth; and only a small minority even of the lucky ones did much more than collect their rents or receive their dividends. Advances or loans might be made to builders and businessmen, but it was usually they who took the real risks and provided the expertise and the day-to-day supervision. What the landlords and their agents did was to make the basic resources available, lay down some of the ground rules, and take their cut. This was increasingly the case from about the 1830s or 1840s, as landowners who had hitherto taken an active interest in mines and urban housing retreated into a more passive role.

The key contribution of the large landowners lay in their willingness to allow their estates to be developed in non-traditional, non-agricultural ways. Even here, however, their record was somewhat chequered. The Earls of Yarborough were strong supporters of railway extensions in Lincolnshire during the 1840s, but opposed railway building on the Isle of Wight, where the family also owned property. Railway proposals which came within a mile or two of gentlemen's seats were usually opposed tooth and nail, especially if they threatened to interfere with hunting arrangements. At Keele Hall (Staffordshire) in the 1820s and 1830s Ralph Sneyd

Box Hill, Surrey, as portrayed by George Lambert in 1733, with the harvest in full swing. This was the landscape that Thomas Grissell sought to protect, more than a century later, from the disruptive impact of the Leatherhead to Dorking railway.

viewed the lucrative spread of mines, furnaces and cottages across his estate with abhorrence, concentrated his energies on landscaping the grounds of the Hall itself, and complained in 1829 about 'the unfeeling decision of my Steward that I am to live like a beggar for several years in order to buy some of the ugliest land I have ever beheld and the filthy coalpit it contains'. But he did not reject the industrial revenues which came to underpin the finances of the estate.

Such seemingly inconsistent responses and contradictory attitudes tell us a great deal about the priorities of large landowners. Their main concern was for the survival and prosperity of the agricultural estate and the life-style that went with it. Non-agricultural sources of income helped to preserve that life-style, and were therefore welcome, provided that they did not interfere with the landowners' comfort and enjoyment. If they did, evasive or preventive action might be taken. Thus in 1848 the 4th Earl of Dartmouth paid £297,000 for Patshull Hall in Staffordshire to take his family away from the industrial grime which was enveloping his existing seat at Sandwell Park, West Bromwich, largely on account of industrial development on his own estate. The newest land-

be made to retain the goodwill of tenants or neighbours. This helps to explain some of the aristocratic support for railway lines and other disruptive innovations. Such considerations also set limits to the extent to which it was politic to raise the rent of a good tenant, or to demand his political support at election time. They further ensured that *noblesse oblige* would make the great estates take a leading role in giving to charities and good causes; and such attitudes often extended to the urban and industrial parts of an estate. But this was, ultimately, an ideal based on the rural idyll, the country house, and the pleasures of the chase and the landscaped garden. This ideal remained pervasive even in the late nineteenth and early twentieth centuries, when landowners were beginning to diversify their investments into assorted shares and bonds, and their pleasures became as international as their portfolios.

The ideal of the country-house idyll was one of the cohesive forces in the culture of the aristocracy and gentry; and it remained so. There were many other widely shared experiences and preoccupations which pulled the landed élite together: they included education, electioneering and the exercise of power at local and national level, and the problems of estate management. The gulf between the aristocracy and the county and local gentry may have widened in this period, and especially in the century after 1750, as Professor Lawrence Stone has suggested; and this chapter has made much of the sub-divisions within this remarkably resilient ruling class. But we need to look more closely at what this vitally important stratum of the privileged and the powerful had in common. The next chapter will look at this important question, starting with the shared experience of the country-house life-style, and working outwards into the world beyond the park railings and the estate boundary.

owners could be tenacious defenders of their amenities: thus the railway contractor Thomas Grissell was a formidable adversary for the promoters of the Leatherhead to Dorking railway when they threatened his new-found romantic seclusion at Norbury Park in Surrey, and his hard bargaining did much to preserve the scenery around Box Hill (NT) for posterity, as well as for his own enjoyment.

The country house and its estate remained the hub of the aristocratic and genteel way of life. What mattered most was to present to the world, and to enjoy, an appropriately opulent house, with suitable furnishings, gardens and park, and to exercise visible influence over servants and dependent tenantry. At times, adjustments had to

CHAPTER THREE

Country Houses
and
Country Living

By 1750 the substantial country mansion, with its gardens, park and surrounding agricultural estate, was an almost ubiquitous feature of the landscape of England and the Scottish Lowlands. There were perhaps 5000 such houses in England alone, a figure which seems to have remained roughly constant from the mid seventeenth century to the First World War. In addition, there were the numerous smaller houses of the lesser gentry, and the often imposing rural retreats of bankers, merchants and industrialists, which were proliferating in Victorian times. In favoured areas, country mansions could be remarkably thick on the ground. On the 1930 edition of the 1-inch Ordnance Survey map, covering the Hereford area, John Harris counted 'seven large houses in great parks, about seventy with parks of varying size, and at least twenty small but notable houses with only a garden', in an area measuring 25 by 28 miles.

This chapter will concentrate on the first two of these categories: houses which display the power, opulence and character of owners who seek not just to spend time in the country, but to participate in, and to some extent shape and control, the life and landscape around them. It will concentrate on houses which formed the core of a landed estate, whose rents generated most or all of the householder's income. Some big houses with small estates and industrial or commercial sources of income will fall into the net, but the country mansions of the landed aristocracy and gentry will dominate the discussion.

Country houses varied in size and degree of grandeur, reflecting different levels of wealth and personal priorities, and also changing architectural fashions and social preferences. At the top of the scale were the real 'stately homes', the palatial houses of the aristocracy, with their suites of state rooms, scores of bedrooms, troops of servants and expansive acres of manicured parkland: houses of the overwhelming immensity of Chatsworth, Cliveden (NT) and Culzean Castle (NTS), of Penrhyn Castle, Petworth and Powis. Then there were the mansions of the greater gentry, titled and

otherwise, which were only slightly less magnificent in scope, as at Attingham Park (NT), Tatton Park (NT) or Wallington. Some might be a little wayward in their architecture, such as Florence Court (NT) in County Fermanagh, which has been described as 'endearing rather than fine', with a 'gauche' and even 'quite crazy' main front; but generally these houses were on a par with the top tier in terms of taste, awareness of fashion and opulence of decoration. Then there were the manor houses, squirearchical homes of less daunting proportions, but still several bays long, complex in layout, with elaborate decoration and (often) accumulated treasures, and shielded from the outside world by landscaped grounds: places like Arlington Court, Farnborough Hall (NT) or Gunby Hall (NT).

This is not a perfect classification: some houses would fall between these categories, and others, especially in the nineteenth century, lie outside them. The newly-built mansions of financiers and industrialists, which were often florid and opulent, full of assertive display, are a law unto themselves. Cragside is a good example, of course, but so are the Rothschild houses in Buckinghamshire, such as Ascott and Waddesdon. The hunting-boxes, Georgian 'villa' retreats and later *cottages ornées* which aristocrats built as holiday homes are country houses which lack the social, economic and political roles of the centre of a great estate.

It may seem strange that the century of the Industrial Revolution saw an almost unprecedented spate of country-house building in England and Wales; but this was the case, and it suggests interesting things about attitudes and aspirations at the time. Professor Stone found that in Hertfordshire, Northamptonshire and Northumberland there was 'a second major wave of building' during the century after 1780, which found its only English historical parallel in the Tudor and Jacobean 'building spree' which had followed the Dissolution of the Monasteries. The new surge of activity was especially pronounced at the top of the scale, as really large houses proliferated. This remarkable development initially coincided with a sustained rise in farm rents and other sources of landed income between 1770 and 1815; but the trend continued in the agriculturally difficult decades after the close of the Napoleonic Wars, and even accelerated after 1840. These were not necessarily typical counties, but the findings are quite convincing.

Lower down the scale, the squires seem to have been less ambitious; but a more general survey of

PREVIOUS PAGES *Cliveden, Buckinghamshire, rebuilt after 1850 to Sir Charles Barry's designs as the 2nd Duke of Sutherland's Home Counties residence. Its idyllic position above the Thames, and its confident architectural allusions to the wealth of Italian merchant princes, attracted the Duke of Westminster and Viscount Astor, also prominent among the Victorian super-rich, as later purchasers.*

strip the house of everything saleable, leaving an enduring ruin. Absurdities of this sort were rare, however, and most of the disappearing country houses were lost for reasons other than overweening ambition. Most of the lost houses of Hertfordshire were given up because their owners had more than one seat, and had no use for outdated or inconvenient surplus houses. The threat to privacy and amenity from urban expansion and (in some parts of the country) industrial development also took a toll. But losses seem to have reached a peak in the late eighteenth and early nineteenth century. After about 1830 a growing respect for the past, extending increasingly to the Elizabethan and Jacobean as well as the medieval, made it more likely that old houses would be modified and rescued rather than abandoned; and this was the frame of mind that ensured a plentiful supply of work for architects who could offer to recreate an idealised past in a more comfortable and sanitary present.

This helps to explain the surprisingly low mortality rate for country houses in the late nineteenth and early twentieth century. An authoritative (though admittedly incomplete) listing suggests that fewer than two dozen houses were demolished or allowed to become ruinous in the whole of England between 1875 and 1914, although a further dozen were not replaced after being burnt down. Even in agriculturally-depressed Essex there were only two casualties, one from a fire; and in Scotland and Wales together only eleven houses were lost, most of them being fire victims. This evidence casts the losses of the inter-war and post-war years into very sharp relief.

Fashions in building changed strikingly over the period. In the mid eighteenth century the preferred architectural style for country houses was classical and symmetrical, featuring imposing entrance porticoes and formal arrangements of columns, pedimented windows, sometimes decorative pilasters and occasionally a top-lighted dome under which statues might be displayed. This remained the dominant idiom until well into the nineteenth century. It evolved in important details, as first-hand knowledge of Roman buildings became more widely diffused among those who had gone on the Grand Tour, while intrepid travellers to Greece and the eastern Mediterranean brought back more informed ideas about the architecture of older classical civilisations.

There was some scope for eccentricity, as at West Wycombe (NT), in Buckinghamshire, where Lord Le Despencer, politician, scholar and lover of wine and women, presided over the creation of a remarkable house. The asymmetrical east front is upstaged by an eleven-bay, two-storey colonnade stretching the length of the south façade which has to be seen to be believed. At the turn of the century the extraordinary oval houses commissioned by Frederick Hervey, 4th Earl of Bristol and Bishop of Derry, at Ballyscullion in Northern Ireland and at Ickworth (NT) in Suffolk, were otherwise based on classical assumptions. Indeed, Hervey, like Lord Le Despencer, was a formidably well-travelled scholar and collector (it is said that most of Europe's Hotels Bristol are named after him); and the idiosyncrasies of their houses were founded on the confidence which went with a consciousness of wealth, power and cultural superiority.

These, of course, were the messages that the classical country house sought to convey. Its scale, its formality, its assertive symmetry, the very quality of the materials and their working, spoke of the power to command skills and resources: power over people and power over nature itself. This was exemplified, though in extreme form, by the construction of Castle Coole for Lord Belmore, who imported Portland stone by sea to Ballyshannon, whence it was taken to Lough Erne, shipped across the lough and transported the last 2 miles by bullock cart. Lord Belmore also imported English plasterers: in England itself, of course, many of the craftsmen were Italian.

The landscaping of parks, which often involved the creation of lakes and the movement of hills, and sometimes the demolition of churches, the re-routing of roads and even the reconstruction of whole villages, served to reinforce the message about power. Parks also demonstrated an ability to consume land conspicuously for pleasure rather than profit (although they often used land which would have been of little value for agriculture); and they expressed the cultural separateness of those who insulated themselves from their neighbours by these ostentatious expanses of ornamental space. The classical house reinforced this message. The understanding of classical architecture was part of the expected cultural repertoire of the gentleman, and the classical house expressed his claim to kinship with, and understanding of, the civilisations of Greece and Rome. In this idiom, the country house paraded the superior education and understanding of the aristocrat and gentleman: a sense of superiority which came increasingly to be identified in other minds with aloofness, insensitivity, overweening pride and the abdication of social responsibility.

By 1750, the gothick taste already provided an established alternative to the classical idioms of country-house building. At Castle Ward, County Down, in the 1760s the differing merits of the two styles provoked a domestic dispute between Bernard Ward and his wife, Lady Anne Ward, which had to be resolved by compromise. The north front of their new house was treated in the gothick of the time, according to Lady Anne's wishes, while the south front followed Mr Ward's preference for classical sobriety.

But, at this stage, the real differences between the styles were not nearly as sharp as this unique example might seem to suggest: indeed, the very fact that they could be juxtaposed in this way shows that they had important things in common. Culzean Castle (NTS), which perches so dramatically above the breakers of the Firth of Clyde, is a case in point. It presents itself as a romantic medieval fortress, with round towers, stylised

battlements, machicolations and all the appropriate paraphernalia. It even has a west wing which renders the showy north front picturesquely asymmetrical. But the main body of the building is basically symmetrical, its rhythms are classical, and its windows are straightforwardly Georgian. Its architect, Robert Adam, who designed so many country houses in Scotland in the later eighteenth century, did most of his work in the classical idiom, and his interiors at Culzean do indeed perpetuate the style on which his fame rested, as at Kedleston, Osterley and Hatchlands (all NT). It was free, flexible and undoctrinaire, borrowing from Greek, Roman and Etruscan influences; but it was classical all the same.

In this vein, the castellated country houses of the late eighteenth and early nineteenth century conveyed similar messages to those of their classical contemporaries. The grandest examples, like Lowther Castle in Cumbria, now so imposing in its dereliction, add a threatening, overbearing dimension to the general message about power and authority. The occasional neo-Norman mansion develops the imagery of feudal authoritarianism to an even more daunting extreme, as the forbidding exterior of Penrhyn Castle demonstrates.

Significant changes were becoming evident around 1830. The preferred style for country houses ceased to be classical, although the supply of new houses in this vein did not dry up overnight. Perhaps one-third of early Victorian country houses in England used classical styles, mostly Italianate in the manner of Osborne House on the Isle of Wight. By about 1855, however, the appeal of the classical was almost exhausted. Styles which harked back to earlier epochs in English history, which had been gaining ground since the 1820s, now dominated the field, and continued to do so into the twentieth century. Tudor compositions in brick and stone were consistently popular, as were various kinds of English gothic, but there were also Elizabethan and Jacobean revivals. All these idioms were pursued in increasingly scholarly ways, with more attention to contemporary detail and even, where the money ran to it, to contemporary modes of construction. This trend was also apparent in the occasional Victorian castles, such as Peckforton in Cheshire and the Marquess of Bute's reconstruction of Castell Coch on his Welsh estates.

But this was far from being the whole story. The Rothschilds brought French Renaissance châteaux to Buckinghamshire in the 1870s and 1880s; and this kind of ostentation had a mid Victorian vogue among the newly rich as well as for these cosmopolitan international financiers. In the later nineteenth century, on the other hand, English architects looked to the vernacular and, led by Norman Shaw and W. E. Nesfield, developed a relaxed, informal 'Old English' style, with tile-hanging, tall idiosyncratic chimneys, half-timbering and ingle-nooks, which was widely copied. Scaled-down versions proliferated in suburbia. The freer, less assertive approaches of Voysey or Lethaby, building further outwards from Tudor or Jacobean idioms, followed on from this at the turn of the century. But there was also a revival of 'English Renaissance' at this time, and Shaw himself was at the forefront of a Georgian resurgence, as discipline and symmetry made a comeback, exemplified by Bryanston in Dorset, 'an enormous, belated grandee mansion' in 'swaggering English baroque'. Scotland, meanwhile, had its own idiosyncrasies: classical country houses were built in significant numbers much later north of the border, alongside a distinctive form of Scottish baronial architecture which corresponded roughly to English gothic.

All this means that, for example, Sir Charles Barry's rebuilding of Cliveden in Buckinghamshire for the 2nd Duke of Sutherland in an Italian Renaissance mode was a belated essay in a declining fashion, while the Tudor revival used by Burges at Knightshayes in the early 1870s and the Jacobean reconstruction of Lanhydrock (NT) in Cornwall after the fire of 1881 stood much closer to the mainstream of Victorian country-house taste. Shaw's 'Old English', transplanted from the Home Counties whose vernacular provided so many of its details, finds a particularly spectacular expression at Cragside in Northumberland, while in West Sussex Philip Webb's Standen (NT) of the early 1890s goes further along the road towards relaxed, eclectic borrowing from a variety of local building traditions. Wightwick Manor (NT) in Staffordshire is a much bolder variant, with an exuberant use of half-timbering which reflected the prevailing local Tudor idiom. But the commissioning of Castle Drogo in 1910, with its 6-foot-thick granite walls, and in less extravagant vein the creation of Lindisfarne Castle (NT) in Northumberland, remind us that even in Edwardian England the attractions of the sham castle could still exert a powerful influence on aspiring country-house owners and their architects.

What are we to make of the Victorian and Edwardian cornucopia of styles, the pageant of borrowed motifs from distant times and different cultures? In part it was a product of the rise of the architectural profession and the growing scholarship and versatility of many of the architects themselves. Most could turn their hand to a variety of styles rather than being identified solely with one in particular; and the burgeoning architectural press and publishing industry soon made new ideas widely accessible. Sometimes, no doubt, architects steered uncertain clients in the direction of the styles they themselves preferred. But most clients were capable of making their own choices; and what they preferred may tell us something about their social attitudes as well as their aesthetic predilections.

A cosy corner of a magnificent room: the fireplace and ingle-nook in the Great Parlour at Wightwick Manor, Staffordshire, built in the late nineteenth century for Theodore Mander, a Wolverhampton paint and varnish manufacturer who had read his Ruskin and wanted an Old English house with Victorian comforts.

Some historians have suggested that the movement towards Tudor and gothic styles for country houses expresses an enhanced sense of social responsibility. Instead of seeking to overawe the lower orders, and distance themselves from them, country-house builders were identifying with an idealised version of an earlier, happier England, in which property-owners acknowledged their responsibilities as well as asserting their rights, and the lower orders knew their place and accepted it gladly as God-given and naturally justified. So the country house was to be lived in; hospitality was to be dispensed from its hall; its owner was to take a personal interest in his tenants and dependants, to be active in local government, in charities and in religion, and to be a generally benevolent, paternalist influence on his territory.

There is some evidence that such things were actually happening during the second quarter of the nineteenth century, after a period in which these duties had been neglected. The rise of the London season and the attractions of the spas and

other new leisure towns had made country living seem unattractive in the later eighteenth century, when transport improvements were sufficient to make the towns accessible but not to allow easy to-ing and fro-ing. So the great houses of the aristocracy, at least, lay empty for most of the year. But the 1810s and 1830s, in particular, saw sharpening social and political tensions in country as well as town, and a gathering impetus towards social and political reform from sections of the prospering urban middle classes, as well as from the beleaguered wage-earners. The special social position of the aristocracy and gentry came under challenge. The 1840s saw Thomas Carlyle's widely-read declamations in support of a revived hierarchical medieval society led by patriarchal hero-figures. This was also the decade of Young England, with its advocacy of aristocratic paternalism as the way to heal society's wounds. Several other influences, from the revived religious seriousness of the Church of England to the early novels of Charles Dickens, pointed in the same nostalgic direction. More mundanely, the repeal of the Corn Laws in 1846 opened arable agriculture to foreign competition and set a stronger premium on active, efficient estate management. The spread of the railway network made it easier for aristocrats with urban interests to keep in regular personal contact with their estates, and fox-hunting was making country living more sociable, more exciting and more attractive.

So the trend towards old English styles of country-house architecture can be seen as part of a pattern: the revival of an ideal of concerned rural landed paternalism. There is something in this, but it is not a simple matter. Some of the key trends, like a spreading interest in agricultural improvement, and indeed the rise of fox-hunting, were already well under way by the later eighteenth century. Game preservation, which also made rural life more attractive, was itself socially divisive, pitting landlords against tenants and labourers. Moreover, Tudor and Gothic, or Elizabethan and Jacobean, houses were not the sole prerogative of the established landed families which might have been expected to respond to this ideal: they were also built for rising commercial men and industrialists, whose motives may have been rather different. An appeal to history through the architecture of a new country house was often part of a search for legitimacy and acceptance on the part of the newly wealthy. More generally, an appeal to the imagined stability of the feudal past had obvious attractions at a time of seemingly

unprecedented social change and political turmoil. Nor should we discount the possibility that people chose a certain style of house because it was thought to be the fashion, or just because they liked it.

The Rothschild invasion of Buckinghamshire illustrates some of the cross-currents. It was not all French châteaux: Mentmore was mock-Elizabethan, largely modelled on Wollaton Hall in Nottinghamshire; Aston Clinton was a rambling Italianate structure; and Ascott was 'an immensely overgrown half-timbered cottage, designed from the first to be smothered in creeper', by an architect who specialised in creating houses which seemed to have grown by accretion over the centuries. It was here that Leopold de Rothschild took on 'the role of bluff country squire', and the nature of the house may have reflected his identification with the rural pursuits of the established gentry. But the other Buckinghamshire Rothschilds were not far out of line. They hunted; they built estate villages of model housing; they patronised local good causes with appropriate munificence; and they worked their local political influence as to the manner born. A château from Touraine, in yellow Bath stone, might strike an incongruous note in the Vale of Aylesbury; but it was capable of coexisting with aspects of the traditional way of life of the great estate, as well as with the peculiar brand of high living which the Rothschilds made their own.

Clive Aslet has identified two distinctive styles of country-house living which came to the fore in the late nineteenth century and the Edwardian years, and made their mark on some of the new houses of this period. The 'smart' or 'social' country house built on established themes: it was a well-appointed gathering-place for the rich and aspiring, the powerful and the power-hungry, and the leaders of fashionable society. It combined ostentation with the most advanced domestic technology: marble halls with central heating. Polesden Lacey (NT) in Surrey, at which Mrs Greville played hostess to Edward VII and those who moved in his orbit, is an impressive example, rebuilt and greatly extended for an Indian civil servant in 1902–5 and magnificently redecorated after the Grevilles moved in in 1906. At the other extreme from Polesden Lacey, so conveniently sited in Surrey commuterland, was Lindisfarne Castle. This exemplifies the 'romantic' country house, which set a premium on isolation, closeness to nature, traditional craftsmanship, fresh air and simplicity. Its remote Northumbrian location, accessible only by a tidal causeway, made this ruined fortress on a rock irresistible to Edward Hudson, owner of *Country Life*, and his architect Lutyens, who produced 'a vision of passages hewn into the rock, of large vaulted chambers, of short strong circular pillars and low arches, and of beamed ceilings'. Furnishings and decoration were spartan, and the house was stronger on atmosphere than comfort, provoking extreme reactions of delight or dismay in visitors.

A romantic attachment to old buildings and their traditions was attracting growing numbers of affluent professional families, the Victorian and Edwardian intelligentsia, towards this mode of living. William Morris's acquisition of Kelmscott in Oxfordshire in which to live out his version of an ideal rural existence was close to the fountainhead of this trend. The Edinburgh professor who

adopted the almost ruinous Kellie Castle (NTS), in Fifeshire, as a summer home for his family, and rescued it from dilapidation, is a less famous example.

In these cases, and in most examples of the newly-built 'romantic' country house, there was no landed estate to speak of. Hudson rented a few fields near Lindisfarne Castle, but was more interested in protecting rabbits than growing crops; and most of the 'romantics' were likewise playing at country living. Not that the 'smart' country-house owner had much affinity with, or dependence on, the life of the land. Polesden Lacey had about a thousand acres of land, and some members of the house parties took an interest in the home farm; but this was an optional recreation rather than a central concern. At both ends of the spectrum, these were 'houses in the country' rather than country houses in the traditional manner, or even the manner of the Rothschilds.

Lindisfarne Castle and Polesden Lacey are such extreme examples of the 'romantic' and the 'smart'

The drawing-room at Polesden Lacey, Surrey, epitome of the 'smart' country houses of the Edwardian plutocracy and the circles in which the King himself moved.

COUNTRY HOUSES AND COUNTRY LIVING

that they come dangerously close to caricature. There was an extensive middle ground, and a formal style of architecture did not necessarily go with a formal style of life. But what the new country houses of the turn of the century had in common was a detachment from agriculture and the wider life of rural England which cut them off from some of the roots of older landed attitudes and ways of life. They shared to the full in the idea of the country house as a centre for leisure and enjoyment; but they did not embody the local powers, responsibilities, economic decisions and administrative burdens that went with the management of a landed estate.

Country houses of all kinds responded, above all, to the tastes and preferences of their occupants, and to changing fashions in the enjoyment of the leisured life-style which was the most universal distinguishing feature of country-house living. George Lucy of Charlecote Park (NT), Warwickshire, expresses many of the enthusiasms of the later eighteenth century. He was no intellectual or arbiter of taste, but his European travels and sociable visits to London and the spas left their mark on his house, inside and out. He sat for his portrait to Pompeo Battoni in Rome, where he also commissioned a poor relation to copy Old Masters for him. He brought back twenty views of Italian scenes, and some marble busts, 'copies of the antique'. Mr Lucy also had his portrait painted by Gainsborough at Bath, and ordered 'a pair of large gilt mirrors of Chinese design' from Chippendale's for his bedroom. In the 1760s he took out 'all the old wainscoting' from the main rooms, and redecorated in accordance with the taste of the time, with generous use of stucco, gilding and white paint, and elaborately carved mouldings for doors and window frames. There were external transformations, too: the seventeenth-century geometrical water-garden and formal avenues of trees were swept away, and the park was remodelled by the ubiquitous Capability Brown, with the usual changes of level, careful scattering of groups of trees and the conversion of the Avon into a series of small lakes.

These were representative changes: they had contemporary counterparts all over Britain. Not that Charlecote provides a microcosm of a universal experience. At one extreme, George Lucy did not share the immense resources and

George Lucy, the easy-going bachelor squire of Charlecote, Warwickshire, as painted in Rome by Pompeo Battoni.

obsessive drive to accumulate treasures of a William Beckford. Nor was he as uncaring of the dictates of fashion as the first Simon Yorke of Erdigg, who left the house much as he found it after 34 years' residence. But Charlecote's experience is valuable because it was close to the mainstream. Its owner was neither an adventurer nor an innovator: he was amiable, sociable, undemanding, a follower rather than a leader, and descriptions of Charlecote show us what such a man enjoyed, and what he thought was expected of him. It was the requirements of people like George Lucy, and of landed society in general, often indiscriminate and catered for by remote control through agents, that led the production in Rome of classical statuary and busts to assume 'almost the character of a factory industry'.

Two generations on, Charlecote produced another squire whose tastes were strikingly representative of his time. Where George Lucy had been a bachelor, George Hammond Lucy, who succeeded in 1823, had already married into the Welsh gentry and was to bring up a considerable family. His undergraduate travels in Europe had stimulated an urge to collect works of art, and in 1823 he spent £3400 on items from Beckford's collection at an auction at Fonthill. He dabbled in heraldry and genealogy, and did his house up internally in neo-Elizabethan style, with elaborate heraldic stained glass, new wallpapers, light oak doors and hot-air heating. He and his wife collaborated in reorganising the garden in a more formal style, and in the early 1840s they made an exhaustive, and exhausting, cultural tour of Italy and France, returning with new marble fireplaces, pictures, 'Graeco-Roman vases' and furniture. In the early years of their marriage, especially, the Lucys participated in the gaieties of the London season, and they mingled in the social round of the upper reaches of Warwickshire county society. The combination of romantic attachment to family history and Tudor roots, with a persisting interest in the antiquities and works of art of Italy, was a general theme of the aristocratic culture of the time; and in this case, as in many others, it coexisted with a concern to build up and sustain good relations with tenants and neighbours. The experience of George Hammond Lucy in the second quarter of the nineteenth century ran parallel to that of many of his contemporaries of similar status.

After the mid nineteenth century it becomes harder to find a notional mainstream in the tastes of country-house owners. Between the Rothschilds at

Mentmore or Waddesdon with their collections of French furniture, pictures and porcelain, displayed in marble halls, and the Old English and 'arts-and-crafts' interiors at Wightwick or Standen, yawns a gulf across which it is difficult to generalise. Within their shared frame of reference, too, there are important contrasts between Wightwick and Standen. The former glows with the rich medievalising stained glass of Kempe, and boasts elaborate panelling, fireplaces and plaster friezes. It presents a 'wealth of patterns, in Morris designs, Oriental carpets, plasterwork, inlaid furniture and tiles', as well as 'a multitude of hangings, embroideries and coverings from the Morris workshops'. Standen is altogether more austere, as befits the character of its architect, Philip Webb. There are Morris wallpapers and curtains, but otherwise patterns are simple. The windows have leaded lights, and white paint and panelling are much in evidence. The idiosyncrasies of the architect are modest and understated. Nothing could be further in spirit from the Rothschild palaces, or Polesden Lacey, or even the sumptuous upstairs drawing-room at Cragside with its monstrous marble fireplace, which mocks the domestic, rustic overtones of the ingle-nook which shelters incongruously beneath it. The contrasts were not just a matter of different levels of financial resources: they were matters of taste, even of philosophy, as well.

What the vast majority of country-house owners did have in common was a deep interest in the maintenance and embellishment of their homes. Only the small minority who opted out of the social obligations of mutual entertainment which generally prevailed in county society failed to make some adjustment to changing fashions. Calke was just about unique, and Erddig unusual, in the extent to which they were allowed to slumber in the later nineteenth century. House and grounds, decoration and furnishings were, after all, visible embodiments of the family's prestige and wealth.

Significantly, improvements in domestic technology were taken up less enthusiastically than new forms of display and decoration. Hardly any innovations in such vital matters as heating and plumbing made an impact on country-house life in the half century after 1750, and when central heating systems and efficient water-closets became available at the turn of the century, they were adopted slowly and patchily. Oil lighting was preferred to gas in the vast majority of houses throughout the nineteenth century. Even in new houses, bathrooms were provided sparingly; and

even where partial central heating was installed it might, as at Mentmore, fail to overcome the chill blast of the fierce draughts which could make the most palatial room uncomfortable. Plumbed-in hot and cold water, and bedroom wash-basins, were rare luxuries before the First World War; and electric light and external telephone lines also remained unusual. Jill Franklin tells us that 'some of the older great houses' of Edwardian England 'had often changed little for a hundred years' in these respects, and 'the visitor could still encounter icy corridors, hot water in cans and candles to light him to bed'. Many of the newer houses did manage to combine warmth, fresh air and safe sanitation, but improvements were, at best, 'patchy'. Cragside, above all, felt the benefit of Armstrong's technological expertise and resources: in 1880 it became the first house in England, and perhaps the world, to have an effective electric lighting system, and Armstrong's professional concern with hydraulics had spin-offs at home in the form of hydraulic lifts, a hydraulically-turned spit in the kitchen, and even hydraulically-powered central heating.

Cragside was a generation ahead of almost all other country houses. Most aristocrats and gentry probably put show before comfort. Inured to draughts and cold baths by their experience of public school and university, the men of the house were suspicious of expensive palliatives against privations, and perhaps distrusted technology as they despised the wrong kind of luxury. There were also good practical reasons for the slow adoption of domestic improvements among families whose material resources were so impressive. New technologies were often visibly unreliable and, in the case of early electricity, dangerous. It was often unclear for many years which of several alternatives was going to be the best answer to a particular need. Almost all country houses, too, were beyond the reach of the increasingly efficient municipal gas and electricity services of the late nineteenth and early twentieth centuries. A few, such as Castle Ward, Mount Stewart and The Argory in Northern Ireland with their gas plants, manufactured their own power supply, but the vast majority did without. But perhaps the most important brake on technological innovation in country houses before the First World War was the ready availability of cheap domestic servants. With plenty of muscle power available to fetch luggage, carry hot and cold water, make fires, clean grates and empty chamber pots, there was often little incentive to mechanise or innovate, except where

chimneys smoked or corridors were Arctic in their iciness.

The country houses employed a minority of Britain's astonishingly numerous and steadily growing population of domestic servants; but they provided the best working conditions and promotion prospects, and were able to recruit without much difficulty even in the Edwardian years, when the demand for domestic servants was visibly increasing faster than the supply. At their late Victorian apogee, some of the great estates had several hundred servants if outside workers such as grooms and gardeners are included. At Welbeck Abbey in Nottinghamshire at the turn of the century there were about 320: 'more like a principality than anything else', recalled one footman, and certainly equivalent to a sizeable village. Between twenty and forty was more usual: Mentmore had 34 indoor servants in 1871, and Calke showed an unusual degree of continuity, with 25 in 1737 and 27 in about 1910. The lesser

The domestic staff at Cragside in 1886: five men and eighteen women, beautifully turned-out and gazing confidently into the camera, as befitted people who were accustomed to looking after international financiers and crowned heads from all over the world.

gentry might make do with much smaller numbers.

These establishments were big enough for elaborate hierarchies to develop below stairs. At the top were the house steward, in really big establishments, or the butler, and the housekeeper, whose duties were mainly ceremonial, supervisory and administrative. The cook, who presided over the kitchen maids, and the coachman also held positions of seniority, skill and responsibility, as might the head gardener and the gamekeeper. The larger country houses were unusual in employing significant numbers of male servants, who were more expensive and more difficult to manage (it was thought) than the young women who predominated. The trend of the later eighteenth century to employ ever-growing numbers of strapping footmen in elaborate liveries, mainly for purposes of competitive display, was not sustained far into the new century, although adult males remained a highly visible minority of the domestic workforce in most country houses until their numbers declined sharply in late Victorian times. Each department of the household had its own social pecking order, with the governess occupying a difficult intermediate position because of her often superior social origins. The divisions below stairs were expressed by the elaborate rituals of dinner in the servants' hall, which the 'upper ten' of senior servants formally vacated after the first course to finish their meal elsewhere.

In many houses the servants' world became increasingly segregated from that of the family, especially in the nineteenth century. A growing concern for privacy relegated the servants to separate service wings, which were so arranged that they could not look out over formal gardens or family rooms. Back stairs and special corridors were introduced to keep servants out of sight as far as possible. Sir Vauncey Harpur Crewe of Calke, who often communicated with his servants only by letter, was not unique in his eccentricity, and some noblemen would sack any servants they saw above stairs without having been summoned. There was a pervasive fear that servants might gossip about family secrets, and this may explain the widespread tendency to recruit from a distance, rather than relying on the village. This was not universal, but where it occurred it must have reduced the social contact between the big house and the local community.

The trend towards social segregation coexisted with a paradoxical, countervailing trend towards growing concern for the moral welfare of servants, which was especially apparent in the early and mid Victorian years. Thus the new service wings separated the women's sleeping quarters from the men's, and efforts were made to keep them as far apart as possible during the working day. Family prayers included the servants, and some employers took an interest in their education. In the early 1880s the Countess of Aberdeen set up the Haddo House Young Women's Improvement Association for servants over a wide area of Aberdeenshire, and there were other such initiatives. Most houses had an annual Servants' Ball, at which the master and mistress customarily led the dancing with the

housekeeper and butler, and some had regular entertainments through the year. Members of the family might captain a house cricket team or otherwise take an active interest in the servants. Sometimes, of course, relationships between male family members and female servants became sexually exploitative, and this was a recurrent fear. But in many houses genuine attempts were made, throughout the period, to build up a paternal relationship between employer and employee, incorporating a moral ascendancy on the part of the former.

In this context the famous case of Erddig is interesting in several ways. The Erddig tradition by which successive squires commemorated servants with commissioned portraits and affectionate verses was most unusual; and the servants here do seem to have stayed longer, and to have been succeeded or supplemented more often by relatives, than in most places. But even here relations were sometimes strained, and the Yorkes did not always know their servants as well as they believed. Some were conscious of being comparatively badly paid, and tried to make it up in illicit ways. Others were more straightforwardly dishonest. But even Erddig's attics were much more spacious than a working-class bedroom in the outside world, and, as elsewhere, servants had access to ample supplies of food and drink, and could sometimes save remarkable sums from their wages. For those who could cope with the feeling of dependence and the lack of autonomy, service could provide security and quite high material living standards. Its decline came when, especially after 1914, a growing proportion of young people began to put independence before security, and to revolt against the patriarchal regime of the country house. The Achilles' heel of the country house was its need for a sustained supply of tolerably cheap, discreet, trustworthy and uncomplaining servants. The eventual failure of this supply played a significant part in bringing down the whole system.

What all country-house owners had in common was the experience of managing the labour of a substantial number of resident workers, often equivalent to a small factory. Styles of management differed, as did the extent of delegation through the

Philip Yorke's estate carpenter, Edward Prince, painted at Erddig in 1792. This was the beginning of the family tradition of writing and displaying affectionate verses about their servants.

One lab ur more, thou muse of mirth
That brought down our birth
And before you leave us enter
To record our old Carpenter.
'Tis thirteen years, then young in grammer
When here, at first, he held an hammer
Under his Father; dead long since,
Who was entitled The black Prince.

A Raiser this indeed, of Houses,
That has already had four Spouses,
And if the Present, don't survive,
Hopes to rebuild them up to five:
From their bold strokes, architecture
Of Princes, to adorn the place,
Who thrive beneath their parent stock,
And make good Chipps from that old block.

*Under the drawing
Spalive Sister of the
mine.

Ed Prince A t 75 1790.

Old Charle Prince the present
Ed's Father was the Carpenter
at Eeting in Mr Miller's time
who was used to call him the
black Prince, being a Thick build
dark complecioned Man.

This carefully-posed picture of the Erddig staff, taken for the last Simon Yorke's coming-of-age party in 1924, gives a completely misleading impression. Only a handful of permanent servants remained at this time, and most of the maids had been hired specially for the occasion. Hence, perhaps, the widespread air of embarrassment and uncertainty.

senior servants, but the experience was general, and it must have helped to form atttitudes and broaden horizons, although it may also have confirmed stereotypes and created unrealistic expectations about the working class at large. There were no trade unions in stately homes. Just as important, however, was the role of the country house as élite social centre; and the physical expansion of many country houses through the period owed as much to the need to accommodate the parties of visitors which helped to justify their

existence, as to the need to expand and rearrange the servants' quarters. The exchange of hospitality with people of similar status was an essential basis of country-house life, and Theodore Mander's decision, in 1893, to build the delightful eastern extension at Wightwick in order to house visitors for cricket weeks was unusual only in the very specific reason behind it.

As Mark Girouard put it, towards the middle of the eighteenth century 'one result of the nobility and gentry becoming more mobile and mixing more together was new kinds of parties'. Balls and assemblies came to be held in country houses as well as in the town, and they escaped from older formalities to combine dancing, tea-drinking, conversation and card-playing as well as a supper or dinner, while the festivities might spread into half a dozen adjoining reception rooms rather than being confined to one or two. As the countryside became more accessible and more attractive, and the landscaped parks tamed the threatening aspect of Nature while providing circuits of follies, temples and viewpoints to enjoy, as at Stowe and Stourhead, extended house parties became regular features in the country-house calendar. They were useful for bringing powerful men together to discuss and arrange politics, and many country houses attracted particular political labels. They also oiled the machinery of the marriage market, enabling suitable young people to be thrown together with opportunities for flirtation. These were recurrent themes.

But the serious business was seasoned with enjoyments. From the 1770s onwards there were amateur theatricals: the first Philip Yorke put on *Henry V* at Erddig after taking part in performances at nearby Wynnstay, and in the next generation the 4th Earl of Aberdeen formed part of an eager company of aristocratic players at the Duke of Abercorn's Bentley Priory. The new Evangelical seriousness soon took its toll of plays and players, but failed to make inroads into the passion for fox-hunting and the mass slaughter of pheasants, partridges and moor game which gained rapidly in popularity in the later eighteenth century and sustained itself thereafter. It was accompanied by a growing interest in the selective breeding of animals: thoroughbred horses, and sporting dogs such as the Clumber spaniel, as well as more utilitarian beasts like cattle and pigs. People with pride in their pedigrees demanded animals to match.

Women were not excluded from these interests, and some distinguished themselves on the hunting field; but the internal arrangements of houses developed to cater for a separate masculine society in the billiard room, the smoking room and to some extent the library. The women had their own preserves for music, needlework and conversation, and the mingling of the sexes was reserved for prescribed times and territories. But conventions of all kinds were thawing to an altogether novel extent in many late Victorian and Edwardian households, as tennis, croquet and golf provided mixed outdoor pursuits, and a few new houses even acquired swimming-pools. Even in the most formal and restrictive settings, the shared culture and enjoyment of the country-house party helped to fuse and sustain a sense of common identity among the British upper classes.

The amusements of the big house were not always confined to the charmed circle of the owners and their guests. They could build bridges to the outside world of the village, the tenantry and the labourers. Cricket is an obvious case in point, and

The garden furniture at Stourhead, Wiltshire, includes a medieval cross from Bristol, an obelisk, a Temple of Flora and a gothick cottage, as well as the grotto over which this river-god presides. He was sculpted by John Cheere in 1751.

examples of social mixing in country-house teams run right through the period. Fox-hunting, a much more regular event over most of lowland England, involved the active participation of tenant farmers. Their co-operation was needed in preserving foxes and allowing ready access to the land they farmed. But the gentry did the organising and had the best horses: a good showing in the saddle was important for prestige. Social divisions were expressed in turn-out and performance, and labourers followed on foot. Villagers could participate more directly in shoots organised at the big house, with the need for beaters to flush the game birds and sometimes loaders; and game was given away to local tradesmen and tenants as a mark of favour. But this was a controversial area: where game was preserved, farmers grumbled about damage to their crops, and poachers proliferated. Parts of England saw violent conflict on this issue for years at a time.

More convincing and direct as attempts to maintain the loyalty of tenants and dependants were the grand ceremonial events which brought the tenantry into the great house for feasting and dancing on special occasions. Such events were being revived here and there in the late eighteenth century, celebrating political successes, national events such as victory in battle, and the births, marriages and coming of age of members of the squire's family. By the second quarter of the nineteenth century they were becoming more widespread and more frequent, and the vogue for the building and refurbishment of gothic halls was often associated with this kind of hospitality.

These joint celebrations, which brought together whole village communities, were important to the social order of the countryside. They were aimed at identifying tenants, labourers and neighbours with the joys, sorrows, interests and fortunes of the local landed family. In 1811 the enormous sum of £1709 2s 8d was spent on the 6th Duke of Devonshire's coming-of-age party at Hardwick Hall. The result was something of an orgy, in which two people were accidentally killed and a gatecrasher described drunks lying around the park 'like the slain on a battlefield'.

Victorian celebrations tended to be more decorous and controlled. Thus the twenty-first birthday of John Elliott Boileau of Ketteringham, Norfolk, was marked by a week of celebrations in the autumn of 1848. There were illuminations and fireworks in the park, which was thrown open to the villagers; dinner for the tenants in the recently-built Great Hall; roast beef and plum pudding for the labourers and cottagers; a servants' ball; and games for the village children, including such evocatively archaic pursuits as climbing a soapy mast for a shoulder of mutton. This was an unusually elaborate programme, expressing the paternalist aspirations of a new squire; but such activities were expected of most self-respecting Victorian aristocrats and gentry. The tenants, in their turn, knew what was expected of them. In 1876 the future Sir Vauncey Harpur Crewe and his bride found 'flowers, flags and triumphal arches of evergreen' displayed, and enthusiastic crowds lining the streets, as they toured the family's estates on a ceremonial journey from Derby station to Calke. In 1902 the second Philip Yorke and his

second bride were similarly welcomed back to Erddig, and in a characteristic gesture 'the Erddig servants unharnessed the carriage horses and themselves dragged the vehicle up the hill leading to the house'.

Exactly what these displays of mutual affection meant to the participants is open to question. The novelist Surtees provided a cynical portrayal of Squire Jawleyford, trotting out the expected rhetoric about his tenants being as dear to him as his family, but really interested only in the rents which his steward Mr Screwemtight extracts from them before the festivities. On the other hand the tenants and villlagers may merely have gone through the motions of grateful endorsement of the social order, basing their participation on fear or cupidity rather than genuine affection, just as the labourer's tugged forelock may have masked apathy or bitterness. The surface rhetoric of social conventions need not tell the whole story. Even at the Ketteringham coming-of-age celebrations, the squire noticed the absence of one farmer with whom he was in dispute, while another, whose continued tenancy was under a cloud 'because he is a disgrace to the estate', lowered his stock still further by getting drunk. Even on the most elaborate set piece occasions, designed to present a façade of hierarchical unanimity, social friction and dissent might not be far from the surface.

Genuine harmony between the big house and the village or estate was more likely to be sustained where the 'ceremonial régime', as E. W. Martin called it, was underpinned by regular residence and attention to the needs and problems of the locals. The ideal landlord encouraged or enjoined his tenants to improve their farms, and invested directly in the land himself; he refrained from putting rents up to the highest level the markets would sustain, and looked favourably on son succeeding father in the same tenancy; and he was prepared to reduce rents, or to wait a long time for them, in hard times. In return, the landlord might expect his tenants to vote for his preferred candidate at election time; but such support was supposed to derive from goodwill and a sense of the seemly, rather than from threats; and tenants' expectations of political independence steadily expanded through the nineteenth century. Some landowners – a highly visible minority – went so far as to provide model dwellings for tenants and labourers. From the Georgian terraces of Blanchland in Northumberland, through the carefully-contrived irregular rusticity of the almshouses which cluster picturesquely at Blaise Hamlet (NT) near Bristol or the distinctive 'garishly coloured tile-hanging' of Ilam (NT) in Staffordshire, to the substantial late Victorian thatched cottages built for the Wantages at East Lockinge in Oxfordshire, improved rural housing was being created throughout the period by landowners in most parts of Britain. But it was difficult to let such cottages at economic rents: they were expensive to build, and subsidies were necessary to bring them within the grasp of labouring families. As at Blaise Hamlet, too, the picturesque effect was often achieved at the expense of internal comfort and convenience. Aesthetic considerations, the dictates of fashion and the need to be *seen* to be making improvements too often outweighed the provision of light, space and warmth. The surest way to good relations between landlord, tenant and labourer lay through

the kind of financial management that matched the prevailing popular ideas of fairness and generosity.

An active landlord would also devote time and attention to the administration of justice and of local government more generally, and to the spiritual welfare of tenants and neighbours: or at least, to the provision and upkeep of churches and clergy. Some of these roles could generate conflict, or exacerbate it, as when landed Justices of the Peace tried and convicted poachers summarily in the kitchen of the big house, or took a severe line against petty thieves or rioters, or administered poor relief in a harsh or penny-pinching way, or used their position to divert old rights of way from their parks or out of their line of vision. Even the rebuilding or improvement of churches was not always straightforward, especially where it was associated with changes in traditional ways of conducting the service, or with the introduction of a vainglorious display of family heraldry and memorials. Sometimes a secular motive was especially prominent. Lord Le Despencer's opulent rebuilding of the West Wycombe estate church in the 1760s was more the creation of an

Cottages at Blaise Hamlet, on the outskirts of Bristol, designed by John Nash in 1811 to accommodate 'old retainers' of the estate's owner, the Quaker banker John Harford.

extravagant piece of park furniture than a display of piety or social concern. It was alleged that he held drinking parties in the golden ball at the top of the tower. A century later the majestic and wonderfully-decorated gothic church at Studley Royal (NT) in North Yorkshire, with its dramatically imaginative stained-glass scenes from the Book of Revelation, commemorated the violent and untimely death of Frederick Grantham Vyner, and enhanced the scenery of a famous landscaped park. Public worship must always have been a minor consideration. These were not the only buildings or rebuildings of churches which put aesthetic and familial considerations a long way ahead of the religious or social needs of tenantry and villagers.

Landlords often held the right to appoint the parson, especially in Scotland, although here the congregation also had a say and often asserted its wishes in opposition to those of the laird. Aristocrats might have a score or more 'livings' in their gift. Sometimes they nominated a relative, concentrating local power and resources. Often they took the opportunity to nominate a clergyman whose religious views were congenial; and Nonconformists might find it difficult to secure a meeting-place on an estate whose owner was a staunch Churchman. Occasionally squire and parson were one and the same, as at Hampton Lucy, next door to Charlecote, in the mid nineteenth century. Here the hard-drinking, stern, awe-inspiring Revd. John Lucy ruled his villagers fiercely, terrorising backsliders while spending long days hunting and shooting, and announcing forthcoming meets from the pulpit during Sunday service. This was an arresting but unusual kind of regime: such local power was rarely concentrated into a single individual.

All these aspects of the local power and influence of landed society varied widely in the ways in which they were exercised, depending on the personality of the landowner and his agent, and on how often he was in residence. But all substantial landowners had not only to concern themselves with the economics of running their estates, however much they might try to delegate such matters to a steward or agent; they were also expected to hold unpaid local offices of various kinds, to give active support to the influence of the established Church, and, ideally, to take some responsibility for the morals and social welfare of their underlings on the estate and in the village. Some were keener to do this than others: some neglected their responsibilities, some delegated them in large measure to the ladies of

their household, some exercised them with an enthusiasm which verged on the tyrannical. But a central aspect of the distinctive common culture of the aristocracy and gentry was a shared awareness, however distant and unwelcome, of the duties which went with the running of a great estate, and a shared knowledge of how these relationships worked.

Beyond the exercise of local power, the great landowners dominated the operation of national politics almost throughout the period. The House of Lords remained a landed stronghold, despite a late Victorian and Edwardian infusion of unlanded industrialists, and its power to block legislation was not significantly reduced until the eve of the First World War. A substantial proportion of the seats in the unreformed Commons lay in the gift of peers and other large landowners, and in many others a magnate could expect to see his chosen candidate returned. Small boroughs with few electors were especially vulnerable to aristocratic control. In 1807 peers could expect to dominate or control the election of 236 MPs, not far short of half the House of Commons. Reform was slow, and the famous 1832 Reform Act by no means completed the process. Even after the Second Reform Act of 1867, about one-eighth of the seats still came under aristocratic patronage. The direct representation of the landed gentry and sons of the aristocracy remained strong into late Victorian times. In 1880 322 MPs owned 2000 acres or more apiece, and in 1895 60 per cent of MPs were 'gentlemen of leisure, country squires, retired officers and lawyers'.

Landed domination of the law-making processes was not seriously threatened until the late nineteenth century, with the coming of the secret ballot in 1872 and the extension of household suffrage into the county seats in 1884. Landed control of county government, with its important control over spending on road and bridge improvements, the police, prisons and lunatic asylums, was only challenged after the introduction of elected county councils in 1889, and even then large landowners had considerable influence on the new bodies. The spreading influence of the towns, and the rise of the professional expert in local government as well as in the national civil service, also undermined the influence of the traditional social leaders. By the turn of the century power beyond the village and estate was visibly passing to the middle classes, though not in any direct sense to the working class.

Parliament and local government were among several institutions which helped to form the

Summary justice in the squire's hall: Sir Charles Abraham Elton, Bt., of Clevedon Court, interrogates a suspected poacher.

shared culture of landed society. Formative educational influences were vital: during the century after 1750 or so a steadily rising proportion of aristocrats and gentry sent their sons to the so-called 'public schools', especially Eton and Harrow. Here they formed friendships with boys of similar standing, picked up at least a smattering of Latin and Greek and (from the mid nineteenth century) were given liberal doses of muscular Christianity and team spirit through compulsory Chapel and organised games. The public schools were spartan in more ways than one, but they formed a distinctive set of shared experiences which helped to mark off the aristocracy and gentry from the rest of society. Where university followed, English grandees usually sent their sons to Oxford or Cambridge, even when provincial alternatives appeared during the nineteenth century. The aristocratic colleges were Christ Church in Oxford and Trinity in Cambridge, and the development of social skills and cultivation of social contacts were generally (not universally) regarded more highly than academic attainments. This is probably why the great landowners of Scotland generally ignored the four long-established Scottish universities, and sent their sons to Oxford or Cambridge, after a stint at Eton, Harrow or Rugby, for most of the nineteenth century. Only Edinburgh was attractive enough to stem this tide a little, and only in a small minority of cases. As the nineteenth century proceeded, the sons of farmers, clergy and the solid middle classes increasingly penetrated the public-school world and added to their social acceptability accordingly; but most of them colonised the lower divisions of the developing public-school hierarchy, and in Scotland most remained loyal to their established educational institutions.

Travel, especially to the great cultural centres of Mediterranean Europe, was a further distinguishing feature of the culture of landed society, providing a further frame of reference and assumed common ground in conversation. For younger sons, especially, a spell as an army officer was a common formative experience; and as with the public schools, there was a hierarchy of fashionable regiments, with tests of social acceptability being applied by those at the top of the scale. The rise of London clubland, especially in Victorian times, provided meeting-places for older members of the élite, enabling them to segregate themselves according to politics and interests, but within a common framework of institutions. The peculiar inheritance practices of landed society, especially the complicated means by which estates were held together and passed on intact from one generation to the next, also furnished common ground and helped to shape this distinctive élite culture.

Most of these institutions and preoccupations excluded women, or pushed them to the margins. Girls' public schools began to develop from the 1870s, as did higher education for women, which was well established by the 1890s; but these innovations affected only a minority, and home tuition by governesses remained the rule. The growing respectability of nursing, where Florence Nightingale's initiatives made an impact from the 1860s onwards, took a few women out of mainstream upper-class culture rather than offering a securer place within it. Women's clubs were developing in the last quarter of the nineteenth century, especially in London, for conventional ladies of leisure as well as feminists and graduates; but they did not add up to an equivalent of the masculine world of clubland, and there was no female counterpart to army life. Women in aristocratic families were excluded by rigid conventions from gainful employment, and were left to supervise their households (sometimes no mean managerial task), to display ornamental accomplishments, to dispense charity and to be custodians of etiquette. The rise of the London season, with its rituals of balls, court presentations and marriage-broking, became an acceptable focal point for female attention, especially when daughters were marriageable; and the rituals of morning calls, leaving cards, exchanging tea and deciding who could mix with whom, on what terms, were female spheres of influence. The proper role of an upper-class woman was defined in such a way as to rule out wider public activity, whether political or professional.

Within the shared culture of the masculine upper class, the combination of leisure, wealth and power enabled a myriad of contrasting life-styles to flourish and be tolerated. There were Whigs, Tories, supporters of the French Revolution in the 1790s, Victorian Radicals of various hues, even the occasional Socialist. There were ostentatious big spenders and miserly recluses, country lovers and metropolitan socialites, obsessive sportsmen, notorious rakes, staunch Evangelicals and dedicated Roman Catholics. There were those who straddled some of these apparent contradictions, like the 1st Marquess of Ripon, a Christian Socialist turned Gladstonian Liberal, leading Freemason turned Roman Catholic, Cabinet minister and Governor-General of India, and always an earnest paternalist. There were eccentrics like Sir Vauncey Harpur Crewe of Calke, who spent much of his time shooting birds and collecting butterflies on his estate in the company of his head gamekeeper, and 'made off into the woods' when his wife entertained, 'setting his coachman to keep watch and tell him when the intruders had departed'. And there were also those who used their wealth and leisure to pursue and support science and the arts: men like the 4th Earl of Aberdeen, who combined his rise to become Prime Minister in the mid 1850s with being, at various times, President of the Society of Antiquaries, a Trustee of the British Museum and a Fellow of the Royal Society.

Such men were a minority, but an important one. The complete range of possibilities open to an aristocrat was perhaps best exemplified by John Bowes of Streatlam Castle, County Durham. He was the illegitimate son of the 10th Earl of Strathmore, inherited the Earl's extensive estates and coal mines after the inevitable lawsuit, was a conscientious (though silent) MP for South Durham for fifteen years, after being elected in 1832 at the age of 21, and a friend of the novelist Thackeray. He owned four Derby winners, and was a well-known figure on the Turf; owned and managed a theatre in Paris for several years; married a Parisienne who acted in his theatre; gave generously to a wide range of Durham charities and dependants; and, most famously, put together the remarkable art collections which he and his wife housed in a specially-built museum, a French château improbably sited on the outskirts of Barnard Castle and erected to French designs by a local builder.

Bowes is a unique and engaging figure; but his career helps to explain the resilience of the English landed ruling class. Even when distracted by London politics and Paris theatricals, he kept in close touch with the business of his estate, and he held the local offices which were expected of him, as magistrate, sheriff and Lieutenant-Colonel of

The star turn of John Bowes' collections at the Bowes Museum: the Silver Swan, an astonishingly lifelike automaton which was displayed at the Paris International Exposition of 1867. Mark Twain wrote that the swan had 'a living grace about his movements and a living intelligence in his eyes'.

the county militia, even when this involved him in basic military training and the prospect of public embarrassment. In Parliament he was careful to look after local interests, and he was generous to tenants and former servants. In the eyes of almost all his contemporaries, these virtues were sufficient to justify his wealth and position; and indeed, his support for the first Reform Act and for the secret ballot made him a popular figure in unexpected circles. There were enough men of this stamp in landed society, even in the difficult early decades of the nineteenth century, to ensure its survival as a ruling class; and the ready co-option of new industrial and commercial wealth into the ranks of the 'gentlemen' provided important reinforcement. But not every country village had its resident squire, and no set of rural relationships was conflict-free. In order to provide a more balanced picture of rural society, the next chapter will look more closely at the farmers, tradesmen and village labourers, and see how they fared during this period of unprecedented change in the countryside.

CHAPTER FOUR

The Farm and the Village

Life in the countryside remained important throughout the period, despite the impressive statistics of urban and industrial growth. It was not until the 1860s that the population of rural England ceased to grow, and began a long decline. At about this time, too, the urban population came to outnumber the rural for the first time; although both these statements depend on rather arbitrary distinctions between rural and urban, for many people lived in settlements which could have been described either as large villages or as small towns, depending on how you looked at them. But by 1891 nearly two-thirds of the inhabitants of England and Wales lived in towns of more than 10,000 people. Even in the early twentieth century, however, a very large – though unknowable – number of town and city dwellers had migrated from the countryside, and many more had rural relatives with whom they kept in touch. The countryside was especially important as a reservoir of domestic servants, labourers, police and transport workers, and its influence remained pervasive even in the heavily industrial Britain of the early twentieth century. It was itself increasingly open to urban influences, but its importance, and the persisting contribution of agriculture as industry as well as way of life, should not be underestimated.

Throughout the period, the vast majority of British farming was done by tenant farmers who paid money rents to the owners of the land they occupied, although payment in kind and labour services was not extinct in northern and upland areas in the later eighteenth century. The landowner supplied the buildings and paid for major improvements like enclosure and drainage, hoping to recoup the expenditure by charging higher rents in the long run. The tenant was responsible for implements, seed, stock, manure and general running expenses. Nearly nine-tenths of the cultivated land in England, Wales and Scotland was farmed on this system in 1887. This figure would have been smaller in the mid eighteenth century, because there had been a steady decline in the number of owner-occupiers: small landowners who farmed their own estates. In the eighteenth century the more substantial of these people were known in England as the 'yeomanry', a term which gradually faded from use as it became nostalgically identified with an archaic way of life. The traditional yeomanry were presented by those who mourned their passing as the embodiments of old-fashioned hospitality, unpretentiousness, thrift, hard work and good neighbouring. But to agricultural improvers they were identified with backward, slovenly farming methods, shortage of capital, ignorance and poverty. The optimistic view was probably based on prosperous Kentish hop-growers or substantial northern families with deep local roots, like the Brownes of Troutbeck. It was also based on a romanticisation of rustic virtues which said more about the needs and values of the commentators than about rural realities. But the owner-occupier did not disappear: he survived tenaciously in southern and eastern counties like Norfolk and Kent as well as in the Welsh and Cumbrian uplands and Southern Scotland, although the balance of his economy tilted steadily away from subsistence towards farming for the market.

Even in Cumbria, which included some of his last English strongholds, the owner-occupier farmer was in steady decline for most of the period. But the results of this attrition were not dramatic, for the way of life of the farmers changed relatively little. When the old yeomanry sold out, their lands tended to go to small purchasers: often industrialists from further south who wanted a stake in the Lake District landscape they had come to love. Beatrix Potter's purchase of Hill Top Farm (NT) at Sawrey in 1905 may stand for a number of similar transactions: she kept the existing occupants as her tenants, and allowed them to continue farming much as they had done hitherto, despite her alterations to the house and eager attention to the garden. The farmers of Torver or Dunnerdale might be less likely to own their land in 1914 than in 1750, but the continuities in their agricultural practices and routines were far more important to their lives than the gradual and unobtrusive divorce between landownership and farming which quietly spanned so many generations, and remained incomplete on the eve of the First World War.

Below the yeomanry there were smaller landowners still, whose holdings were insufficient to keep a family without extra sources of income. They eked out the bare living provided by a few acres and a cow or two by practising a trade (as did many yeomen), sending their children out to service or as

---

PREVIOUS PAGES *The stacking of hay could be a major operation on a large farm, as this picture makes clear; and it was a highly-skilled task, as the threat of spontaneous combustion had to be minimised. The regular farm-workers would be supplemented by migrant labourers for the hay harvest, and work would continue from dawn to dusk through the long daylight hours of early summer.*

labourers, or hiring their own labour out to farmers at busy periods like haytime or harvest. They often depended on customary rights to pasture animals and take turf and brushwood from the common. The enclosure of these open spaces, which were converted into the private property of individuals in a way which failed to compensate most cottagers and smallholders for lost rights of access and use, contributed to the continuing decline of small landowners during the century after 1750. The loss of rural industries and the lure of towns and urban industry also played their part. After the mid nineteenth century the small landowners who survived were increasingly likely to be market gardeners on the urban fringe, or specialists catering for urban markets, such as fruit farmers, rather than the traditional semi-independent husbandman (a word which declined in parallel with the use of 'yeoman') or cottager.

By the mid nineteenth century all who worked the land as owners or tenants, almost everywhere, were coming to be known simply as farmers. But this word covered an enormous range of experiences. Not only did it embrace owner-occupiers as well as tenants; it also included everyone from the occupier of hundreds of acres on a great estate, to the smallholder who depended solely on family labour and could barely scrape a living by adding extra sources of income.

The early Victorian censuses counted about a quarter of a million farmers in Britain (excluding Ireland); but fewer than 20,000 occupied large farms of 300 acres or more in 1885, and the vast majority had less than 50 acres. Throughout the late nineteenth and early twentieth century the average size of farm in England and Scotland was about 60 acres; in Wales it was just under 50. Farm sizes did not increase much over the whole period, except on some of the great estates. Even in a supposedly 'advanced' agricultural county like Norfolk, which was in the forefront of innovation in the late eighteenth century, more than half the farms in 1850 contained less than 100 acres.

There were good reasons for this. Tempted though improving landlords might be to concentrate their farms into the hands of large farmers with abundant capital and an incentive to adopt up-to-date methods with maximum efficiency, they knew that such men were in short supply. Smaller farms attracted a much wider range of potential takers, and the security of knowing that land could be let usually took precedence over the ideal of large farms and economies of scale. In any case, reorganising the farms on an estate was expensive

and disruptive. It required rearranged fields and tracks, new farm buildings and more imposing farmhouses. It might also involve evictions, which would be bad for the estate's image. Only the self-confident proprietors of the great estates could cope with all this, and not all of them chose to do so. It was much easier to lead by example, and an estate's Home Farm, like the one at Tatton Park (NT), could act as a showcase for new ideas and practices which tenants could be encouraged to emulate.

Farming could be big business, especially at the peak of mid Victorian prosperity. When Lodge Farm, at Castle Acre on the 2nd Earl of Leicester's Holkham estate in Norfolk, changed hands in 1878, the stock of the outgoing tenant was sold. The catalogue lists 24 cart-horses, 5 riding- and carriage-horses, 74 cattle and 1017 sheep. There were 30 ploughs and harrows and, among other things, a reaping machine, a threshing-drum, several turnip cutters, 15 wagons, 11 tumbrils, and a 9-horse-power portable steam-engine. All this was probably worth between £4000 and £5000, not including seed, manure and cattle feed. A farmer of this standing would keep four or five domestic servants, and employ up to 120 people to get in the harvest. He needed as much capital and labour as a substantial industrialist.

This was most unusual. The Holkham estate was famous for its high standards. By 1850 it included six giant farms like Lodge Farm with more than 1000 acres, and twenty-eight with more than 500. The tenant, John Hudson, was a leading member of the Royal Agricultural Society and an eager experimenter with manures and cattle-cake. Holkham's influence rubbed off elsewhere in Norfolk; on the Felbrigg estate (NT), for example, William Howe Windham strove to emulate it in the 1830s and 1840s by improving his farm buildings, draining and planting, marking each new piece of building with a stone tablet bearing his initials and the date. But much more typical, especially of upland northern and western England, were the mid Victorian farmers of Danby-in-Cleveland, in North Yorkshire. Here, the vicar reckoned that perhaps six or eight farms occupied more than 100 acres, while the rest, excluding smallholdings, 'scarcely average seventy-five acres each'. Many of the older farmers were still illiterate, and lived largely off their own produce. There were improved breeds of cattle, sheep and horses, and a few other innovations; but farmhouses were small and sometimes overcrowded, and in general traditional ways died hard. Some large landowners attempted to improve matters where outlying parts of their estates displayed such symptoms of backwardness. Thus Sir George Crewe of Calke tried from 1830 onwards to bring 'moral and economic enlightenment' to the 'backward and benighted people' of his Staffordshire moorlands estate, beginning with a general distribution of blankets and warm clothing and proceeding with a programme of moorland enclosure, and the building of churches, chapels, schools and parsonage houses. Likewise, from early in the nineteenth century the 4th Earl of Aberdeen took pains to rebuild farmhouses and impose improved farming methods on his extensive estates around Haddo House, which had been neglected by his predecessor.

Changes of this kind were most in evidence over much of southern, eastern and midland England and southern Scotland. In these areas the century after 1750 saw the emergence of growing numbers of substantial farmers, living in neat Georgian or Victorian Tudor farmhouses, employing increasingly sophisticated methods, developing aspirations to a genteel life-style and forming a rural middle class of considerable prestige and power. This was a minority experience, but a highly visible and important one.

The mixed farms of the Scottish lowlands also saw a rise in farming prosperity and farmers' pretensions, as did parts of Northumberland. Farms were rebuilt on a grander scale from the late eighteenth century onwards, and the 'steadings' or outbuildings were extended to accommodate more workers, plough horses and machinery. In the Lothians, farm-workers' accommodation was concentrated increasingly into the farm itself, and the detached cottages of semi-independent workers with their own plots of land disappeared from the landscape. Many farm settlements became almost self-sufficient on their isolated sites. But whereas large, highly-commercialised farms became completely dominant in East Lothian, smaller holdings remained numerous in the cattle and corn districts of north-east Scotland, where the older ways in general survived longer and more tenaciously.

The Highlands and Islands saw even more far-reaching changes. The defeat of the Jacobite army at Culloden in 1746 was the prelude to the wholesale dismantling of the clan as a military organisation based on kinship loyalties, and the introduction of an English-style system of estate management in which land was no longer farmed communally through a complex pattern of sub-tenancies, but divided up and let to the highest bidder. This suited the old clan chieftains, who needed extra cash to finance their expensive life-styles in Edinburgh, London or Paris, but it had dire implications for their dependants. The 'tacksmen', kinsmen of the chief who had been responsible for managing the estates to assure an ample supply of soldiers rather than cash, had no place under the new system. Increasingly in the late eighteenth century they found their farms let to outsiders and their traditional social position destroyed. Many emigrated, taking their sub-tenants and dependants with them in their embittered flight. Meanwhile, the old system of semi-subsistence farming and cattle rearing was abolished, and estates were carved up into enormous sheep ranches, run by outsiders and requiring very little labour. The redundant clansmen were uprooted from their ancestral lands, which they occupied by custom rather than by law, and decanted on to tiny plots of infertile land in new coastal settlements. Here they were expected to eke out a living by fishing and gathering seaweed to make kelp for sale to the growing chemical industries of the Lowlands and England.

This transformation was well advanced by the early nineteenth century. The evictions, and the setting up of the new coastal settlements of 'crofters', have become infamous as the 'Highland Clearances'. Their apologists claim that they 'modernised' and 'civilised' the Highlands, and prevented a disastrous famine of Irish proportions. But the cost in human suffering – including famine – was immense. Fishing was a terribly insecure operation, and the demand for kelp collapsed calamitously in the mid 1820s, leaving the crofters to depend on the potatoes which enabled them to scratch a living from their little plots. When the potato blight appeared in 1846, thousands of families were left to try to survive on shellfish, sand eels and whatever relief could be gleaned from landlords and central government. A further round of evictions and enforced emigration followed, while many of the old chieftains' families went bankrupt and were replaced by speculative outsiders. In less than a century a whole social system had collapsed, and the Highland landscape and way of life had undergone a drastic and irreversible revolution.

Those crofters who endured saw the great sheep ranches pass away in their turn, undermined by the fall in the price of wool in the late nineteenth century. Where the terrain was suitable, they gave way to deer forests, a profitable way of parting aristocrats and industrialists from their wealth.

Georgian country-house landscaping at its finest : the Pantheon at
Stourhead, Wiltshire, beautifully picked out by slanting sunlight
across the lake.

LEFT *The gothick east front of Castle Ward, Co. Down, an odd combination of battlements and pinnacles with classical symmetry and urns. The second-floor windows to left and right have delightfully eccentric tracery.*

BELOW *The Great Parlour at Wightwick Manor, Staffordshire, with its sumptuous display of patterns, textures and designs on walls and ceilings, and in the enormous fireplace with its cosy ingle-nooks on either side.*

RIGHT *The morning-room at Standen, West Sussex. Philip Webb's austerity is tempered by the glories of the 'daffodil chintz' wall hangings, from one of the last designs of William Morris.*

BELOW *The grand manner of the 'smart' Edwardian country house : the drawing-room at Polesden Lacey, Surrey, with its ostentatious gilding and displays of French furniture and oriental porcelain.*

ABOVE *Elswick Works,
Newcastle upon Tyne, in
1886 : this vast industrial
complex generated most of
the money which supported
Sir William Armstrong's
life-style at Cragside.*

*The real Cragside is solid
and substantial, despite its
unlikely setting halfway up
a Northumbrian hill ; but
this delightful water-colour
turns it into an ethereal
fairy palace, which might
vanish with the passage of a
cloud across the sun.*

There is nothing ethereal about the overwhelming marble chimneypiece in the drawing-room at Cragside : it is a blunt expression of command over wealth and materials, and pride in possession.

One of the treasures which flowed into Britain with the returning 'nabobs' of the East India Company : Mir Kalan Khan's depiction of a lion hunt, from the Clive Museum at Powis Castle in north Wales.

RIGHT *Almost the ultimate location for a 'romantic' country house : Lindisfarne Castle, Northumberland, perched on its rock overlooking the monastic remains on Holy Island, which is connected to the mainland solely by a tidal causeway.*

INSET RIGHT *The Ship Room at Lindisfarne Castle, showing the starkness and limited array of creature comforts in this austerely renovated Northumbrian fortress.*

OVERLEAF *The interior of Sir John Soane's great barn at Wimpole, Cambridgeshire, designed as part of the Home Farm complex of 1794, showing some of the carts and farm machinery which are displayed there.*

Ulster's small farms required hard physical work from all members of the family. This picture shows young women breaking clods before setting seed potatoes at Glenshesk, Co. Antrim.

Meanwhile, the crofters themselves were becoming a political force, and trying to gain a measure of security against rising rents and the threat of eviction. They also began to agitate for the restoration of their lost rights and lands. From 1882 onwards, conflict on these issues was endemic in many parts of the Highlands and Islands. It was palliated, but not resolved, by the Crofters Act of 1886, and bitter disputes continued beyond the First World War.

Ulster was different again. Holdings remained very small: throughout the later nineteenth century nine-tenths of the farms had fewer than 50 acres. For most of the century after 1750 most families combined farming with linen or cotton weaving, and from the 1830s shirtmaking became important around Londonderry. Farmers sublet even smaller plots to 'cottiers' until the famine of the later 1840s reduced pressure on the land. The farmers themselves, who depended almost entirely on family labour, survived the famine and the subsequent decline of most domestic manufactures, and benefited from legal changes in the later nineteenth century. The layers of middlemen who had taken their profit on the administration of the gentry estates were gradually displaced by salaried stewards, and the 'Ulster custom' guaranteed an unusual degree of security of tenure and the right to pass the tenancy on for a cash payment, which was usually not the case in the rest of Britain. Legislation from the 1880s made it easier for Irish tenants to buy their farms, and this was widely taken up in Ulster. In the province as a whole, more than two-thirds of the farmers were owner-occupiers by 1913, in remarkable contrast with the rest of Britain.

In Britain as a whole, substantial farmers prospered for most of the period. For more than half a century after 1750 agricultural prices were buoyant, although some farmers suffered from runs of bad harvests at the turn of the century. Population growth outstripped expanding production, and imports were restrained by the steady tightening of the Corn Laws, protecting arable farmers from foreign competition. Meanwhile wage levels were held down by rising rural population. There were bad years after the end of the Napoleonic Wars in 1815, especially for farmers who had borrowed excessively to extend their cornfields into places that had never been cultivated before and were never to grow crops again. But there were renewed good times in the early and mid Victorian years, as railways and steamships opened out new markets and landowners invested confidently in their estates. The repeal of the Corn Laws in 1846, as Free Trade ideas became dominant, opened the way to imports of foreign grain, but the full impact of these was delayed until the great influx of North American wheat began more than a generation later.

Only from the late 1870s did a sustained fall in farmers' fortunes begin, with the so-called 'great agricultural depression', as imports flooded British markets. The worst sufferers were the wheat farmers of the south and east, who were undercut by the new producers of the Great Plains. There were many bankruptcies, rents fell sharply, and arable farms reverted to grass under the canny management of Scots from Clydesdale and Ayrshire.

Pastoral farming came under much less pressure, as the prices of high quality meat and dairy produce held firm, and cattle-feed costs actually fell. The sustained optimism and confidence of the 1850s and 1860s was never to be repeated, but until the late nineteenth century British farmers in general were doing very well indeed, as was shown by the queues for vacant holdings, which only fell away in the worst years of the depression in those places which were most badly affected, such as Essex. Unless they were demonstrably incompetent, farmers could expect to be helped through hard times by rent rebates and permitted arrears from landlords who also provided much of their improvement capital; and wage costs remained low despite rising productivity. Over most of Britain, for most of the period, farmers contrived in large measure to have the best of both worlds, and they prospered accordingly.

Some of this success was achieved at the expense of the rural labourers. They suffered as agriculture prospered and, in seeming paradox, their fortunes did not improve until the price of necessities began to fall under the same influences that brought about the late Victorian 'agricultural depression'. In southern and eastern England, especially, a grim conspiracy of changes forced living standards down between the later eighteenth century and the 1830s. Population growth and sharpening seasonal fluctuations in the demand for labour enabled farmers to pay starvation wages, lay men off when they were not needed, and abandon the practice of boarding labourers in the farmhouse. Workers were kept on the land by making up their income to the barest possible subsistence through the Poor Law. Women's work opportunities declined, and the loss of access to commons and woodland for grazing and fuel made its mark. The old routes to a smallholding and a measure of independence were sealed off.

These changes removed the opportunity to save and the incentive to defer marriage, and created a climate of apathy and demoralization, as large families depended on parish poor relief for their survival through the long slack periods of the farming calendar. Many labouring families in these areas survived on bread, 'tea kettle broth' (hot water with a flavouring of herbs or bacon) and weak tea (sometimes simulated by the use of burnt toast to colour the water). What little cheese and bacon there was went to the man to sustain him, inefficiently, in his outdoor labour. Housing was appalling, and the damp, overcrowded hovels bred rheumatism as well as infectious diseases. The widespread decline of cottage industries made matters even worse, and the New Poor Law of 1834, with its threat to incarcerate the unemployed in workhouses and break up their families, was almost the last straw. Fortunately, it was not carried out to the full, as the farmers who ran the rural Poor Law found it cheaper to relieve the able-bodied in other ways, and workhouse populations continued to be dominated by the sick and elderly.

The decline of farm service over much of lowland England was part of this pattern. Farm servants who lived in, as opposed to day-labourers who lived in cottages, were usually hired for six months or a year. They were paid their keep, plus a lump sum, agreed when they were hired, at the end of their term of engagement. Most were young, and the vast majority were unmarried. On the credit side, such workers were assured of their keep, and were able to save during the year. On the other hand, it was difficult to escape from a bad employer, and farm servants had little time they could with certainty call their own, coming as they did under the paternal discipline of the house-holder.

The day-labourer in his cottage received a much higher proportion of his wage in cash, and in theory this gave him more choice about how to spend it. Marriage was also a practical possibility. But income was unreliable: the demand for labour varied with the agricultural calendar, and labourers were often laid off when the weather was too bad to work outside. Shorter daylight hours meant lower wages in winter, too. So the cottager had more freedom in theory, but less security in practice; and his income was seldom enough to bring up a family without spells of hunger and dependence on charity or poor relief, or to make provision for the most basic of subsistence in old age.

There were several reasons for the strongly marked transition from farm service to day-labouring, especially in southern and eastern England, in the later eighteenth and early nineteenth century. Rising grain prices meant that it cost the farmer more to feed the labourers in the farmhouse than to pay a money wage and let them fend for themselves. Increased specialisation in wheat-growing meant that labour needs were concentrated more into certain parts of the year, so there was no need to employ such a numerous permanent work-force as before. Hiring for the year entitled servants to poor relief from the farmer's parish, and threatened to put the rates up, though some farmers solved the problem by hiring for 51 weeks instead of the whole year. Prospering farmers with pianos, idle daughters and social pretensions increasingly preferred to safeguard their privacy by banishing their employees from their homes; and the greed and snobbery of a new generation of farmers was blamed by many, in the 1820s and 1830s, for deepening problems of poverty and social conflict in southern and eastern England.

By 1850 farm servants were a small minority in lowland England. Living in, and the security that went with it, became the preserve of key workers, especially horsemen: wagoners, carters and plough-men. These were men with scarce skills which

The business part of a Victorian hiring fair at Burford, Oxfordshire. There would be livelier times ahead in the evening, with drinking and dancing into the small hours.

were needed throughout the year, and in Kent, for example, they continued to be boarded in the farmhouse right up to 1914. For Jack Larkin, who was lucky in his employer, this meant a comfortable living:

We used to have our meals in the farmhouse and there was a bit of an old cottage attached to it and we used to sleep in there. The farmer always had a barrel of beer in and we used to have small beer for breakfast, ale for dinner and small beer for tea. . . . For breakfast . . . was a darn great lump of fat pork, half a loaf . . . and, if they'd got plenty of milk, a jolly great bowl of bread and milk. That was something to go to work on.

For labourers in general there was little improvement in rural living standards in the south and east until the 1870s. The inmates of workhouses and prisons enjoyed a better diet and warmer winter quarters than many labouring families. The model estates were too few and too scattered to address the housing problem, and sanitation and water-supply remained primitive and dangerous. It took the general cheapening of basic food prices from the late 1870s, together with accelerating migration off the land (enabling wages to rise) and the increasing accessibility of urban shops and travelling vendors, to raise living standards so that meat could be eaten more than occasionally. But a survey of rural England on the eve of the First World War showed that only in the north did agricultural wages suffice to keep an average family in a state of 'merely physical efficiency', if nothing was spent on drink, tobacco or other frivolities.

Throughout the period conditions on the land were much better in the north and west of England (Devon excepted) and the Scottish lowlands. Wherever pastoral or mixed farming provided regular year-round employment, farm service survived, and nearby industries offered competition for labour which pulled wages up, the labourer's lot was tolerable and the cost of poor relief was correspondingly low. In upland areas members of the farmer's family increasingly did most of the work on small pastoral farms. In late Victorian Wales and Cumbria half of the male farm-workers were family members, and in Ulster in 1913 three-quarters of those who worked the land were farmers themselves or relatives who lived with them. All too often such labour was exploited and relatives were badly underpaid, but at least the family offered subsistence and mutual support in most cases.

Diet in most of these areas was based on oatmeal and milk rather than wheaten bread and weak tea,

and was more nutritious and sustaining. Many Scottish labourers were able to keep a cow. In much of Wales and Scotland, too, wages continued to be paid partly in kind. These payments were being traded for cash in the late nineteenth century, when white bread and jam began to oust porridge from the affections of Scottish labourers. But the rural workers of northern England and most of Scotland were consistently better nourished, taller and stronger than their southern counterparts. Housing was slow to improve. Single-roomed cottages with box beds and no amenities remained standard in the Borders and Lowlands, and labourers were expected to provide 'their own oven, copper, grate, shelves . . . partitions and window frames, and some sort of substitute for a ceiling', which they took with them from hiring to hiring. The bothies and chaumers in which farm servants lodged in north-eastern Scotland were notoriously spartan. But in general the contrast with Norfolk or Dorset was sharp. Labourers in the Highlands and Islands could challenge the poverty of the south: the 'scallags' of Harris, for example, who lived in portable sod huts and were effectively slaves, paid in kind, for the duration of their hire. But these were a small and remote minority in an area where most farm work was done by family labour.

Agricultural work had its own hierarchies of skill, payment and respect. Alun Howkins tells us that, 'At the top of the farm workforce in Norfolk stood the man who worked the horses, the teamman . . . under horse culture even a relatively small farm of 100–150 acres employed two or three teammen'. Within this group, there was a further hierarchy, as Bert Hazel remembered:

When we were working in the plough teams (the head team-man) would take the lead, and nobody would dare to leave the yard until he'd got onto his horse, and he'd go in front. He'd be followed by the second team-man and then subsequently down the line.

The same custom prevailed in Aberdeenshire. The ploughing contests which spread through arable Britain bore witness to the pride these highly-skilled men took in their craft and their mastery of their enormous horses. Dairymen and shepherds also had an acknowledged expertise and independence which set them above the ordinary farm-worker.

But to speak of 'ordinary' farm-workers is to devalue them. They might be badly paid, and looked down upon as slow and ignorant by townsmen and employers, but they had to acquire

the ability to use a wide range of tools quickly and safely. The skill and stamina required to wield a sickle or scythe through the heat of the harvest day illustrates this point. One of Alun Howkins' interviewees gave a less glamorous example of unsung skills at work, in the autumn and winter root harvest:

You grasped the leaves of the mangold with the left hand. . . . You pulled (it) out of the ground, swung it upwards, and at the right moment slipped your knife blade through the leaves where they joined the root. Then, if you had judged it correctly, the mangold flew into the cart and you were left with the leaves. . . . You dropped them, and stooped to pull another. The whole process took the labourer one second.

This was in mild weather: this back-breaking work became another matter when the mangolds froze in the winter earth. And one miscalculation or lapse of concentration might mean a lost finger or thumb.

Migrant workers also made important contributions. These included independent craftsmen, such as hedgers or thatchers, who did contract work for a variety of employers. But there were also bands of itinerant harvesters who followed the hay and grain harvests, or went hopping or fruit-picking. The Scottish Lowlands saw annual influxes of Irishmen and Highland women, trying to sustain the marginal economies of their families back home. Spinners, weavers, colliers and even schoolteachers from nearby towns might swell the numbers. In England, too, the Irish were ubiquitous. But there were other sources of harvest labour. Southern labourers might travel north to join the later harvests in Yorkshire, and all the large

93

A striking photograph of horse husbandry on a Derbyshire farm, just before the advent of the tractor.

towns and industrial districts sent out harvesters and haymakers. The annual exodus from London's East End to the Kentish hop-gardens was paralleled by the mass migration of Black Country metalworkers to the fruit-picking in the Vale of Evesham and the hopping in Herefordshire. Sheffield lead-workers, Lancashire weavers and miners everywhere might be lured away to haymaking, often in their old home villages. In winter, with little agricultural work available, there were reverse migrations, like those of East Anglian farm-workers to the Burton-on-Trent breweries. All these exchanges of people helped to maintain contact between country and town: they did not exist in separate, isolated compartments.

Women's work was important at harvest time, as was their contribution to agriculture more generally. But the range of jobs they did narrowed sharply in southern and eastern England after 1750. As K. D. M. Snell says, their work had extended to 'reaping, loading and spreading dung, ploughing, threshing, thatching, following the harrow, sheep shearing and even working as shepherdesses'. By the early 1840s they were largely confined to weeding, stone clearing, helping with haymaking, and the dairying and poultry work which remained a female preserve. In the west, increasing concentration on milk, butter and cheese gave women a higher profile, whether as farmers' wives, working daughters or farm servants. And in Northumberland and the mixed farming areas of southern and eastern Scotland, women continued to perform a very wide range of activities. They were particularly important in the economies of fishing villages, performing such

Adolescent boys might be expected to do adult work at an early age: this is another view of farm life at Glenshesk, Co. Antrim (see p. 89).

tasks as gutting and cleaning fish and mending nets, and following the herring boats southwards for the autumn season.

But all farm work with horses was a male prerogative, and the northward spread of the scythe, a heavy implement which was thought unsuitable for women, reduced the importance in the harvest field of the sickle, the 'heuk', and the women who wielded them. More generally, new technologies came to be defined as men's work. On the other hand women continued to be attractive as employees because they were cheap (half the wage of a man) and easy to control. Only at the very end of the nineteenth century did long hours and low wages begin to take their toll, as women in lowland Scotland followed their English sisters into the towns, and field-work came to be seen as a coarsening and improper activity for delicate and vulnerable females. This point of view had already hardened into an orthodoxy in mid Victorian England, where cheap and abundant male labour left little room for women on the arable farms of the south and east, although innovations like potato-digging machinery continued to create new possibilities for women's work in places long after this period.

Farm-workers' children began work early. Contributions to the family budget were urgently needed. The most infamous use of child labour in rural areas was the gang system which flourished in the mid nineteenth century, especially in East Anglia. In areas of large arable farms and scattered villages, men contracted to supply and supervise women and children for weeding and stone-

picking. Children of five years old might be
required to walk several miles in bitter cold to and
from work, with a long day of strictly-supervised
toil in between. When serious abuses were exposed
in 1867, legislation followed, and the under-eights
were banned from the gangs. But children
continued to be used as bird-scarers, animal
minders, or helpers at the plough or at harvest. The
need for a child's wage took precedence over school
or play in much of England, even when attempts
were made to impose compulsory schooling from
the 1870s. This did retard the starting age for full-
time work, and the late Victorian depression in
arable farming led to untidier fields and less work
for children as farmers economised on labour. But
children's work remained an inescapable necessity
in most rural labouring families.

Children also worked in rural cottage industries:
not just spinning and weaving, which became so
important on the Pennine uplands and elsewhere,
but also stocking-knitting in the East Midlands,

*Children's work at harvest time was a serious business, as
these preoccupied faces show.*

straw-plaiting and pillow-lace making a little
further south, and many others. Most of these
industries dovetailed with small-scale agriculture
until at least the early nineteenth century, and
many miners and metalworkers also had small
farms. The divorce between farming and industry
was gradual and piecemeal. The same applied to
the relationship between fishing, farming and
domestic manufacture in many coastal villages. By
the 1830s and 1840s most of the older crafts were
declining or being transferred to urban factories,
while once-thriving rural societies like the lead-
mining and cowkeeping smallholders of the windswept northern Pennines were being threatened by
foreign competition. But for much of this period
mining and manufacturing had an important

The house and workshop of the village souter, or cobbler, at Kirkoswald, near Maybole, Strathclyde. John Davidson, the 'Souter Johnnie' of Burns' Tam O'Shanter, *lived here.*

presence over wide tracts of British countryside. Most of the early textile factories had rural settings and a high proportion of the children who worked in early water-powered cotton mills had fathers who worked on the land. Some of these industries left deep and enduring evidence on landscape, experiences and values.

In all but the smallest settlements there were traders, craftsmen and the odd professional to supply and service the farmers and labourers. Thus East Hoathly in Sussex in the 1750s supported a general shop, three pubs, two shoemakers, two tailors, a butcher, a chandler, a schoolmaster, an excise officer, a brickmaker, a postman, a carrier, a carpenter, a miller and the inevitable blacksmith and clergyman. A century later, Elmdon in Essex still had a very similar array of trades. The pattern was only just beginning to change on the eve of the First World War. Such traders often had deep local roots, but they were also important as intermediaries between the village and the outside world at a level below that of the squire and clergy.

There were many varieties of village. At one extreme was the estate village, such as Bradenham or West Wycombe (NT), where the squire and his agent, in conjunction with the parson, were able to exercise extensive economic and moral controls over a largely dependent population. At the other extreme was the 'open' settlement, like Morwenstow or Troutbeck, a straggling village or scattering of farmsteads whose land was divided among many owners. Open villages often supplied much of the labour on nearby large estates whose owners were unwilling to build houses and pay poor rates on their own land. The open village was often a rural slum built largely by speculating tradesmen, but without it rural housing in general, and overcrowding especially, would have been even worse. Many villages fell between the extremes, and full-scale estate villages were always a small minority. As Professor Thompson argues, the paternalism of large landowners 'was restricted and localized in its appearances. . . . Pockets of sheltered, protected and regimented rural communities studded a landscape populated by much more independent, self-reliant and exposed villages. . . .'

Open villages could have very complex economies. Magilligan, on the eastern shore of Lough Foyle in County Londonderry, was owned by large absentee landlords who exercised little control over their tenants and sub-tenants. During the century after 1750 they grew corn, fattened cattle and 'finished' sheep, pasturing them to improve the texture of their wool. There was also some flax-

growing and linen spinning. But the resourceful inhabitants also cultivated rabbits in extensive warrens, distilled illicit whiskey and poteen, sold special honey from their meadows, accommodated wealthy visitors who came for the sea-bathing and to drink the herb-rich whey from the local goats, netted seabirds, fished, made matting for floor coverings from marram grass, and sold oysters and cockles. This diversity was unusual, but it shows that there could be more to rural life than corn and cattle.

But these were the mainstays, and it was to producing more of them that the ingenuity of agricultural improvers was directed. For most of the century after 1750 this meant the more efficient use of the land, and the enhancement of its capacity, through further enclosure, the use of crop rotations which did not exhaust the land, and fuller use of manures and other soil dressings. On the lighter soils of the south and east, especially, clover and other fodder crops were brought into rotations, putting the land into better heart and enabling more cattle and sheep to be kept. These in turn supplied additional manure. These ways of working were not new, but they were widely adopted by improving landowners, who often

A thatched cabin with turf walls at Magilligan, Co. Derry. This kind of dwelling had many counterparts in the Scottish Highlands and Islands as well as elsewhere in Ireland.

imposed them on tenants through clauses in their leases, and by the contagion of successful example. Such techniques were not suitable everywhere, however, and over much of the Midlands 'convertible husbandry' became the rule, in which several years of pasture were alternated with two or three successive grain crops: another kind of mixed farming with a much stronger pastoral element. Again, this was less a matter of the sudden introduction of brand new methods, than the gradual adoption of ways of working which had a long pedigree and were refined and spread over several generations. The impact of the selective breeding of livestock, especially on the small farms of the mainly pastoral north and west, was likewise diffuse and long-term.

Alongside these developments came the further spread of enclosure. Over much of lowland England, especially in the Midlands, the old open fields were rearranged, and the scattered strips were consolidated into separate blocks of land for individual farmers. More generally, common land was also being divided up among those who had a legal right to use it: those whose rights were merely customary lost out. This was a process which continued far into the nineteenth century in the uplands of the north and west, marking the bare fellsides with geometrical patterns of implacably marching, wonderfully-crafted stone dividing walls, as on the National Trust's estates in the Lake District above Troutbeck or Coniston. On the lowlands, the hawthorn or 'quickset' hedge achieved the same results. Enclosure could be traumatic for the smaller occupiers and labourers, but often it was the culmination of a long process of piecemeal rearrangement of the open fields. It expressed a long trend towards more individualist, competitive and profit-maximising farming, away from communal regulation and the sharing out of good land and bad. Often it enhanced productivity and helped to bring prosperity to the larger farmers; but there were costs of many kinds to set against these benefits.

The 1830s and 1840s ushered in new patterns of change. The use of tile drainage improved the intractable heavy clay soils of midland England, and eased the lot of farmers over a much wider area. For the first time, agricultural machinery began to be factory-made in large quantities by firms like Ransomes of Ipswich, turning the village blacksmith into a repairer and servicer rather than a manufacturer in his own right. Reaping-, binding- and threshing-machines spread rapidly, together with seed drills and the new iron ploughs; and

increasingly in the mid Victorian years steam power was harnessed to agriculture, especially in the harvest field and the threshing barn. Some large farmers owned their own steam-powered machines, but most hired from contractors; and even in the prosperous and innovative mid Victorian decades the impact of the high technology of the time should not be exaggerated. Ploughing by steam never really caught on: it was too difficult and too expensive. Small, steep and stony fields remained the preserve of the sickle and the scythe. New technologies had little to offer the small pastoral farmer of the uplands, though primitive milking-machines were available by the 1890s.

Steam's most important contribution was indirect: through the railways which opened out new markets, encouraged specialisation and helped to speed competing imports on their way. Perhaps the most generally important innovations on the farm were the new manures, Peruvian guano and assorted manufactured concoctions; and expenditure on new farm buildings far outweighed spending on technology. Above all, farming remained heavily dependent on the muscle power of horses and people. The replacement of oxen by horses as draught animals had been an important theme of the eighteenth century; and significantly the number of horses used in British agriculture grew even in the last quarter of the nineteenth century, from 1.7 to 2 million. It took the tractor in the inter-war years to make the most dramatic revolution in British farming. Meanwhile, the most important input continued to be cheap labour, for the daily round of farming tasks. The machines that were adopted saved labour where it was most expensive, at seed-time and harvest. Despite the innovations, what counted most, at the end of the period as at the beginning, was the skill and toil of the labourers.

In areas of small pastoral farms, like the Lake District and the Welsh uplands, industry and frugality might be rewarded, as farm servants and labourers could hope to inherit a holding, or save to acquire one of their own. Even in Norfolk a few labourers became small farmers, and others set up as petty traders, hawking shellfish or working as bootmakers or carpenters. But the best escape route from the grinding rural poverty of this period was migration. Some of the rural surplus of births

OVERLEAF *Prospective buyers inspect the finer points of horses in a Welsh market town at the turn of the century.*

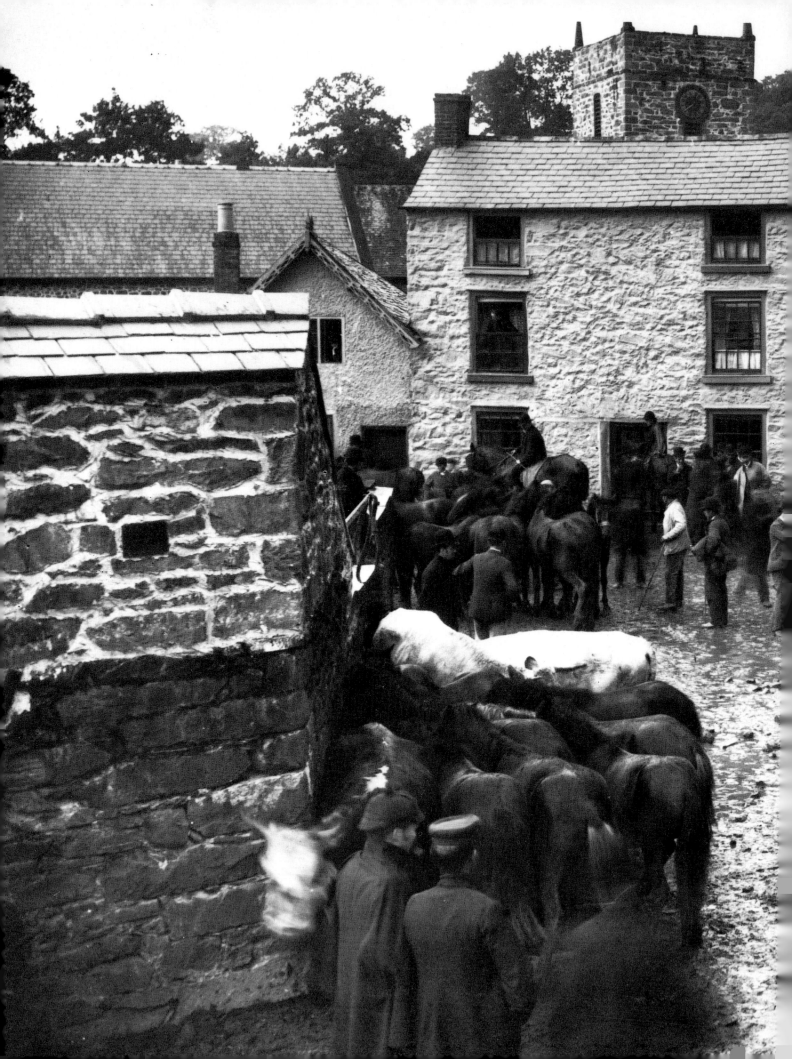

Upland enclosure in Wensleydale: Penhill, between Aysgarth and Wensley, with stone walls reaching almost to its summit.

over deaths was already being siphoned off to the towns in the eighteenth century, and emigration from the Highlands and Islands was beginning in the 1770s, especially to Canada. Men and women from Ulster were joining the Highland exodus to North America in considerable numbers by the early nineteenth century, though many were farmers' sons and craftsmen rather than agricultural labourers.

Migration from the English countryside increased steadily for most of the nineteenth century, culminating in widespread rural population decline after 1851. Part of this 'flight from the land' found its way to the colonies, sometimes with trade-union sponsorship. But by the early Victorian years the most marked aspect of rural migration in England was the extensive employment of teenage girls in domestic service. This followed naturally from the decline of women's work on the land, the poverty of many labouring families and the growing purchasing power of the urban middle classes. By the late nineteenth century many villages, like Flora Thompson's *Lark Rise*, were almost denuded of young women for most of the year. But the men went too, finding that many rural skills, especially involving the management of horses, were also needed in towns. Thus nearly half of the Great Northern Railway's London stablemen in 1906 were former agricultural workers, as were between a quarter and a third of the work-forces of several large London employers. By the turn of the century the exodus was leaving ageing labour forces and a falling birthrate in the countryside, as the liveliest, best-educated and most enterprising left for brighter lights and better opportunities elsewhere.

In much of England this process accelerated the decline of traditional ways of life and patterns of belief. The older rural culture was based on mutual help, reciprocity and participation in the shared rituals of village life. Christenings and burials, especially, were celebrated in ways which involved neighbours and the wider community as well as family. There were shared superstitions among people whose work kept them close to the inscrutably unpredictable ways of the natural world. Boggarts and ghosts abounded, witchcraft was an ever-present threat, and the Devil was quite

likely to appear in person to claim his own. Rituals had to be observed to appease the occult powers which teemed just beyond the range of the conventional senses. In Lincolnshire the cutting of elder wood had to be prefaced by seeking the permission of the 'Owd Gal', the guardian spirit of elder trees. If all else failed, there were wise men or women, learned in astrology and other supernatural lore, within walking distance. This was predominantly an oral culture, within which traditional songs passed from mouth to mouth; and it was a communal culture, as the preference for dances in sets and rounds rather than couples neatly indicated.

These ways were already in decline in early Victorian times. The gentry and larger farmers detached themselves from the festivities and public rituals of the village, withdrawing their patronage and often trying to suppress the wilder or more threatening activities. The rise of evangelical Nonconformity among the labourers undermined beliefs and practices which now seemed to have pagan or immoral connotations. The spread of the printed word, increased literacy and easier mobility played their part in the erosion of a protective core of local certainties. The broadsheet displaced the folk song, although in exchange many folk songs found their way into print. The 'flight from the land' accentuated these processes by inhibiting the transmission of older values to a new and more worldy-wise generation.

Attempts to suppress traditional games and festivities sometimes provoked conflict; and so, at times, did other issues. Relations between landlord and tenant were not always trouble-free; but in England there was rarely sustained or organised discontent about rents and conditions. Most farmers were secure in their occupancy of their holdings. Evictions for voting against the landlord or his candidate at election time were not unknown, but they were always, and increasingly, rare. Tenant farmers were capable of putting their own candidates forward when they felt that their interests were not being looked after, as in Nottinghamshire in the mid nineteenth century when tenants were unhappy about their landlords' position on the Corn Laws. During the troubled decades of the late nineteenth century farmers' organisations did begin to multiply, urging fair rents, security of tenure and compensation on leaving for improvements made to the property. But in general English farmers continued to display an overriding identity of interests with their landlords on the great issues of the day.

But in parts of Wales, the Scottish Highlands and Ulster, tensions sometimes ran deeper and farmers might become militant. This was especially the case in Ulster in the late 1870s and early 1880s, when grievances over rent levels and evictions gave rise to violent assaults, arson, threatening letters and even the occasional homicide. In the Highlands and Islands there were regular rent strikes and forcible occupations of farms and disputed grazing land from the 1880s onwards. The Crofters Land Act of 1886 provided security of tenure and a system for assessing fair rents which was very well received by the crofters themselves; but it did not assuage their land hunger, and the landless cottars remained especially bitter about the expropriation of their forefathers in the Clearances. Thus in Kintail (NTS), which had passed through the full cycle of evictions, the installation of sheep farms, famine and the decline of the ranching economy, twenty cottars occupied waste land near their landlord's residence, Morvich House, in 1886, and began to plough for their own families. Similar activities repeatedly led to confrontations and arrests all over the region. Parts of Wales also saw similar conflicts. These were areas where absentee landlords predominated, and in many cases there were religious, linguistic and cultural divisions between landlord and tenant. They offer a reminder that the experience of the Celtic areas of northern and western Britain could differ very widely indeed from the English pattern.

In England, however, it was the grievances of the labourers that generated the most widespread and endemic conflict, especially in the south and east and the West Country. The worsening circumstances of the rural labour force brought a variety of responses from the victims. Grain riots were frequent in the later eighteenth and early nineteenth century: they were directed against those farmers and speculators who tried to maximise their profits at the expense of the wage-earning consumer. The rioters sought to fix prices at a 'fair', affordable level, and to restrain dealers from removing grain for resale elsewhere in time of shortage. As conditions worsened after the Napoleonic Wars, there were uprisings in East Anglia in 1816 and 1822, and in 1830 renewed disturbances spread across the whole of the south and east, extending tentacles into the Midlands and sparking isolated outbreaks further north. The main target of these 'Swing Riots' was the threshing-machines which were being introduced on growing numbers of farms, depriving labourers of the monotonous, badly-paid but precious winter work of hand-threshing with the flail. Machines were destroyed, ricks were burnt, threatening letters were sent and higher wages were sought during that desperate winter of high prices and little work. Like the grain riots, these were generally disciplined disturbances aimed at specific targets, and some magistrates showed sympathy with the labourers' plight. But the alarm of central government was expressed in a brutal judicial response: 252 of the rioters were sentenced to death, 19 were actually hanged, and 481 were transported to Australia, effectively for life.

This was the 'Last Labourers' Rising'. It was remembered long afterwards in the villages: W. H. Hudson was being told vivid stories about it by aged Wiltshire people nearly eighty years later. Despite the harsh penalties, there were renewed disturbances in opposition to the New Poor Law in the mid 1830s, when a few attempts were also made to form agricultural trade unions. These included the ill-fated venture at Tolpuddle in Dorset, where the famous Tolpuddle Martyrs were transported for allegedly taking illegal oaths: trade unions themselves were ostensibly legal by this time. But from the mid 1830s onwards, a generation of rural labourers suffered in silence and isolation. The crimes of hunger, such as poaching and sheep-stealing, and the outrages of fury and frustration, such as cattle-maiming and especially arson, continued. Not all such crimes were of this nature, of course: there were organised gangs of poachers who made a business of their dangerous calling. But the lack of overt protest from the half-starved labourers of the south and east does not mean that harmony and deference were restored. The labourers might doff their hats and do their work, but the ostentatious refusal of many to help put out barnyard fires was eloquent testimony to their real feelings.

In the early 1870s, agricultural labourers began in earnest to organise into trade unions, in the English midlands and the Scottish lowlands as well as in the south and east. In the nature of agricultural work, strikes were difficult to organise beyond the immediate grievance, the farm and the locality, and the unions lost ground between each burst of activity. Their members were vulnerable to the blacklist, and many had to seek work outside agriculture. But their strength was growing, and their influence spreading into new areas, on the eve of the First World War. For the most part, their quarrel was more directly with farmers and village worthies than with landowners; and throughout

The Swing Riots of 1830, presented by a cartoonist who was sympathetic to the rioters' grievances, as the dialogue to the right of the blazing rick makes clear.

the period the labourers' energies were devoted to trying to improve their lot within the existing system, rather than to change it root and branch. What they sought was fair treatment and a living wage; and their trade-union activists included the most respectable of working men, Primitive Methodist lay preachers and earnest supporters of Gladstone's Liberal Party. Joseph Arch, the hedger and ditcher who led the first National Agricultural Labourers' Union from its foundation in 1872, and became a Liberal MP in 1885, was cast squarely in this mould. The moderation of such people was as remarkable as their dedication; and the rise of the labourers' unions went hand in hand with a steady decline in rural crime, drunkenness, and outrages.

Rural society in Britain was more complex than it might appear at first sight. Not only were there important differences within the ranks of aristoc-racy, gentry, farmers, tradesmen and labourers: there were also variations between regions and types of agriculture, and from place to place. It should therefore not be surprising to find that not all aristocrats were benevolent paternalists, and not all labourers were uncritically accepting of their lot. Many hid their thoughts behind a veil of stolid taciturnity which some outside observers mistook for bovine stupidity and ignorance. Many, no doubt, were outwardly deferential and inwardly angry or contemptuous. Indeed, Patrick Joyce has suggested that the most deferential, unquestioning work-forces in Victorian England were to be found in the textile factories rather than the fields. This may seem paradoxical, in the light of the reputation of factory workers for political radicalism and trade-union activity; and Joyce himself would agree that it is only part of the story. But as we move on to look at the rise of industry in the 'first industrial nation', it may be useful to bear this apparent paradox in mind. There may be something in it, and it may help to explain the remarkable political stability which underpinned the unprecedented economic and social changes in the Britain of the Industrial Revolution.

CHAPTER FIVE

Factories and Industries

The Industrial Revolution was not a sudden event: it was a long process. Historians now agree that the growth of industry and trade in Britain accelerated gently but cumulatively over a long period; that there was no dramatic turning-point in the late eighteenth century, except in a few distinctive industries; that the cotton industry was less important to the economy as a whole than had been thought; that in many respects the most impressive period of growth and change came in the early railway age, the middle decades of the nineteenth century; and that for most of the nineteenth century the workshop remained more important than the factory, the small firm more pervasive than the giant combine. As late as 1870 the steam-engine, that potent emblem of the Industrial Revolution, was so far from being dominant in manufacturing that half the steam power in Britain's factories was concentrated into textiles and ironworking. British manufacturing depended heavily on hand technology until well beyond the middle of the nineteenth century.

The key change in the eighteenth-century British economy was unobtrusive but crucial. It was a shift in the balance of employment and investment from agriculture to trade and industry, accomplished through the gradual spread and accumulation of cottage industries and the multi-plication of small mines and quarries. The multi-storeyed factories, flaring furnaces and deep mines were the impressive exceptions rather than the rule. So the roots of Britain's industrial transfor-mation lie in the eighteenth-century expansion of domestic manufacture, the 'cottage industry' of the weavers, nailmakers and so many others whose home was also their workshop.

We do not know what proportion of Britain's population was involved in domestic manufacture, because so many families combined it with agriculture and fishing. This way of life was declining by the later eighteenth century, as more and more petty manufacturers became landless full-timers; but even in 1850 it was not negligible. Even in the late seventeenth century, little more

than half the labour force in England and Wales can have been engaged mainly in agriculture; and the relative importance of mining, manufacturing and commerce grew inexorably thereafter. By the late eighteenth century, every British region had a substantial proportion of its population heavily involved in manufacture and trade. This was probably the most important difference between Britain and the other developing nations of Western Europe, where agriculture remained much more important.

Textiles were almost ubiquitous. The woollen industry, with its deep medieval roots, was expanding and diversifying its output throughout the eighteenth century, despite set-backs caused by wars and trade depressions. It grew fastest in the West Riding of Yorkshire, but also did well in the West Country and parts of Wales, and in the Norwich area. Linen was even more widespread, with strongholds in East Anglia and north-west England as well as in Scotland and Northern Ireland. Wool was more export-oriented than linen, whose outlets were often merely local; but both industries made rapid headway in the mid eighteenth century, before the coming of factories and major technical advances. It was the cotton industry – growing at an unprecedented rate, far outpacing its rivals, from the late eighteenth century onwards – which pioneered the large-scale introduction of the factory system.

When the transition to the factory eventually came in the older textile industries it was concentrated in Northern Ireland (for linen) and the West Riding of Yorkshire (for woollens), although woollen factories also flourished for a long time in the West Country and around Newtown, in Montgomeryshire, 'the Leeds of Wales'. But these were essentially developments of the nineteenth century.

The earlier expansion of these manufactures was based on 'cottage industry', scattered through populous tracts of countryside. It was organised by urban merchants who bought the raw material and marketed the finished product; but the work was given out and gathered in by a network of intermediaries. Thus in Wales, according to J. G. Jenkins,

In the Llanidloes district . . . raw wool was sorted, carefully packed and strapped to the back of a horse and taken to the country for carding and spinning. Here in each village the clothier had his agents who received the wool and distributed it among the peasantry and received it back as yarn for re-distribution to the weavers.

PREVIOUS PAGES *The first published view of the Upper Works at Coalbrookdale, engraved by Francis Vivares and issued in 1758. The chimneys and coke ovens provide animation without as yet scarring a cheerful and mainly verdant landscape. The horse-drawn wagons show how most goods were transported in the early years of the Industrial Revolution.*

This 'putting-out' system, in which the domestic manufacturer performed an agreed task for an agreed price, using material which remained the property of the merchant, gained ground steadily during the eighteenth century. Only in the West Riding woollen industry did significant numbers of independent craftsmen survive, buying their raw materials where they could and selling them where they chose. Otherwise, domestic manufacturers became increasingly tied by debts and limited opportunities to individual merchants, so that

instead of trading on their own account, they were effectively working for a wage, remote and even invisible though their master might be. Such people might own their own machinery, especially while spinning-wheels and carding equipment remained basic and cheap. The pace and pattern of work, too, was set by the head of the houschold rather than by a factory manager, a foreman and a bell. But the effective independence of this kind of family business was increasingly limited, especially as smallholdings dwindled to the size of potato gardens or disappeared altogether.

For a long time the cotton and silk industries operated on the same principle, as did a lot of metalworking. But the merchants who sat at the centre of these elaborate webs of organisation bccame dissatisfied with the disadvantages they experienced. These scattered, rural labour forces

The cramped and cluttered interior of the loomshop in the hand-loom weaver's cottage owned by the National Trust for Scotland at Kilbarchan, Renfrewshire.

Spinning on the distaff, which persisted into the nineteenth century in the Scottish linen industry, could readily be combined with gossip and flirtation by the fire in the evening.

were difficult to supervise and control. They could not be trusted to deliver on time, and sometimes they embezzled some of the raw materials, sending in a slightly lower-quality product than they should and keeping whatever they saved for sale or for their own use. All this put merchants at risk in competitive markets. They themselves operated on credit, they could not always afford to wait for material delayed in the loom or on the road and substandard goods put their commercial reputation in danger. So they became interested in ever-tighter controls over the manufacturing processes.

It was in cotton, rather than in the older textile industries, that the incentive and opportunity for change came earliest and most strongly. The use of cotton was already well established in south-east Lancashire by the early eighteenth century: it was mixed with linen to form fabrics called fustians and cotton-linens. By mid century, the output of pure cotton cloth was beginning to expand in earnest. The popularity and versatility of cotton generated a rapidly-swelling demand, at all levels of society, at home and overseas; and the output of the raw material could be expanded in step with the needs of the industry. The problems lay in the manufacture, and especially in the spinning of the yarn: for by the third quarter of the eighteenth century the weaving process had become more efficient than the spinning. Merchants were having to pay higher wages to evermore distant spinners, whose reliability and trustworthiness were frustratingly deficient in the eyes of employers who had identified a golden opportunity for profit and expansion.

It was under these circumstances that the factory system was brought in, as inventors struggled and competed to devise ways of spinning cotton faster, more efficiently and on a larger scale, and as merchants eagerly invested in the new technologies. The first of the famous trio of inventions, the jenny, was usable and affordable in domestic workshops, and did not necessarily require a continuous power supply from a water-wheel, although its optimum scale soon increased beyond this basic level. The mule, which could spin yarns of the highest quality, also began life as a hand-operated machine which could be tied into the domestic system; but it soon became harnessed to water, and then steam, in factories of ever-increasing size. But it was the water-frame, the famous invention of Richard Arkwright, that first pulled spinning into the factory on a large scale from the 1770s and 1780s. These were not the first factories: they had precursors, especially in silk-spinning, in the early eighteenth century. But they were large enough, and numerous enough, to impress contemporaries with their novelty and grandeur, with the opportunities they offered and the social problems they posed.

Styal, a few miles south of Manchester in northeast Cheshire, was not one of the very first mills on the Arkwright principle; but in some ways it was representative. It was opened in 1784, and was, says its historian Mary Rose, 'a typical Arkwright type mill which cost around £3000 to build and equip'. This was a substantial sum, but well within the pocket of Samuel Greg, a well-established and well-connected Manchester merchant, credit-worthy and with access to loans from his family. It was not an enormous mill, though larger than most: at first it employed about 150 people to spin coarse yarns which found a ready sale through Greg's merchant house. Like the vast majority of the early mills, it was established in a remote and attractive rural setting: the raw material and finished product could be transported quite cheaply, and the main essential was access to a good and reliable head of water to operate the water-wheel. But this posed problems of labour supply: the local population was insufficient, and displayed a well-established prejudice against the long hours and imposed discipline of factory work, which could look disturbingly like the regime of the workhouse. In the event it was from this source that Greg obtained the cheap child labour that he needed. The Poor Law authorities of many parishes were eager to unload the children in their charge into the care of others, as 'pauper apprentices' who were supposedly taught a trade and kept off the burden of the rates. This captive labour force, drawn from as far away as London and supplemented by local children hired under 'contract' from their impoverished and often illiterate parents, solved one of Greg's problems in a way which had many counterparts elsewhere.

Greg looked after the pauper children carefully, remembering that he had taken on the responsibilities of a parent as well as the rights of an employer. They were lodged in a purpose-built Apprentice House where, as one remembered, 'The rooms were very clean, the floors frequently washed. . . . Our beds were good, we slept two to a bed and had clean sheets once a month, new clothes for Sundays once in two years and new working jackets when those had worn out.' Schooling was provided, but discipline was stern and there was very little free time. Medical attention was also on hand. This was a matter of good business as well as humanity: a healthy labour force was also likely to be more efficient. But not all the early factory masters thought like this: from Backbarrow, in the Lake District, and elsewhere came haunting stories of neglect, disease and unbridled severity. From the beginning Styal's Quarry Bank mill was, in material terms, a good factory in which to work.

It was not until the 1820s that the mill grew to about its present size. It expanded steadily as the capacity and effectiveness of the water-wheel was increased, and by 1833 it employed 380 people, mostly women. Meanwhile, the pauper apprentices were gradually phased out, as new legal restraints made them less available and less attractive economically; and new houses had to be built to accommodate the families from whom a new, expanded labour force could be drawn. Most of the men worked outside the mill; but the whole village came under the paternal oversight of the Greg family. Alcohol was discouraged, as was radical politics, and the 'rational recreations' of reading, music and controlled debate were fostered. Wages were low, but so were rents and other costs, and the employees gained materially and

OVERLEAF *The substantial buildings of Samuel Greg's Quarry Bank Mill, Styal, Cheshire. Factories on this scale were unusual in the era of water-powered industry.*

Be it remembered, IT is this

Day agreed by and between SAMUEL GREG, of Styal, in the County of Chester, of the one Part, and *Joseph Garside Seer and Joseph Garside Junier* — of *Gatley in the County of Chester* — of the other Part, as follows: That the said *Joseph Garside Iun.* shall — serve the said Samuel Greg in his Cotton-Mills, in Styal, in the County of Chester, as a just and honest Servant, *Twelve* — Hours in each of the six working Days, and to be at *his* own Liberty at all other Times; the Commencement of the Hours to be fixed from Time to Time by the said Samuel Greg, for the Term of *Six* Years at the Wages of *Nine pence*

p week the first year & one shilling p week for the remaining part of the Term & M.r Greg Engages to find the said Jo.s Garside with Meat Drink Washing & Lodging Sufficient for one in his Station

And that if the said *Joseph Garside* — shall absent *him self* from the Service of the said Samuel Greg, in the said working Hours, during the said Term, without his Consent first obtained, that the said Samuel Greg may abate the Wages in a double Proportion for such Absence; and the said Samuel Greg shall be at Liberty, during the Term, to discharge the Servant from his Service, for Misbehaviour, or Want of Employ.

As Witness their Hands, this *Second* — Day of *March* 1795

Shoes	4.	6
Stockins	1.	6
Coate	4.	6
Vest	2.	6
Britches	4.	
Shirts	4.	2
hatt	2.	6
	1.3	8

Witness
Matt.w Faulkner

the Mark of Jo.s Garside der +
Joseph Garside Jun.s Mark *Geo*

Apprenticeship contract for Joseph Garside, a child worker at Quarry Bank Mill, 1795. The wage is very low, but it includes keep 'sufficient for one in his station'. Joseph can form à few letters of his name, but his father is completely illiterate.

environmentally while they lost freedom and political autonomy. In these respects Styal was typical of many model villages presided over by factory masters. But it, and its like, were increasingly out of step with the cotton industry at large.

The heyday of the water-frame had seen water-powered cotton mills sprouting on rural sites over a wide area of northern and midland England and southern Scotland. By 1795 there were perhaps 300. Not all employers provided housing, and many workers began and ended their twelve- or fourteen-hour working day with a long walk. Where housing was on offer, it seldom matched the sturdiness and generous gardens of Styal. Some factory villages were severely overcrowded, with whole families occupying a single room, as in the worst of the urban slums. Employers sometimes required their workers to pay extortionate prices and go into debt at the company's monopoly 'truck' shop, and many failed to provide the continuity of employment on which the Gregs prided themselves. Working conditions were often unhealthy and dangerous. The rural 'factory village' was not always as idyllic as some who paid fleeting visits thought.

From the 1790s onwards, the water-powered mills were overtaken in importance by the urban steam-powered factories, using the mule, which became the preferred technology. As the growth of the cotton industry accelerated to hitherto unimaginable levels in the early decades of the nineteenth century, factories became concentrated into towns, where coal was cheap, transport easy and labour plentiful. The size of individual firms and factories was rarely very large. The handful of giant firms who employed over a thousand people apiece in 1841 dated their origins from the earliest days of the industry; and all of them divided their operations between two or more sites. Thus the Gregs employed over 2000 workers by 1833, but this was on five sites; four additional mills had been acquired between 1817 and 1832. This gave one for each of the sons to manage, and enabled a variety of products to be made, some of which were likely to be profitable when others were not. This was quite

exceptional. Most of the early water-powered cotton mills had been unpretentious structures: old corn mills were often converted cheaply, and the standard new mill might be of three or four storeys and measure 70–80 feet long by 35–40 feet wide. The new urban mills were often no larger in the 1830s and 1840s, and many were subdivided among petty employers who hired a room and the use of the power supply. In 1841 nearly half the cotton firms in Lancashire employed fewer than fifty people each. This scale of enterprise was considerably bigger than a domestic workshop, but it should still discourage easy generalisations about the overwhelming dominance of enormous, impersonal 'dark Satanic mills'.

Even in the so-called 'cotton towns', the cotton factories themselves only employed a minority of grown men and women. They had a voracious appetite for the labour of young children and adolescents, although after 1833 legislation began to restrict the use of the former and limit the hours of the latter; but factory work was a stage through which people passed, rather than a lifetime commitment. Moreover, for a long time only the preparation and spinning of yarn, and in some senses the bleaching and printing of the cloth, were taken into the factory. The immense growth in output of yarn and demand for cloth thus had to be met by hand-loom weavers working on the domestic system, whose numbers grew dramatically in the late eighteenth and early nineteenth century. For a brief span, these weavers were well-paid and prosperous; but already during the Napoleonic Wars their incomes were beginning to slide. Yarn was being exported in increasing volume to be woven more cheaply on the Continent when conditions allowed, and the number of weavers had expanded even faster than the demand for their work.

By the 1820s the weavers were well into a grim period of working ever-longer hours for ever-lower earnings per piece of cloth woven; and it was during this decade that the introduction of a workable power-loom began to push this branch of cotton into the factory as well, although hand-loom weavers survived in the cotton industry into the 1860s. Their cottages can still be seen, with cellar windows to light the work of a trade which needed damp conditions, those of the 1820s at Styal being typical examples, although they were never used for this purpose. The fate of the hand-loom weavers is one of the saddest stories of this period. Proud and independent, in many cases, they included self-taught mathematicians, botanists

Surviving machinery at the Wellbrook Beetling Mill, Co. Tyrone: wheel and hammers seen from above.

and geologists, as well as dialect poets, choristers and radical politicians. James Leach published successful collections of his psalms and hymns, and sang as a counter-tenor in Westminster Abbey; and Samuel Bamford, himself a poet and politician, remembered that his father was 'considerably imbued with book knowledge, particularly of a religious kind; wrote a good hand; understood arithmetic; had some acquaintance with astronomy; (and) was a vocal and instrumental musician'. But the last generation of weavers endured the starkest of poverty, and had to send their children into the factories to eke out the barest subsistence.

Some of the power-looms were attached to the big spinning complexes, but most weaving factories were very small. Even in cotton, the coming of the factory was protracted, and the re-

organisation of the industry lasted for a long individual lifespan, from the 1770s to the 1840s. But this was the narrow cutting edge of the Industrial Revolution. Other textile industries grew less dramatically and reorganised even more slowly, and the direct influence of cotton itself was concentrated into limited areas around Manchester, Glasgow and (for a time) Belfast, with a few outposts elsewhere.

Woollens were slower to move into the factory. A burst of factory building in the 1790s mainly involved preparing the wool for spinning, and fulling the cloth. The great multiplication of larger, steam-powered factories using spinning mules came in the second quarter of the nineteenth century, when the independence of the hand-loom weavers began to be undermined, but these were concentrated into the worsted industry, which used long-staple wool and different production techniques from the older woollen fabrics. Hand weaving and domestic production continued in more traditional branches of the industry well beyond mid century, even in the West Riding of Yorkshire where the changes were most advanced.

Factory production came even later and more slowly in linen. The first and last of the processes – scutching (separating the wooden parts of the flax from the fibres) and beetling (flattening the fibre of the finished cloth by beating it with mallets) were mechanised early on, and in Northern Ireland, especially, small water-powered mills proliferated to serve the widely-scattered rural manufactures. The surviving mill at Wellbrook (NT), near Cookstown, was one of many. Bleaching became a large-scale activity, concentrated into the hands of a relatively few firms who could afford the water power, the machinery and the extensive bleach-fields on which the cloth had to be stretched. But with spinning and weaving, which employed the most labour, effective factory machinery was slow to emerge. In Scotland, spinning mills spread slowly after their introduction in 1787, and it was not until the 1820s that the development of the wet-spinning process, which reduced breakages in the yarn, brought about the demise of the hand-spinner, thereby removing a once-important source of earnings for women in the home. In Northern Ireland spinning factories failed to take root until the introduction of wet-spinning in the late 1820s, when many former cotton mills in Belfast switched to linen yarn. Power-looms were even slower to appear. In Scotland they began to spread widely from the 1820s, but as late as 1850 hardly any were in use in Northern Ireland, where the domestic system remained completely dom-inant and wages actually rose sharply after the mass emigration of the mid and late 1840s. So the linen industry, which was centrally important to the economies of eastern Scotland and Northern Ireland, lagged far behind cotton in its transition to the factory.

Domestic manufacture survived just as long in the silk industry, despite the early availability of factory spinning technology. The Spitalfields silk weavers even kept a foothold for the trade in London's East End, where some of the houses in which they worked can still be seen. All this draws

attention to the limited hold of the factory system on Britain's production and work-forces even in the mid nineteenth century. Outside textiles, factory production in the fullest sense was almost non-existent. There were steadily-growing num-bers of extensive workplaces, some of which had imposing buildings and provided exciting spec-tacles of smoke and flame; and the subdivision of tasks into a number of repetitive routines which required dexterity and application rather than craftsmanship and judgement was becoming ever more general and more advanced. But even in the most developed sectors of industry, the pace of work was usually dictated by people rather than machines, handicraft skills were still in demand, and the cost of labour far outweighed that of machinery.

Machine-making itself is a case in point, from the very heart of our ideas about what makes an industrial revolution. The rise of specialist en-gineering firms, especially in the early nineteenth century, led to the displacement of the millwright, an all-round craftsman who could work with a variety of materials and plan the machinery for a whole factory. His skills were fragmented by the development of new kinds of increasingly sophisti-cated and task-specific equipment which furthered the advancement of the division of labour. But all but the most basic and universal of machines continued to be made as one-off projects or in small batches, with very few exceptions. This meant that craft skills remained at a premium, even though each individual had a narrower range of expertise than before; and skilled engineering workers were still expected to serve apprenticeships.

Even the redoubtable James Nasmyth, no friend to the pretensions of skilled workers and the restrictive practices of their trade unions, was unable to break through this barrier. His new Patricroft works, on a green-field site a few miles outside Manchester, was carefully laid out in the late 1830s so as to make possible the assembly-line production of locomotives and heavy plant items. In 1836 he wrote to his partner urging the mass-production of standardised machines for stock, in advance of orders. Despite the use of the most advanced and accurate machine tools, and the issue of a catalogue from which potential customers were encouraged to order, these ideas did not come to fruition. Only a small proportion of the firm's turnover – between one-sixth and one-twentieth – came from the sale of items kept in stock. Even in this spearhead industry, most of the trade was bespoke; and this meant that the skills of the

A hiring market for children at Spitalfields, London, providing cheap domestic labour to sustain the weavers in their workshops. The policeman and street vendor are prominent and characteristic, and so is the shop offering 'cheap funerals'. The railway arches confirm the low status of the area.

workers remained at the heart of the success of the enterprise. They might be numbered in hundreds rather than handfuls, and subjected to the discipline of the foreman and the works' clock, but the prevailing atmosphere was still more akin to the craft workshop than the fully-fledged factory.

In striking contrast, the immense expansion in the making of cheap articles for mass consumption, such as clothing, footwear and furniture, took place through the multiplication of domestic outworkers and the proliferation of fetid little workshops in garrets and cellars. In London, especially, factories would have been uneconomic. Rents and overheads would have been enormous, and the demand for most of the goods concerned was so seasonal that expensive plant would have been lying idle for much of the year. Changes in fashion would have taxed machinery to its limit. But above all, there was a much cheaper and more flexible alternative. The manufacturers found that, with a

seemingly inexhaustible supply of cheap labour, they could expand production most effectively by putting the work out into people's homes. In the overcrowded state of much of working-class London, what resulted was not so much cottage industry as bed-sit industry. In a fiercely competitive atmosphere, the sale of cheap clothing was channelled through a system of warehouses, whose proprietors distributed work at lower and lower prices through two or three tiers of middlemen,

each of whom took a cut. Some of them employed workers on their own premises, charging them exorbitantly for food and accommodation; but most of the work was done at home by families, in which wives and children were increasingly pressed into service alongside the men. The rage for price-cutting, and the intense competition for work, meant that these families were working longer and longer hours in the season for lower and lower returns, as the price per item was reduced. They had to find their own lighting, heating and tools, and some of their own materials. They also had to find some way of surviving during the off-season. It was small wonder that the London docks had an enormous surplus of half-starved casual labourers.

This state of affairs, as it prevailed in the mid nineteenth century, was carefully documented by Henry Mayhew in a famous series of articles in the *Morning Chronicle*. It did not apply to all of London's artisans, for each trade had its 'honourable' sector in which trade-union rates were paid and workers could still take pride in their skill. In contrast with the 'sweated' or 'dishonourable' sectors, this was luxury production for the West End market. Across the board, however, conditions had worsened considerably in the untrammelled competition for expanding markets during the second quarter of the nineteenth century. Even the building trades, in which small firms predominated and traditional technologies prevailed, were being pushed towards a kind of sweating system, as contractors tried to work to impossibly low price margins and rapid schedules, and passed the pressures on to subcontractors and wage-labourers. Conditions were not as bad in the provinces, where rents were lower and other prices cheaper. In Sheffield, for example, the file, scissors and cutlery trades remained the preserve of small craftsmen who maintained the traditions of their trades, although many suffered terribly from occupational lung diseases. But a lower cost of living could help London's competitors to put even greater pressure on the East End: thus the Northamptonshire boot- and shoemakers, in their village workshops, were able to undercut London prices and worsen the conditions of the East End craftsmen. This pattern of cost-cutting by intensifying competition between domestic manufacturers was affecting far more people by the 1830s and 1840s than was the impact of the factory system itself.

The sweated trades were, by their nature, inconspicuous. What attracted much more attention most of the time were those aspects of industrial development which made a concentrated and distinctive impact on the landscape: the iron, steel and chemical works, the mines and quarries. Developments in these spheres were indeed of central importance to the industrial transformation of Britain, although huge firms and enormous factories remained exceptional.

As Barrie Trinder says, 'Iron making was the most awe-inspiring of industries in the eighteenth century, and its products the most spectacular.' Britain's iron output grew fifty-sixfold between the 1780s and 1860. The use of coke rather than charcoal released the furnace owners from dependence on immense expanses of coppice woodland, and the forgemasters from the need to import additional pig-iron from the Baltic. The iron industry became concentrated into distinctive areas where its raw materials were readily available, and parts of Staffordshire, south Yorkshire, Clydeside and South Wales became engulfed in smoke, fire, slag-heaps and industrial pollution. But the first area to develop in this way, and the one most noticed at the time, was centred on the Severn Gorge around what became Ironbridge in Shropshire.

Here, the pioneering ventures of the Darbys of Coalbrookdale became, from the 1750s, the core of an array of interrelated industries: iron, coal, tar, pottery and many others. The famous Iron Bridge itself, an enduring symbol of Industrial Revolution, was the more spectacular of two which were completed in 1780 on a short stretch of the Severn. Other products of the local furnaces and forges included cannon, steam-engine parts, water-wheels, clock weights, frying-pans, cider and cheese presses, soap boilers and threshing-mill castings: a reminder of the ubiquitous importance of the iron trade. Steam-engines, used for a widening variety of purposes, were probably thicker on the ground in 1800 in Shropshire than anywhere else in Britain. The great ironmaster partnerships came to control mines, transport and marketing, and the Coalbrookdale concern was eclipsed by the Botfields of Dawley, who by 1806 had the second largest ironworks in Britain. The impact of all this activity on a famously attractive landscape provoked awe among contemporaries, and the reactions of an Italian visitor in 1787

convey some sense of the way the spectacle affected educated contemporaries:

The approach to Coalbrookdale appeared to be a veritable descent to the infernal regions. A dense column of smoke arose from the earth; volumes of steam were ejected from the fire engines; a blacker cloud issued from a tower in which was a forge; and smoke arose from a mountain of burning coals which burst out into a turbid flame. . . . I descended towards the Severn, which runs slowly between two high mountains, and after leaving which passed under a bridge constructed entirely of iron. It appeared as a gate of mystery, and night already falling, added to the impressiveness of the scene, which could only be compared to the regions so powerfully described by Virgil.

By the early nineteenth century Shropshire was already losing its leading and distinctive position, and the torch was being picked up elsewhere. But its experience draws attention to the central and formative importance of the iron trade, and to the importance of links between local industries and the outside world. The Coalbrookdale complex and its neighbours depended on investment from Bristol merchants and landed aristocrats, on government contracts and on exports to all corners of the known world. Shropshire industrialists developed additional interests in mining, manufacturing and land throughout the British Isles and beyond. Similar webs of connection and chains of causation could be found in the other metalworking industries which began to grow rapidly in the later eighteenth century, just as, of course, they could in textiles.

The Cornish tin- and copper-mining industry provides a good example. These metals were far from being as universally important as iron, and their output grew much more slowly: Cornish tin output nearly doubled between the 1750s and the early 1830s, while that of copper roughly quadrupled between the 1780s and the 1840s. But they were in demand for new purposes. Pewter plates were falling out of fashion, but the tin-plate industry, which coated sheets of iron or other metals to prevent rust or tarnishing, was taking root in South Wales, within easy seaborne access of the Cornish mines. The Birmingham trinket and toy trades, which were expanding rapidly in the eighteenth century, depended on increasing copper production, as did, for example, the brass and wire manufacturers. Copper sheathing came to be used to preserve the hulls of wooden ships.

These developments ensured continuing investment and speculation in Cornish mining, and pushed it to the forefront of eighteenth-century technology. In order to expand output, the mine syndicates were having to pursue the mineral veins to ever-greater depths. At the same time, their costs were being squeezed by the threat of competition from the tin deposits of the East Indies and the copper mines of Anglesey and later Cuba and Chile. So they were prominent among the pioneers of steam pumping engines, while striving to reduce coal consumption to a minimum: for this was the key resource which they lacked, and it had to be supplied, expensively, by sea. They were among the earliest users of the new Boulton and Watt engines, from the late 1770s onwards, and the high premiums which had to be paid to the Birmingham firm to meet Watt's patent rights stimulated local engineers to try to find alternative methods of their own. The key figure was Richard Trevithick, a pioneer of the dangerous but exciting use of high-pressure steam. Working in competition with Arthur Woolf, another experimenter with high pressures, Trevithick helped to spearhead the 'phenomenal developments in Cornish engineering' after 1810, when the increasing problems of deep-level mining stimulated a flurry of invention and adaptation which was soon to bear fruit in the big new engines of enterprises like the Levant Mine (NT) at St Just.

Over the next generation there was a fourfold increase in the average 'duty' (a measure of output and fuel efficiency) of Cornish pumping engines, and the biggest ones could more than double the average. Some of the earlier engines had been enormous, with cylinders up to 7 feet in diameter; but the biggest of the new ones were larger still. Here, as in Shropshire, were potent symbols of Industrial Revolution; and the scores of engines working in Cornwall had helped Harveys of Hayle, by 1840, to transform 'what had once been a blacksmith's shop into one of the greatest foundries in the kingdom'.

This is all very impressive; but two points are worth emphasis. Firstly, actual working and payment methods in the mines changed very little. Secondly, the lack of a local coal supply limited the scope for Cornwall's economic development. It meant that nearly all the copper and tin had to be smelted and manufactured elsewhere, and that the scars of mining were not accompanied by large-scale urban growth and the proliferation of factories and foundries. Cornwall exported raw materials to more developed industrial economies elsewhere in Britain. With the decline of Cornish mining in the later nineteenth century it also

Richard Trevithick, improver of Cornish mine engines and inventor of steam locomotives, dredgers and threshing-machines: 'a restless, inspired genius'.

became an exporter of skilled labour, as miners scattered to South Africa, Australia and the Americas in pursuit of the work they understood.

There were many other major extractive industries, such as the enormous slate quarries at Penrhyn and elsewhere in North Wales, or the slate quarrying and assorted mineral enterprises of the Lake District. But Cornwall's experience underlines the central importance of coal. Its output grew impressively, doubling during the second half of the eighteenth century, then trebling again to over 33 million tons by 1840. Here again, the most important acceleration came in the early decades of the nineteenth century, rather than the eighteenth. In 1800 up to two-thirds of the coal raised was still being used in the home, but by 1840 industry, especially iron, accounted for more than 6 tons in every 10. If metalworking industries had the most voracious appetites for coal, however, its availability was just as important to the cotton industry, and to every process that came to depend on steam-engines, or simply to use a lot of fuel. There were practical limits to the scope for harnessing water power on evermore scattered and remote sites, just as there were limits to the amount of coppice timber that could be grown to feed the furnaces of the iron industry. Coal enabled industry to grow and concentrate in ways which would have been impossible with technologies which depended on wood, water, wind and muscle power.

This great, and vital, expansion of coal production was achieved without major changes in the organisation of the industry, or even in its technology. By 1850 improved forms of ventilation, lighting, haulage and winding had all been introduced, though most innovations spread slowly outside the large mines of north-east England and West Cumberland. The safety lamp, which reduced the danger of explosions, was a particularly important innovation. But, as Christopher Smout says of the Scottish miners, the only novelties which actually affected the physical work itself were steam-engines to drain the mines and lift the coals, and 'the miners themselves went on hewing in the nineteenth century with exactly the same tools as their ancestors had (used) two hundred years before'. This meant that the expansion of production came largely from employing more labour, including (until the 1840s) large numbers of women and children for underground coal carrying and ventilation work. Mines multiplied in number, and large concerns employing several hundred became more common; but the coal that sustained the industrial transformation of Britain was won by the desperately hard physical labour of men who were worn out by their forties, supported by the ill-rewarded toil, in damp and darkness, of their wives and children. In much of Scotland the miners and their families were effectively serfs, bound to serve their noble employers for life and subject to corporal punishment and compulsory return to work if they absconded, until the very end of the eighteenth century. All this drives home the point that much of the economic growth of Britain during the century after 1750 was secured by the multiplication and reorganisation of hand labour, rather than by the introduction of new factories and glamorous inventions.

The economic developments of the years between the 1840s and the First World War continued to be underpinned by coal: indeed, this period saw the steam-powered economy in all its glory. Output trebled again between 1840 and 1869, when more than 100 million tons were produced. The 1913 figure was nearly 300 million tons. The growth of domestic demand was far outpaced by the needs of industry (including gasworks and railways) and the export trade, which was especially important in South Wales. Increasingly the mines were run by syndicates and companies, some of which controlled dozens of pits and dominated the working life of wide areas. But mining technology changed remarkably little: the rise in output was achieved by developing new pits, seams and coalfields (especially in the English Midlands), and by employing more men, rather than by investment in labour-saving machinery.

This is not to deny that there were changes: it is to put them in perspective. There were further improvements in ventilation and safety; underground haulage was mechanised in many mines, and the speed and capacity of winding gear was increased. Electricity was being introduced in the late nineteenth century, and in some places it was applied to coal-cutting machinery. But machine cutting and the use of conveyor belts spread slowly. In 1913 only one ton of coal in every twelve was cut by machine, though in Scotland the figure was one in five. So the skills of the hewer at the coal-face remained crucial to the whole enterprise: under-

The ruined engine house and stack of the Wheal Prosper tin and copper mine, which was abandoned in about 1860, seen from Rinsey Cliff, between Helston and Marazion on the south coast of Cornwall.

Miners at Bargoed, near Cardiff, wait to ascend the shaft at the end of their shift in December 1910, alongside the coal they have 'won'.

standing timbering and the lie of the coal, knowing how to use pick and shovel to best advantage, all the things that gave a sense of pride in work, and an awareness of a hierarchy of skills and esteem. These themes were strong in mining but not peculiar to it. Many of them recur in other sectors of British industry in Victorian and Edwardian times.

The textile industries completed and consolidated their transition to factory production. In cotton, the triumph of steam over water power was manifest by the 1830s, and the average size of spinning factories grew considerably from the 1860s onwards, with a spate of monster mills being built on the outskirts of several Lancashire towns at the turn of the century. This period also saw the old family firms being steadily displaced by limited companies; and these trends may have altered the nature of workplace relations in the cotton industry, making them more impersonal if not more prone to conflict. Meanwhile, power-loom weaving expanded rapidly, especially in the late-developing East Lancashire towns of Burnley, Nelson and Colne. Here the factories remained small, so that working men were still able to make the transition from employee to petty capitalist by borrowing in support of their savings. But this was not an era of major innovations: expansion was based largely on the use of established techniques. Existing machines were worked at higher speeds, and weaving sheds were made artificially damp to squeeze the maximum output from the looms. But the new American technologies, ring-spinning and the automatic loom, were not widely adopted, and then only for the coarsest kinds of yarn and cloth, where their profitability was least in doubt.

These policies were probably soundly based, in the context of the time; but it is interesting to see that Quarry Bank Mill in Styal went against the trend. As a water-powered mill in family ownership, it was increasingly anachronistic, and suffered accordingly in the late nineteenth century. A brief flirtation with ring-spinning, which should have suited the mill's coarse yarns, was a failure; but the introduction of automatic looms in the early twentieth century, which allowed one worker to mind twenty looms instead of four or six ordinary ones, increased productivity considerably in weaving after spinning had been abandoned. In general, however, cotton's sustained expansion in these years depended on the multiplication of factories and workers (especially women) rather than new technology; and here again, the skills and experience of the work-force became important assets.

The cotton industry became firmly concentrated into a small area around Manchester in mid Victorian times; and the wool textile and linen industries also became more localised. Linen became overwhelmingly a Northern Irish speciality, and the Dundee area of eastern Scotland went over to jute manufacture for sacking and other heavy duty products. The West Riding of Yorkshire confirmed its domination of woollens and worsteds, although the makers of West Country broadcloths, at the high-quality end of the clothing market, more than held their own. In these industries, the displacement of the hand-loom was not completed until the 1860s, and the woollen industry, especially, saw important innovations in the later nineteenth century; but the main breakthrough in textiles had already been made by 1850, and the changes thereafter were of lesser significance.

Some of the pioneer industries were thus resting on their technical laurels even as they continued to grow after the mid nineteenth century. This was not so much the case with metal processing and manufacture, in which new techniques succeeded one another in the third quarter of the century. This was true especially of iron and steel manufacture, which spawned whole new towns in the 1850s and 1860s. Barrow-in-Furness and the 'Ironopolis' of Middlesbrough extended grimy grids of working-class terraced housing, with almost unprecedented speed, around the railways and industrial plant which had called them into being, while the old Sheffield manufactures were dwarfed by the immense new steelworks which followed the valley to Rotherham.

Barrow diversified into shipbuilding, but its output was insignificant when set against the daunting tonnages of ocean-going giants which were produced in the great new shipyards of the Mersey, the Tyne, the Wear and the Clyde, and on the artificial islands in Belfast's harbour. Here as in other spheres, the use of iron and steel required new techniques and created jealously-guarded new skills. Alongside these developments came massive expansion in such heavy manufacturing industries as textile machinery and railway equipment, increasingly for export. But much of Britain's engineering industry still dealt extensively in one-off orders or short production runs. Under these conditions, innovations in working practices, such as payment by piecework, were resisted by often well-organised skilled workers, who were particularly anxious to avoid the introduction of techniques which might extend the scope of unapprenticed labour and undermine the scarcity value of the skilled. These attitudes came under sustained attack at the turn of the century, however, and new machinery and working practices were spreading rapidly in the Edwardian years.

The continuing inventiveness and adaptability of some sectors of British heavy industry is apparent in the business activities of W. G. Armstrong, which generated the fortune from which Cragside was built. Armstrong's famous works at Elswick, on the Tyne, began in 1847 by manufacturing his hydraulic cranes, dock gates, and pumping engines; but it also made bridges and a variety of other general engineering products. But Armstrong's inventions were also applied to gunnery, first for the Royal Navy, then for the navies of the world. By 1885 whole ships were being completed at Elswick, including the world's first purpose-built bulk oil tanker. A spectacular event in 1876 illustrates the sheer scale of some of this activity. The Italian vessel *Europa* left Elswick with 31 100-ton guns for the Italian Government, and Peter McKenzie tells us that

She was the first vessel to pass through the Newcastle Swing Bridge channel. The Swing Bridge at that time was the largest in the world. The 100-ton guns were also the largest guns in the world, and the sheer-legs that lifted them were the largest sheer-legs in the world. When the guns arrived in Italy, they were lifted ashore by a 180-ton hydraulic crane that was the largest of its type in the world. All these 'largest in the world' items had been built at Elswick.

This offers a reminder of the continuing fertility of important sectors of British industry: it was not just a matter of 'more of the same'. The rise of foreign competition, which was becoming increasingly assertive in some industries (such as chemical dyestuffs) by the late nineteenth century, was posing visible threats to Britain's world industrial leadership, especially in European and American markets. Contemporaries were well aware of the situation. But until the First World War British industrial dominance, shored up by the protected markets of the colonies, was shaken but not yet overturned.

The second half of the nineteenth century saw the spread of the factory system into new industries. Some, like boot- and shoemaking, were old domestic workshop industries which were transformed by the availability of new machinery and the development of new manufacturing centres in the provinces. But there were also food-processing industries – jam-making, for example – which developed to meet the needs and tastes of urban working-class consumers with increased spending power in the late nineteenth century. Chocolate and tobacco also became major employers. The sweated trades of the mid nineteenth century were still in evidence in the Edwardian years, however, in provincial centres like Leeds and Liverpool as well as in London's East End. The sewing-machine, for example, spread rapidly from the 1860s, but it was well suited to the domestic workshop and the perpetuation of the sweating system. Some trades, too, remained almost untouched by new technology and dominated by small firms. The building industry, a major employer of adult male labour, is an obvious example: 'steam navvies' and other expensive technology were largely confined to the biggest projects and the small minority of giant firms. This was exceptional, however, and the dominant trends of the second half of the nineteenth century were for manufacturing industry to become larger in scale, more urban in location, more dependent on coal and machinery for a wider range of processes, more regular and more disciplined.

These developments were associated with a sustained rise in the living standards of most working people. Until the 1840s, there were more sufferers than gainers from the Industrial Revolution. Some skilled or supervisory workers found regular and well-paid work; but for most the seasonal fluctuations in employment, coupled with the intensifying alternation of boom and slump and the impossibility of saving for a rainy day, meant increasing insecurity and widespread abject poverty. The long working hours and often dangerous working conditions in mines and factories worsened matters; and many families needed the additional wages of wives and small children to make ends meet. After mid century, skilled men in many trades benefited from rising wages, and from the mid 1870s the prices of basic foodstuffs fell steadily, increasing the purchasing power of wages for everyone who remained in work. There were occasional setbacks, and living standards for labourers' families, and in the surviving sweated trades, remained insufficient to sustain health and basic comforts. But for many of the working class, shorter hours, safer working conditions and higher, more regular wages provided more security by the turn of the century, and made it possible to combine the enjoyment of little luxuries like trips to the seaside and visits to the music-hall with some measure of insurance against sickness and unemployment. This in turn helped to create the mass markets which stimulated the growth of industries like confectionery, tobacco and cheap newspapers.

A small minority of industrial employees were housed in distinct settlements built and watched over by their employers, with churches, canteens, meeting-places and allotments provided, and public houses discouraged or excluded. Styal, like Robert Owen's New Lanark, was a famous early example. Many other factory villages were founded throughout the period. Among the best-known were Saltaire, built for the workers of Sir Titus Salt's alpaca mill on the outskirts of Bradford in the 1850s and 1860s, with neat terraces on a grid plan, washhouses, a Congregationalist chapel and a park; and the late Victorian and Edwardian garden settlements at Port Sunlight in Cheshire and attached to the chocolate factories of the reforming Quaker families, the Cadburys and Rowntrees, at Bournville near Birmingham and New Earswick near York.

These essays in industrial paternalism enhanced the living standards of their consumers, for relatively low wages were more than offset by the security and fringe benefits they offered. But they did not always sustain the hopes of their builders, whose motives were invariably mixed. Religious

PREVIOUS PAGES *Titus Salt's mid Victorian model factory settlement at Saltaire, viewed from Shipley Glen, a favourite holiday haunt of Bradford workers. The chimneys of Bradford itself can be seen on the horizon.*

and humanitarian hopes of social improvement and the saving of souls jostled with the realisation that well-housed workpeople in company accommodation were likely to be more tractable, and even perhaps more efficient, than those whose welfare was left to chance in the slum housing of the city centres. These expectations were, on the whole, borne out by events; but imperfectly. Even Saltaire had its strikes, in 1868 and (with some bitterness) in 1876. At Styal the paternal regime of the Gregs lapsed for a time in the late nineteenth century, and it was difficult to revive it thereafter. The residents of model villages were usually more than willing to attend fêtes and parties put on for their benefit, and to cheer their employers when it was expected of them; but some also complained of a stifling social atmosphere and a lack of freedom.

As on the landed estate, the employer was held in high esteem while he continued to deliver the goods; but lapses into authoritarianism, or attempts to cut wages significantly below the going rate, did not go uncriticised. Such were the limits to deference even in the most tightly-controlled model factory villages. Employers who offered less than this, received less loyalty in return; and the acid tests involved wage rates and job security. Employers who tried to play the paternalist by offering occasional parties and trips to the seaside were as vulnerable to strikes as their rivals. The factory owner as industrial squire, presiding over a loyal, deferential and politically supportive workforce, was quite a common ideal, but the reality was difficult to sustain even for those large firms which had the money and the will to invest in it. Most people worked for small firms, changed their jobs frequently, lived beyond the ken of their employers, and enjoyed a distinctive working-class life-style of their own.

Most of the industrial paternalists were family firms, like Salts or Cadburys; but the biggest organisations of this kind in Victorian Britain were the railway companies. The nature of their operations made it vitally necessary for them to have a disciplined labour force, and they developed a complex hierarchy of ranks and promotions, expressed in uniforms and privileges, to reward obedience and good behaviour. Some went further than this, and expected their employees to support the company's preferred political party, as with the London and North Western's pressure on the Conservatives' behalf at Carlisle and Crewe. The major companies also presided over substantial towns which developed around their workshops, as at Ashford (Kent) and Swindon as well as Crewe. All this illustrates the central importance of the railways to the economy of Victorian Britain, and, by extension, the role of transport in economic and social change through the whole period. The impact of railways, shipping, turnpikes and canals is a major theme, and merits a chapter to itself.

CHAPTER SIX

Transport, Travel and Trade

Improvements in the speed and capacity of the transport network were necessary to sustain, and sometimes to stimulate, economic and social change in Britain. In this respect the contrast between the mid eighteenth century and the early twentieth can be sharply etched. At the beginning of the period transport was based on wind, water and muscle power: sailing-vessels, horse-drawn boats on navigable rivers, pack-horse trains, carts and wagons, a few lumbering stage-coaches and ramshackle horse-tramways, and a great deal of exhausting human legwork. We cannot measure the amount of farm produce carried to market, or manufactures carried to warehouses, or goods peddled around the countryside, on the backs of those who could not afford a horse; but any such measurement would produce impressive results. And even where, as with the cotton hand-loom weavers of Godley (Cheshire) in the late eighteenth century, a donkey was kept to carry the 'cuts' of cloth to the putting-out master on 'bunting day', the owner would walk alongside. Migrants might walk hundreds of miles in search of work and adventure, and those who had moved shorter distances were willing to tramp 20 or 30 miles to see relatives and former neighbours on high days and holidays. Among the lower orders of eighteenth-century England a great deal of travelling, for business and pleasure, involved foot-slogging; and this is often forgotten by historians of transport who concentrate on the more formal, organised and measurable forms of travel.

Walking was much less important by the early twentieth century; and one indicator of this is the extent to which it was being enjoyed as an end in itself, rather than endured as an inescapable necessity. But the obvious transformations in transport have a much higher profile. By 1914 the steam railway network was almost at its most extensive, stretching from Penzance in the far west of Cornwall to Wick and Thurso on the coast of north-east Scotland and extending its tentacles into improbable rural fastnesses in Wales, the Scottish Borders, the Highlands, Londonderry

RIGHT *St Giles's Circus from Tottenham Court Road, London, June 1912, showing the rapid advance of the internal-combustion engine in the streets of the capital just before the First World War.*

PREVIOUS PAGES *The famous 'five-rise' stairway of locks at Bingley, on the Leeds and Liverpool Canal: one of many bottlenecks on the trans-Pennine canal system.*

and Donegal. Steam also ruled the waves, although the sailing ship fought a stout rearguard action which continued beyond the First World War. The bicycle had given human legs the wings of the wind, or so it must have seemed. Over the last generation electric tramways had made cheap, clean, quiet travel available over short distances to millions of city dwellers; and more recently still, the internal-combustion engine had begun its remorseless advance. Enthusiastic private motorists raised the dust and created novel hazards on country roads, while in a few short years before 1914 the horse was practically banished from London's road passenger transport by the motor bus and the taxi. But the horse was harder to replace for road freight haulage, remaining very important over short distances in cities and to and from railway stations. Indeed, the number of horses used in road transport was still growing at the turn of the century. This evidence of the continuing importance of animal sinews is a reminder that, massive and far-reaching though the changes in British transport had been, they were neither as complete nor as all-embracing as a casual glance might suggest. Moreover, the application of steam power to transport, which is certainly the most impressive of the changes in its overall impact, did not begin on any significant scale until the 1830s. How, then, did a transport system which still depended on wind, water and muscle power cope with and sustain the major economic and social changes of the earlier part of the period?

The canals of the later eighteenth and early nineteenth centuries made more obvious and lasting imprints on the landscape than any transport developments between the Roman roads and the railways. Partly as a result, no doubt, they have attracted considerable attention from historians. Above all, they eased and cheapened the transport of heavy bulk commodities whose cost was disproportionately inflated by being moved more than a few miles along eighteenth-century roads, and whose impact in turn caused roads to become impassable and repair costs to soar to intolerable heights. Contemporary calculations suggested that a single horse could carry one-eighth of a ton on a pack, and haul five-eighths of a ton in a wagon on a soft road; but it could pull 50 tons in a barge on a canal. This advantage over road transport was particularly important in the case of coal: new mines could be opened out, steam-engines could be supplied in new places, and domestic fuel supplies could be guaranteed for swollen urban populations. But canals also greatly eased and cheapened the supply of grain and building materials to the growing towns; they provided marl, manure and limestone for agriculture; and they made it possible to bring together a wide range of bulky raw materials, from iron ore to china clay, for the increasingly complex industrial processes of the time. In these respects, above all, canals were invaluable. The industrial developments of the period could not have taken place, on anything like the same scale, without them; and some would argue that the populations of the new manufacturing towns could not have been fed, with potentially disastrous results.

The canal, as a current-free inland navigation which used locks to negotiate changes in the lie of the land, was not a new invention. The novelty lay in the development and rapid extension of a canal network, and in the sheer scale and expense of the works involved. The first canal of the new era was opened in Northern Ireland in 1742, linking Lough Neagh with the coast at Newry to ease the transport of coal from County Tyrone to Dublin. Unlike the canals which followed in England, this waterway depended on the State for its funding, but its close relationship with a coalfield, albeit an unsuccessful one, anticipated events in England, and it supplied the engineers for the pioneer English canal of the 1750s, the Sankey Navigation, which took St Helens coal to the River Mersey and onwards to Liverpool.

It was the opening of the Duke of Bridgewater's canal, from his Worsley collieries to Manchester, in 1761 that really impressed contemporaries and stimulated a burst of canal promotions which changed the transport geography of England within a generation. The Duke's canal not only halved the cost of coal in Manchester but also featured spectacular innovations. The subterranean mysteries of the canal workings under the mines had their own horrid fascination, but it was the Barton aqueduct, on which coal-barges would float grandly above the River Irwell, that really provoked astonishment. And there were earthworks, embankments, flights of locks and crossings of seemingly impossible terrain. The Duke's enormous gamble, the extension of his canal to open out a new route between Liverpool and Manchester by 1776, showed the practical possibilities for the creation of a national canal system, and smoothed the way for subsequent imitators.

Many further canal schemes were already well advanced by the mid 1770s. Amazement and derision had given way to shrewd and eager calculation, and landowners and merchants began to see the wisdom of investing in canals to serve their areas. The last quarter of the eighteenth century saw the completion of routes linking Trent and Mersey, crossing the Pennines between Yorkshire and Lancashire, and opening out the West Midlands around Birmingham and the Black Country. The early 1790s saw a burst of promotion and speculative investment, the so-called 'Canal Mania', in which optimistic schemes to open out remote rural areas were floated. Some were never completed, and many proved unrewarding to their investors. But the successful industrial concerns could be extremely lucrative; and the self-confidence of the canal engineers was expressed in increasingly costly and monumental projects. Thomas Telford's magnificent cast-iron and masonry aqueduct at Pontcysyllte in North Wales, whose 19 spans cross the River Dee at a maximum

height of 127 feet, illustrates the resources which canal builders could command and the ingenuity which their requirements could stimulate. Many of the skills, techniques and approaches of the railway builders were prefigured in the great canal projects, whose labourers, the 'navigators' or navvies, were a race whose successors gained greater notoriety in the railway age.

OVERLEAF *An artist's portrayal of the Barton Aqueduct on the Bridgewater Canal, showing a vessel sailing gracefully above a remarkably enticing River Irwell.*

BELOW *Thomas Telford's aqueduct at Chirk, on the Ellesmere Canal, built between 1796 and 1801: a major work of its time. The larger railway viaduct behind it is a routine piece of Victorian railway architecture, and bears witness to the ever-growing scale of the projects and ambitions of nineteenth-century civil engineers.*

The canal-building boom continued into the early nineteenth century, but it was petering out by the last years of the Napoleonic Wars. One of the last extensions of the system was the southern section of the Stratford-on-Avon Canal (NT), which was built between 1812 and 1816. It had been promoted twenty years earlier as part of a furious struggle between warring companies in the Birmingham area, in the hope of providing a direct link between the Black Country, the East Midlands and possibly London itself; but its completion had nothing to do with these now-forgotten battles. It was part of William James's visionary scheme to make Stratford into a nationally important transport centre, with the canal linking up with a railway to London. James was, at best, ahead of his time; but the canal was actually built, descending through 13 miles and 36 locks to join the River Avon at Stratford. It has three cast-iron aqueducts (one second only to Pontcysyllte in length), unusual lock-houses with barrel roofs, and over-bridges of innovatory design. Canal engineering was, indeed, still developing in the 1810s and 1820s; and some of the very last canal works, on the eve of the railway age, involved prodigious feats of tunnelling and cutting, as the limitations of earlier schemes were made good and capacity was expanded to cope with enormously increased traffic.

At its peak the English and Welsh canal network extended over 2000 miles with an additional 200 miles or so in Scotland, as well as the Crinan and Caledonian ship canals. Its importance is undeniable, but we should not make too much of it. In the first place, the canal was not as sharply innovative a development as the steam railway or the internal-combustion engine. By 1750, well over a century of river improvement, involving the straightening and deepening of difficult sections and the use of locks to bypass rapids and shallows, had brought some of the benefits of water transport into much of the heart of England. Some of the river navigations were major transport arteries, like the busy and prosperous Aire and Calder system in the West Riding of Yorkshire; and they were improved further in the canal age. So the canals extended an existing system, improved it, and provided links between its outliers, rather than providing something completely new.

Inland navigation had its drawbacks, too. Canals were very slow, especially when traffic was heavy and locks were numerous, as queues of boats formed among much bickering and acrimony. Tunnels were notorious bottlenecks, boats having to be 'legged' laboriously through most of them by bargees lying on their sides and pushing against the tunnel wall, as there was no towpath. Water supplies were often difficult to sustain; canals had to be closed, or loads limited, in time of drought, while frost frequently interrupted traffic during the winter. The Huddersfield Canal was an extreme – and unprofitable – case, but it is still revealing to learn that it had 74 locks in 20 miles, and that it regularly froze up in winter, being out of action for seven weeks in 1837–8. Moreover, much of the canal system, especially in the Midlands, was built to a narrow gauge which cut costs but also limited payloads. The standard lock on the Midland canals was only about 7 feet 6 inches wide, and the 'narrow boats' which were developed to cope with these conditions had a maximum capacity of about 30 tons. All this worsened the congestion as traffic increased. Under these conditions it was difficult to introduce steam power, and horses remained an essential feature of most canals after a disastrous early experiment on the Forth and Clyde Canal revealed the steam tug's propensity to wash away the banks. Canals further limited their productivity by shutting up shop at night, and until the very eve of the railway age their slowness left them unimportant as passenger carriers.

Perhaps most important of all, canals did not always go where the traffic flows went. The early routes were often circuitous, as they followed the contours to minimise the number of locks and conserve their water supplies; and some of the key routes took an inordinate time to complete. There was no direct water route from Manchester to London until 1805, and Pickfords used the Trent and Mersey Canal for part of the journey, then transferred their cargoes to wagons and completed the task by road, avoiding the meanderings of the waterways *via* Oxford and the Thames. The Leeds and Liverpool Canal, a vital trans-Pennine route, was begun in 1770 and not completed until 1816. So, at the turn of the century and beyond, canals were often used in conjunction with roads for inland trade, and on some journeys there was still no real alternative to road haulage. Where they existed, too, the cost advantages of canals were reduced or even negated by the inconvenience and damage caused by carriage to the canal basin, by the danger of theft from warehouses or on the often protracted journeys, and not least by the tendency of waterway proprietors to exploit any advantage they might have by raising tolls to the highest level the law would allow and the traffic would bear.

Thomas Rowlandson brings to life the busy traffic of a country market town on the eve of the railway age, with cattle drovers, pack animals, carriages of all shapes and sizes, and stage-coaches setting off in every direction.

These defects and limitations of canals must be considered alongside their advantages; and they help to explain the continuing vitality and popularity of road transport. Not only did roads account for almost all the vast increase in commercial inland passenger transport between the 1750s and the 1830s: they also took a substantial share of the freight, especially where goods were expensive, fragile or perishable, and where tight delivery deadlines had to be met.

Improvements in stage-coach schedules were revealingly dramatic. Between 1750 and 1811 the fastest scheduled journey between London and York fell from 84 hours to 27½; between London and Shrewsbury, from 75 hours to 23, and between London and Bath, from 36 hours to 14. Improvements in the provinces were slower, and fares remained high at the top of the market; but the number and variety of services grew enormously, especially in the late eighteenth century, and costs were cut because fewer meals and overnight stays had to be paid for on the road. There was also a remarkable expansion from the late eighteenth century onwards in London suburban coach services for up-market commuters. The road freight haulage industry showed similar vitality, from firms like Pickfords developing national coverage at one extreme, to a proliferation of local carriers operating out of every market town at the other. The flexibility, availability, speed and reliability of road transport gave it the preference for all but the heaviest and least urgent cargoes.

So improvements in road transport were shrinking the real size of England during this period. This effect was especially marked from a London perspective, and in the south and east, but it applied to some extent everywhere. How was it done? In England and Wales, the key innovation was the spread of the turnpike system of road maintenance to become the norm on English main roads (and many not-so-main ones), especially during the second half of the eighteenth century.

The establishment of a Turnpike Trust took the responsibility for maintaining a stretch of road out of the hands of the parishes through which it passed, and passed it over to a group of (usually) local property-owners, who were granted the power to levy tolls to pay for the improvement and upkeep of the road. During the seventeenth century a growing number of parishes which were unlucky enough to have main roads passing through them were showing reluctance to expend the labour and money which the law required of them. The turnpike system transferred most of the cost of main road repairs from local inhabitants to road users while providing (at least in theory) roads of improved quality in return. Turnpikes spread steadily from the late seventeenth century onwards, and by 1750 there was already an extensive network radiating from London, supplemented by knots of local undertakings in areas of mining or burgeoning local trade, such as the Severn Valley and the West Riding of Yorkshire. The Great North Road was turnpiked almost to Berwick on the Scottish border, with a small gap in the North Midlands; the roads to Chester and Manchester were almost complete, and that to Bristol was turnpiked throughout. From this firm basis, the 1750s and 1760s saw a remarkable and unprecedented expansion and consolidation of the network, which extended by 1770 throughout the West Country and into much of Wales, and into the remotest fastnesses of the Lake District and the Scottish Borders. After this, the rate of development slowed down, although growth continued into the nineteenth century in the industrial areas of the north and Midlands.

It is one thing to point to the rapid spread of turnpikes in England and Wales: it is another matter to show how they actually affected the quality of the roads. The verdicts of contemporary travellers confirm that by the 1770s most main roads were being reasonably or even well maintained; and this is what we should expect in the light of the increasing volume and speed of traffic. Trusts were becoming more professional in their repair policies, as more of them employed professional surveyors and experience taught better ways of forming surfaces, laying foundations

Thomas Telford's suspension bridge at Conwy, completed in 1826. The thickness of the suspension cables is a reminder of the novelty of this technology. The gateway displays the Prince of Wales' feathers.

and draining. Long before the well-known activities of Telford and MacAdam in the early nineteenth century, there was a piecemeal spread of practical improvements.

Not only were existing roads improved: in some parts of the country new ones were also being created, sometimes on a very ambitious scale. The Shrewsbury-Holyhead and Chester-Holyhead roads, which by the early nineteenth century carried the Irish mails, were completely remade under the supervision of Thomas Telford, with finance from central government. The sweeping curves of the present A5 in North Wales are one result of this: but the crowning glory of the scheme was the great Menai suspension bridge to Anglesey, which dwarfed all previous bridges. It opened in 1826, a few months before its smaller sister bridge (NT) at Conwy on the Chester road. Here Telford acknowledged the picturesque proximity of Conwy Castle by designing suspension towers which mimicked castellated medieval gateways: a motif which later recurred at the entrances to railway tunnels, and showed the

engineers' awareness of the historic significance of their undertakings.

Central government money was also forthcoming for transport improvements in other remote areas which were too impoverished to make their own arrangements. Between 1803 and 1821 the ubiquitous Telford presided over the making of 875 miles of road and eleven major bridges in the Highlands, and in 1822 the Caledonian Canal was opened, linking the east coast with the west through the Great Glen. This investment was

RIGHT *The George Inn, Southwark, the last survivor of London's galleried coaching inns, which looked after stage-coach travellers in the same way as motorway service stations now cater for drivers on long journeys.*

BELOW *The prevailing techniques of road repair at the beginning of the nineteenth century, as illustrated in Pyne's* Microcosm, *which contains similar material on trades and crafts of all kinds.*

aimed at stemming the tide of emigration and stimulating the Highland economy; and the roads alone provided work for an average of 2700 men in each year. All this activity was particularly remarkable in an age when the dominant creed of economists and 'practical men' sought to reduce the role of the State in the economy to a minimum. Similar pump-priming took place in Northern Ireland, where the legacy includes the Antrim coast road, which clings precariously to a rugged, breaker-pounded shoreline and could never have been financed by the locals alone.

It was under circumstances like these, especially in the Highlands, that the social and economic impact of transport improvement in this period was most obvious and dramatic. The new roads eased the passage of seasonal migrants, cattle drovers and commercial travellers. They brought Inverness into daily contact with Aberdeen, and Wick into daily contact with Inverness. They brought tea, tourists and tobacco to Skye, while the island's eggs began to find unsuspected markets in the outside world. They brought agricultural improvement, money and a market economy, while they raised material living standards and eroded traditional ways of life. They were, in the widest sense (and with losses to set alongside the gains), harbingers of modernity.

In most of England, the results were less arresting. Turnpikes improved existing roads, rather than allowing wheeled transport to penetrate where none had gone before, except in a few upland or otherwise difficult areas. Their contribution is harder to disentangle from the many other changes which were also going on. But important developments can be clearly related to their influence. Corridors of enclosure and (less commonly) market gardening followed the turnpiking of rural roads, and forest and heath were converted into arable when the better roads made markets accessible for produce which had to be carried as well as for beasts which could walk. The larger market towns became readily accessible over a wider area, and grew partly at the expense of their smaller neighbours. Industries found easier access to the home market, and to the ports for export. The burgeoning road transport industry brought prosperity to innkeepers at staging-posts on the turnpikes, and generated employment for inn servants, ostlers, and all who dealt with horses and conveyances. The turnpike approaches to the larger towns became lined with the residences of prosperous commuters, and by the 1820s London stockbrokers were regularly commuting to the City

by stage-coach from Brighton. The improved roads became efficient distributors of news, fashions and ideas, to the dismay of some socially-conservative commentators; and they began the long and never-completed process of smoothing out the peculiarities of the English regions.

All this sometimes generated social conflict. Turnpikes meant that the King's Highway was no longer free to all users: in a sense, they privatised sections of road, for the benefit of those who could afford the tolls, and to the disadvantage of more marginal and impoverished travellers. By aiding the transport of grain to London, the big towns and the ports, they pulled prices up and sometimes induced local shortages, or the fear of shortage. So, not surprisingly, turnpike gates were sometimes attacked by hostile crowds, and food riots also seem to have followed in their wake. Given the importance of turnpikes, it is not surprising that their progress brought suffering to some as well as benefits to others; and they made their contribution to the general economic trends which enriched so many farmers at the expense of their labourers during this period. All this further emphasises their fundamental importance.

Turnpikes, like canals, were being improved right up to the railway age. There were widespread accelerations in services during the 1820s and 1830s, as more road surfaces were 'macadamised' and stage-coaches acquired more sophisticated springing and braking arrangements. Attempts were made to apply steam power to road carriage, but with no more success than on the canals. The transport system of the 1820s still depended on animals and the elements. As in most of the economy, there had been a spate of small innovations, and one or two major new departures; but it would be stretching matters to call the results a 'revolution'. The coastal and overseas shipping trade also depended on the weather, and adverse winds could paralyse a harbour for weeks at a time. The most significant changes in the long run involved the application of the steam-engine to transport, as well as to mining and manufacturing; and it was the combination of steam power and railways that made the crucial difference.

The use of wooden rails to ease the transit of horse-drawn heavy goods, and to reduce wear and tear on trackways, was widespread from at least the early seventeenth century to move coal from upland mines to industry or waterways. By the end of the eighteenth century extensive networks had developed in mining areas where there was little scope for the extension of water transport.

Complex patterns of wagonways and tram-roads trailed across the maps of Tyneside, the Swansea Valley and the Vale of Neath in Glamorgan, for example. By this time iron rails were being introduced, and the early nineteenth century saw increasingly determined attempts to use cheap pit-head coal to run the traffic by stationary and then mobile steam-engines.

The first real breakthrough came in the 1820s, when the Stockton and Darlington line attracted attention by running locomotive-hauled trains interspersed with its horse-drawn traffic, and offering access to its services to the general public, a practice which had been spreading since 1801.

But these early engines were painfully slow, and it was not until the Liverpool and Manchester Railway's famous Rainhill Trials in 1829 that the superior speed and pulling power of the newest kind of locomotive was clearly demonstrated. The steam railway as a practical proposition outside the grimy precincts of the Tyneside mines, and as a potential agent of social and economic transformation, began with Stephenson's *Rocket*.

As early as the mid 1820s, the potential attractions of long-distance railways were becoming apparent enough to induce a brief flurry of speculative promotions; and when the Liverpool and Manchester line opened in 1830, enormous publicity was generated for the new form of transport. The great novelty of the Liverpool and Manchester was its striking financial success as a passenger carrier: indeed, in the early years merchandise receipts were dwarfed by the passenger revenues, as businessmen in the two cities seized the opportunity to do business face to face without significant loss of time. By the mid 1830s, the lessons had been digested, and a new spate of

One of the earliest effective mobile steam railway engines: George Stephenson's locomotive at Killingworth Colliery, with the inevitable train of coal wagons.

serious projects was launched, often based on ludicrously optimistic expectations of profit, but undoubtedly meaning business. From this time on, the development of the British railway network was inexorable, punctuated though it was with bursts of unsound speculation (most famously the 'Railway Mania' of the mid 1840s), followed by periods of lost confidence and doubt. The continuing improvement of the locomotive, so that gradients which seemed impossible in 1840 were mastered with ease a few years later, and the development of goods traffic, cumulatively provided an added impetus.

Between the mid 1830s and the early 1850s the main inter-city railway lines of Britain were almost all completed. By 1854 there were 6000 miles of line in England and Wales alone, and 92 million passenger journeys were made on them in that year: half of them third class or at a penny a mile in the 'Parliamentary' trains which had been legally imposed on all British railways in 1844. Despite the immense passenger traffic, goods receipts were growing even faster: in 1852, for the first time, they outweighed the passenger revenue. But railway building did not stop at the completion of an obviously lucrative basic main-line network. In the 1860s and 1870s large numbers of feeder and branch lines were built, and new cross-country links were developed, sometimes through apparently unpromising tracts of territory such as central Wales. Some duplicates, or near-duplicates, of existing main lines were also opened. The expansion of the system continued to the turn of the century and beyond, as branch lines were built to penetrate any rural backwater from which traffic might be generated. At its peak in the early twentieth century, the network included more than 20,000 route miles. Even Northern Ireland, with its scattered rural population, had more than 2000 miles, many of them cheaply constructed on a narrow 3-foot gauge. The steam train had become an almost universal influence on lives and landscapes.

Most of these railways were financed initially by local landowners and business interests: people who would benefit from the improved communications and access to markets that a railway would provide, even if the company itself failed to pay a dividend. But the early trunk routes, especially, also drew funding from speculative investors who lived at a distance and hoped to get a good return on their capital. Liverpool merchants in the 1830s and 1840s thus put enormous sums into railway schemes as far apart as East Anglia and

Northern Ireland. By the late nineteenth century the big, established railway companies which had developed out of the amalgamation of many smaller ones were coming to be seen as safe places for the savings of small investors; but the initial risks were taken largely by substantial landowners and the business community.

The astonishing extent of the Edwardian railway system arose largely from the competitive framework within which the railways developed. There was no overall state master plan, as there often was in Europe. So, increasingly, lines were built primarily to compete with existing routes; and this led to further spending on cut-off lines to shorten the distance between major centres. Branch lines proliferated partly because of the need to placate local opinion – and many were, in the first place, locally promoted by small independent companies – and partly out of fear lest a rival company should step in and take the traffic. An example from Devon brings these themes together. In 1859 an independent company brought the railway to Tavistock by building a short branch line from the South Devon Railway. Six years later another small company extended the route above the Lydford Gorge (NT) and across the Cornish border into Launceston. All this was typical of much else. But a decade later the London and South Western Railway, swollen from modest beginnings by a series of amalgamations, sought access to Plymouth in competition with the Great Western. To this end it built a new main line from Exeter through Okehampton, which met the Launceston line at Lydford, with the result that this sleepy rural backwater was transformed, and the Lydford Gorge echoed to the pulsating excitement of London expresses working hard to beat their rival's performance between Plymouth and the capital.

In a period when the railways had effectively no competition for what traffic there was, not all rural lines were unprofitable, and in any case the companies themselves seem to have had no idea of measuring the economic performance of individual routes and stations within their empires. Once opened, however deeply a line might slumber, it was kept open, although very little might be spent on it. Railway closures before the First World War were almost unknown, although rolling-stock on some of the Irish lines, especially, became increasingly archaic. At least two passenger services, that from Fintona Junction to Fintona in Northern Ireland, and the Port Carlisle branch in Cumberland, were still horse-hauled on the eve of the First World War.

Mining technology applied to railway building: the top of the Great Shaft at Kilsby Tunnel during the construction of the London and Birmingham Railway in 1836.

Railway building also depended for a long time on manual labour, one of the last lines to be completed without mechanical aids of any kind being the Settle to Carlisle line of the 1870s, across some of the bleakest and most isolated terrain in England. The bulk of the railway system was created with pick, shovel and wheelbarrow, by men who performed legendary feats, under sometimes appalling conditions. But the image of the navvy as a drunken, disreputable social outcast living in primitive hut encampments by the trackside is at least partly misleading. Most navvies lodged in houses close to the works, and many had wives and children with them. Their numbers included a leavening of skilled construction workers such as blacksmiths and stonemasons. The work was arduous and often dangerous, but it did not somehow turn the railway labourers into a race apart.

As the railways became more firmly established, they became major employers of permanent labour in their own right. In 1847 there were 47,000 men on their payrolls; in 1873, 275,000. The wide range of railway employees included professional engineers, who could attain immense authority as locomotive superintendents or traffic managers; an army of supervisors and routine clerical workers; the labour aristocrats of the footplate, the express passenger engine-drivers; the signalmen, who might have awesome responsibilities at busy junctions; and a numerous ill-paid rank and file of porters, platelayers and engine cleaners. What all railway workers had in common, in return for an unusual and envied job security, was the experience of autocratic management with necessarily high expectations of discipline and conduct, and a less necessary tendency to insist on

very long hours under often spartan conditions. As the railway historian Jack Simmons remarks, we should not forget the unsung heroes of the system. He instances the Midland Railway goods guards who, night after night, were effectively in sole control of the brakes on the London to Manchester express freight, at an average speed of 28 miles an hour, on a route which included a switchback section through the Peak District, where the slightest miscalculation might mean disaster. This one example, which had its counterparts all over the country, shows the level of skill, concentration and endurance which could be required of railway workers.

The wider economic impact of the railways is easier to suggest than to calculate. Professor Hawke has argued that by 1865 the railways had effectively augmented the national income by about 10 per cent. They were especially valuable in cutting the cost of coal and mineral transport, although they also achieved significant reductions in freight rates on other goods.

But there is more to the story than this. As the railways spread, they increased the carrying power of the transport system, at a time when a lack of additional water resources made the further extension of canals in the manufacturing districts increasingly costly and difficult. The railways thus enabled the system to break out of what could soon have become a stifling constraint on further growth. They greatly increased the speed of goods transport, opening out new markets for perishables like fresh fish and milk, and cutting farmers' and manufacturers' overheads. They enabled new sources of raw materials to be exploited on a large scale, and encouraged the rise of new towns to process them. In industrial areas they broke the canals' lucrative monopoly on heavy goods, although they often substituted new monopolies of their own which provoked angry complaints from customers. They were heavy users of iron, steel and construction materials in their own right, and they generated employment at a time when population growth was threatening to outrun the economy's need for workers, bringing stark threats of spreading poverty and political unrest. They pioneered the rise of large companies with extensive territorial ramifications, recruiting their investment capital from large numbers of individual shareholders and needing new systems of management and accountancy. In all these ways they were vital to the continuing growth of the Victorian economy.

Even more significant was the railways' influence on the way of life of the British people. Above all, they provided new opportunities. Their relative cheapness, in money and time, encouraged people to journey further and more often. Additional encouragement came from the comparative comfort of rail travel. The engineer Joseph Mitchell, a seasoned traveller, professed to enjoy the overnight journey on top of the stage-coach from Edinburgh to Inverness:

Being an old traveller I dozed, well protected by greatcoats, between two less prudent passengers. I like to ride outside, if well protected, on a summer night, the pure morning air being so fresh and grateful.

But this was a summer luxury; and so were the later Victorian revivals of stage-coach services, with nostalgic amateur drivers, on the London to Brighton route. Most people preferred a closed railway carriage and, if necessary, a footwarmer. The late Victorian development of corridor trains with lavatories and restaurant cars made long-distance travel a still less daunting prospect, and even a pleasure, for the public at large.

All this led to an enormous increase in personal mobility. Long-range migration was eased, and excursion trains broadened the horizons of working-class people. New kinds of outer suburban living became possible. The railways furthered the commercialisation of sport: horses were ferried to distant race-meetings and excursions took crowds to all manner of attractions, from pugilism to professional football and brass band contests. Information flows travelled even faster than the trains, as the electric telegraph followed the tracks across an evermore accessible countryside. The shrinkage of Britain continued at an ever-increasing speed as more powerful locomotives and improved tracks and signalling cut journey times again and again. Perhaps the best indication of the pervasive importance of the railways, especially as passenger carriers, was the growing interest taken by central government at a time when it was most unwilling in principle to interfere in the workings of private companies. Not only did it require the running of 'Parliamentary' trains. It also legislated to impose a standard gauge

---

PREVIOUS PAGES *The first girders for the Midland Railway's enormous train shed at St Pancras Station, London, are set in place. The finished building, which was opened to traffic in 1869, is still the most dramatic and atmospheric of London's termini.*

(in response to the problems caused by the Great Western company's insistence on being different), imposed compulsory inspection of tracks and operations and inquiries into accidents, and restricted the level of railway dividends and the scope for mergers and price-fixing. Here was a business which had become too important to leave to the businessmen; and this point of view predominated whatever the political colour of the government.

Some of these developments had already been presaged by the turnpikes and inland waterways; but steam railways brought about a change of scale, speed, volume and reliability which added up to an unprecedented transformation. It affected, in a direct and positive way, a much higher proportion of the population than had any previous transport change. There were casualties too, of course: towns which were bypassed, bereft innkeepers and stage-coach proprietors, and distinctive occupational groups, such as the cattle drovers whose displacement by the trains left the ancient green-roads on which they had travelled silent and deserted.

But the triumph of steam was not just a land-locked phenomenon. These same years saw a vast increase in steamship tonnage, with similar consequences for the swelling volume of international trade to those of the railways inland. Steamers took Welsh coal to distant markets; they brought grain and cheap meat from the Americas to boost working-class living standards and threaten the prosperity of English farmers; they sped emigrants on their way, and eased the creation of a transatlantic economy; and they provided exotic destinations for wealthy pleasure seekers. Within Britain, the coasting trade remained a real competitor with the railways for some cargoes, on some routes; paddle-steamers criss-crossed the Thames Estuary and the Bristol Channel, took Glasgow holiday-makers to the Clyde resorts and the Isle of Man, opened out the Western Isles to intrepid tourists, and brought Ireland closer to England; and lake steamers, like the National Trust's *Gondola* on Coniston Water in the Lake District, enhanced the enjoyment of mountain scenery for the less adventurous. Here again there were losers, as the ideal size of seagoing vessels increased and trade became concentrated into the larger ports, with proper docks and cargo-handling facilities; but the steam revolution on water was just as far-reaching in its implications as the railway revolution on land: more so, perhaps, if we take account of the role of the steamer and the coaling station in the making and sustaining of the Empire.

On land, the dominance of the steam railway was just beginning to be challenged by the turn of the century. The bicycle was offering growing numbers of young and healthy town-dwellers cheap access to the countryside, playing its part in the early stages of female emancipation in the process. It also increased the mobility of farm-workers, many of whom still lived a fair way from the nearest market town and station. The steam tram, from the 1870s, and especially the electric tram from the 1890s, became more flexible competitors for the custom of the suburban, and even the inter-urban, rail traveller. From about 1910 the motor bus offered even more flexibility, although it was still short on reliability. The motor car was still mainly a short-haul vehicle for the wealthy, despite attempts to bring it down-market in the Edwardian years. Steam still ruled in 1914, with the horse as its handmaiden; and over the past eighty years or so it had transformed the social fabric of Britain. Nowhere was this more apparent than in the towns, and in the ways of life of their inhabitants; and throughout the period urban growth embodied and stimulated some of the most interesting and dramatic aspects of social and economic change. Transport developments contributed inescapably to the rise of urban society, but the process had a dynamic of its own. The next chapter explores this further.

CHAPTER SEVEN

Towns and Cities

The years between 1750 and 1914 saw unprecedented urban growth in Britain. British society was already highly urbanised by comparison with nearly all of Western Europe in 1750, but the developments that followed filled contemporaries with pride, exhilaration, alarm and outrage. The new urban societies offered alluring opportunities for wealth, social advancement and civic amenities; but they also threatened crime, disease, social conflict and revolution. The historic dominance of London was challenged by proud, self-confident provincial metropolises, each with its smoky corona of subordinate towns. The old provincial hierarchy, with York, Bristol and Norwich as the regional capitals of England, was disrupted and then subverted by the rise of new ports, industrial towns and leisure and retirement centres. In Scotland, Edinburgh's leading position was threatened and then overtaken by Glasgow, whose commercial predominance in the late eighteenth century was reinforced by industrial growth. By 1821 Glasgow's population had surpassed Edinburgh's, and by 1901 it was more than double that of the Scottish capital. Meanwhile, Belfast was ousting Dublin as the commercial capital of much of Ireland, and the rise of Cardiff, Swansea and the coal and iron towns of the South Wales valleys completely altered the urban geography and population distribution of Wales.

In some ways, town growth stimulated other economic and social changes on a broad front. In other ways, changes in the size, nature and organisation of towns reflected developments in the wider society. None the less, urban expansion in this period clearly changed lives and transformed landscapes, and much of the legacy of the Georgian and Victorian town builders is still there to be looked at, and lived in. Why this massive inheritance of brick, stone and slate? And what was life like in these towns?

The variety of urban experiences was ever-widening, as new kinds of towns appeared, and established places grew, stagnated, declined or changed in character. At the beginning of the period the great seaports were prominent among the most dynamic of British towns, and some sustained their momentum for much longer. This reflected the persisting importance of overseas trade, and indeed coastal shipping, to economic growth. The fastest-growing port was Liverpool, which overtook Bristol as Britain's most populous provincial port in the 1780s and vied with Birmingham, Glasgow and Manchester in the Victorian and Edwardian years for the title of second city of the Empire. All these cities had populations of over 700,000 in the early twentieth century. Liverpool's growth was based on servicing an extensive and diverse hinterland, which extended to the Potteries, the Birmingham area and North Wales as well as the Cheshire salt industry and the coal, cotton and chemical areas of Lancashire. Hull's less famous rise from obscurity was similarly broadly based, and Bristol's role as the 'metropolis of the west' continued to depend heavily on its maritime connections with the Severn Valley and the Bristol Channel.

Other substantial ports relied mainly on exporting one or two staple commodities: coal on Tyneside and later at Cardiff, grain at eighteenth-century King's Lynn and Great Yarmouth. In such cases growth might be limited by the difficulty of obtaining return cargoes if local industries and populous hinterlands failed to develop. The classic case was Whitehaven, in West Cumberland. Here a brief foray into tobacco importing, for redistribution along the coastline, could not disguise the town's dependence on exporting local coal to Ireland. When tobacco was lost to Glasgow, the impenetrable mountain fastnesses of the western Lake District set strict limits to the growth of a hinterland. The patronage of the redoubtable Lowther family, who had invested heavily in mines and docks, was no match for the brutal facts of geography; and Whitehaven lost its buoyancy at the end of the eighteenth century, to stagnate for many years. This lack of nineteenth-century development left the town's grid-plan of Georgian streets largely intact, along with the harbour works of what was once one of England's top five ports in shipping tonnage, and the chimneys, ventilation buildings and wagon-ways of the mines which adjoined the harbour.

The warehouses and dock installations of the larger ports were even more arresting. In 1841 it was said that Liverpool's fourteen docks, opened at regular intervals since the early eighteenth century, 'probably contain more masonry than the pyramids'. Four years later the Albert Dock followed. Professor Pevsner called it 'the unquestionable climax of Liverpool dock-architecture': the most overwhelming expression of the dock engineer

---

PREVIOUS PAGES *Albert Dock, Liverpool, completed in 1845: the masterpiece of the town's dock engineer, Jesse Hartley, and one of the most powerful displays of commercial architecture in Europe.*

Jesse Hartley's preference for assembling blocks of granite in 'rough Cyclopean masses'. This example of 'architecture for giants', surrounded on all sides by five-storey warehouses with classical detail, was far from being the last of Liverpool's docks; but it embodies the pride, prosperity and self-confidence of mercantile Liverpool in its early Victorian glory.

Alongside the rise of giant seaports which threatened to absorb the trade of whole regions, many smaller ports survived and even prospered modestly, while new ones continued to be created in the canal and railway eras. At Goole on the Humber, Ellesmere Port and Runcorn on the Mersey, and at Grangemouth in Scotland, small towns were planted where goods were transferred between inland waterways and seagoing vessels, while Stourport in the West Midlands grew up as a transfer point between the Birmingham canal system and the Severn estuary. The railway age spawned many more newly-built harbour towns, from Fleetwood to Fishguard to Felixstowe.

These newly-planted ports often presented an imposing face to the waterfront, with warehouses, classical dock offices, and perhaps a Georgian customs-house. Public opulence was a general feature of the business end of seaports, though it was often compromised by the assault on the senses entailed by the unloading of guano or animal hides. Set back from the quays in the larger ports there would be streets and squares of substantial houses for prosperous merchants, bankers and solicitors, such as the eighteenth-century Maister House (NT) in Hull's old High Street. But port life generated a seamy underside. The contrasts between public opulence and private squalor, between elegant displays of wealth and miserable dens of abject poverty and vice, were nowhere more stark than in towns that lived by international commerce.

The waterfront provided abundant but intermittent work for dockers, carters and seamen. Dockers were hired by the day or half-day, if they were lucky enough to be hired at all: for the demand for their labour varied according to season, wind and tide. There were almost always more men than jobs. This led to chronic insecurity, graft and corruption, and heavy drinking while waiting for work. Moreover, dock work was demanding and sometimes dangerous. Experienced dockers specialised in particular kinds of cargo, and took pride in their expertise. The potential agonies of the job are shown by this description of the unloading of Welsh building slates at Runcorn:

There were twenty-four standard sizes and slates were a cruel cargo to unload for they had to be discharged by hand being thrown up from the hold of the coaster to be caught by men on deck who then passed them to others on the quay. Every slate in an eighty or ninety ton cargo was landed in this way.

Most dock work, throughout the period, involved this kind of sustained hard manual labour, with little mechanical assistance except with really large items like heavy machinery.

Sailors encountered their own hazards. The dangers of the sea were all too real, especially in the age of sail. Arrival in port meant exposure to different snares. Seamen who had just been paid off after a long voyage were easy targets for dishonest lodging-house keepers and prostitutes. These occupations, in turn, were among the few means of gainful employment for women in towns whose economies were dominated by heavy manual labour which was defined as men's work. There might be opportunities in import processing, such as making tobacco into cigars, and the sweated clothing trades took advantage of the availability of cheap female labour. There was laundry work, domestic service and the drink trade, but very little else. All this made for a dockside culture of poverty, insecurity and endemic violence. Matters were worsened by the pressure on housing created by the need of waterfront labourers to live close to their work. Overcrowding in the older dockside slums was among the worst in Georgian and Victorian Britain, with many families existing in damp, dark cellars in the 1850s and beyond, and substantial proportions of the population living at two or more to a room.

Liverpool provided the most daunting example of this complex of social problems, but all ports knew them to some extent, although the new promotions of the railway age were less crowded and cramped. Whitehaven's Georgian streets concealed severe overcrowding in handsome houses which were divided into one-room tenements shared by whole families. A government inspector in the mid nineteenth century, case-hardened by many such assignments, commented that 'Few persons would believe the human wretchedness that exists in Whitehaven.' One extract from his survey gives the flavour of conditions which were all too common:

Caledonia . . . (has) 12 tenements let off, and those that occupy two rooms generally have an Irish family living with them; chimney sweeps and vagrants of all classes live and lodge here, many of those have a bull-dog or

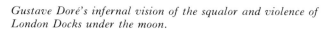
Gustave Doré's infernal vision of the squalor and violence of London Docks under the moon.

two, which is kept in a cupboard or pantry; underneath there is a number of nailmakers' shops, as dark as a dungeon, and the smoke goes from floor to floor through the whole building. There is no water supply to the place, or other convenience.

There were always better-off workers, in building and shipbuilding or repairing, for example; and the range of opportunities widened in the larger ports in the later nineteenth century with the growth of relatively secure white-collar work in banking and insurance and the increase in railway and local government work. Everywhere, too, there was the usual urban lower middle class of shopkeepers and tradesmen. But it was still in the ports that the contrasts between rich and poor were widest and most glaring.

The leaders of port society were the great overseas merchants and shipowners. By the later eighteenth century some were being drawn into banking, too, as provincial banks developed to ease the complexities of credit in a system which had depended on promissory notes and personal reputation. Such people were far enough removed from the often grubby sources of their wealth to occupy the very highest rungs of non-landed society. Some of these merchant princes acquired country estates. Many more moved out to villas in attractive districts of the hinterland. The élites were very small and snobbish; in Hull in the late eighteenth century the best circles embraced perhaps a hundred families. But seaport high society was always open to new money in sufficiently copious quantities. The rise of the fortunate gamblers among the early Liverpool steamship owners, often from humble Scottish origins, bore eloquent witness to this.

The counting houses, offices and even town residences of these ultimate beneficiaries of the commercial revolution were seldom far from the teeming slums of the docks, but their lives might have been conducted on a different planet. Lower down the scale were a larger number of struggling and aspiring merchants and professionals, many of whom played the commodity markets which were becoming increasingly sophisticated by the nineteenth century, their growth accompanied by the opening of provincial stock exchanges. The propertied were protected from too disastrous a fall by the safety net of insurance, the division of risks through the issue of shares, the availability of loans from relatives and allies in times of crisis, and ultimately the coming of limited liability.

The social contrasts between rich and poor were less vivid in the manufacturing towns whose growth accelerated dramatically from the late eighteenth century onwards. The rich were less bloated, there were fewer of the very poor, and there were more layers in between. According to the 1851 census, which surveyed urban growth over a frenetic half-century, the 'manufacturing' and 'mining and hardware' towns had grown faster than the 'seaports', although the 26 largest of these had trebled their population. Only the spas and seaside resorts set a hotter pace than the industrial centres, and the figures for these are suspect. The most dynamic kinds of manufacturing town specialised in iron, cotton, pottery and hardware, in that order. This put the spotlight on the East and West Midlands, south Lancashire, the West Riding of Yorkshire, Tyneside and the central Scottish Lowlands.

The census classification was too simple: ports like Bristol were also manufacturing centres, and county towns like Nottingham and Preston kept older guises as administrative towns and meeting-places for polite society alongside their textile, lace and hosiery industries. Some of the largest industrial towns were regional capitals in their own right, whether they had grown into the role, like Manchester, or kept it despite the decline of traditional industries, like Norwich or Exeter. Such places offered commercial facilities, financial expertise, shopping and leisure for extensive hinterlands, and their trading and professional middle classes were far more numerous than in the really specialised industrial towns. But the overall pattern is not seriously misleading.

After 1851, and especially after 1881, industrial towns in general grew more slowly. There were mid Victorian late developers, iron, steel, railway and chemical towns like Middlesbrough and St Helens, and some older-established coal and textile towns, including Wigan and Bradford, put on a new spurt. But really rapid development in late Victorian times became more the preserve of dormitory towns and resorts. Some older industrial centres, as in the Black Country or Lancashire's Rossendale Valley, were already stagnating or beginning a long decline. So there were many kinds of industrial town, and a multiplicity of experiences.

The most arresting of the industrial towns of the late eighteenth and early nineteenth century were those which emerged in empty countryside or coalesced from scattered hamlets. Merthyr Tydfil, in South Wales, was perhaps the most remarkable of these, expressing within its sprawling boundaries all the most potent visual and moral images of Industrial Revolution. Merthyr's great ironworks, which included household names like Dowlais and Cyfarthfa, brought men in their thousands to colonise the windy hillsides which surged in barren splendour towards the towering summits of the Brecon Beacons. The clangour and roar of the heaviest industrial processes invaded the solitudes of buzzard and kite, and two worlds met.

Within Merthyr itself there were deep social differences, and not just those between the ironmasters and their workers. The Guests of Dowlais and the Crawshays of Cyfarthfa presided over contrasting communities, and their lesser rivals had peculiarities of their own. Dowlais was a paternalist régime, notorious for requiring its workers to buy their goods at Company shops, a 'truck' system which drove them into debt and dependence. But the Guests provided schooling, churches and chapels, and welfare facilities to go with the company housing. The Crawshay regime, by contrast, was less prone to interference in the lives of its workpeople, unusually tolerant of trade unions, opposed to hierarchies and established powers, and concerned to achieve good labour relations by maintaining production and employment during hard times. The Dowlais community tended towards Chapel and respectability, although the pub was almost inescapable in Merthyr before the 1840s, while the Crawshay culture inclined towards beer and hedonism. Merthyr's notorious red-light districts, including 'China', the no-go area for police and respectables which had its own 'Emperor' and 'Empress', huddled by the Taff bridges close to Crawshay territory.

The predominantly Welsh labour force, which had imported its language and its customs from the countryside, defied easy labelling: it supported harpists, balladeers, exponents of traditional Welsh verse, self-taught mathematicians, champion runners, gamblers and poachers. The town long remained a face-to-face society, rich in nicknames. It was presided over by resident ironmasters, whose symbols of authority stood out in the landscape. They were English, and most had ties with the county gentry; but they were not altogether cut off from their work-forces. There were many intermediate layers between ironmaster and labourer; managers, subcontractors, skilled and supervisory workers with an intense pride in their craft, and a ramifying group of prospering shopkeepers and tradesmen. This complex society harboured fierce political cross-currents, and from the 1790s especially it developed a radical democratic political tradition, and a propensity to riot in defence of living standards in the recurrent hard times which struck the iron industry. In 1831 a full-scale uprising was suppressed by a Highland infantry regiment after four days and many deaths. Merthyr thus pulled together the many strands of urban problems and opportunities in the period, and its frontier situation and minimal local government institutions helped to generate a lively and distinctive kind of urban society.

Merthyr Tydfil was unique in the detail of its experience, but many of the themes recurred elsewhere. A comparison with Oldham, another frontier town with a reputation for political radicalism and labour unrest between the 1790s and the 1840s, will emphasise this point.

Oldham, an eastern outpost of Lancashire high in the Pennine foothills, became a distinctive success story of the cotton industry. Indeed, it adapted to the new conditions of the later nineteenth century more convincingly than Merthyr, and sustained its dynamism into Edwardian times while Merthyr retreated into a narrower concentration on coal. In the late eighteenth century Oldham had been a scattering of upland hamlets among the scrubby pasture of the Pennine foothills, where small farmers doubled as domestic manufacturers. Its houses spread higgledy-piggledy across this untidy countryside, and even in the 1830s, when steam-powered mills were proliferating, the map showed pock-marks and blotches of settlement around a thickening urban core, rather than the relentless grid pattern of the later industrial town. Most of its factories were small and its factory-owners self-made, sprung from the rough, assertive, insular local stock; and its people cleaved to their customs with determination, though not always with success, as their world changed around them.

Towards mid century the pace of growth quickened, and Oldham was transformed into the world capital of coarse cotton spinning. At the same time, its subsidiary industry of making beaver hats gave way to the manufacture of textile machinery. The mid Victorian years saw the multiplication of cotton mills on a new scale, many-bayed and multi-storeyed, owned by limited companies whose capital came mainly from local

tradesmen and the skilled and supervisory layers of the working class. Family firms were outfaced and outnumbered, but few had sought a wider influence on the life of the town. At the same time the radical political traditions which had seen Oldham become a stronghold of the Chartists in the late 1830s were withering on the vine. Oldham's growth continued in a similar vein into the new century, its skyline dominated by the towers and chimneys of its mills, with little sense of visible civic pride or architectural display. This was industrial townscape at its most determinedly businesslike: the town not so much as machine for living, but as machine for manufacturing coarse yarns and dividends.

Successful on its own terms, Oldham was only one variant of the cotton town species, although all such towns contrasted sharply with the coal and hardware towns in the amount of waged work they offered for women and children, making for very different family economies and even affecting the balance between the sexes. The cotton towns almost certainly saw less drunkenness and prostitution than the centres of heavy industry. But there were many differences between individual cotton towns. Rochdale, Oldham's neighbour, displayed much more civic pride and municipal initiative, symbolised by a magnificent town hall. So did Bolton, which had its own specialisation in spinning the finer yarns, and retained its family firms, with their paternalist policies and dependent settlements, beyond the First World War. The later-developing weaving towns of Lancashire's northern frontier were different again: among other things, they offered higher wages for women than any other urban economies in late Victorian and Edwardian Britain. Within this framework, towns like Burnley, Nelson and Accrington differed remarkably in topography, building materials, social institutions and politics. The superficial similarities of the 'cotton towns' disguised considerable social diversity.

Macclesfield exemplifies another kind of textile town experience. It lived by the silk industry and by the 1820s could claim to be Britain's premier silk town: two-thirds of the town's work-force were spinners or weavers of silk. Macclesfield was never dominated by mills, as Oldham was. It retained its older role as a market town and shopping centre: and, like many industrial towns, it had a preindustrial past. Its growth as a manufacturing centre was concentrated into the century after 1750, when mill architecture was less overwhelming in scale. Moreover, the transition to power-

Leeds Town Hall, as completed to the designs of Cuthbert Brodrick in 1858: one of the most dignified and sumptuous of many similar essays in mid Victorian civic pride. It was politically easier to build magnificent town halls than to invest in the improvement of working-class housing conditions.

163

loom weaving in silk was very protracted, especially for the more elaborate fabrics and designs. While the town was studded with symmetrical, pedimented mills, with their clocks and cupolas, and its industrialists invested lavishly in churches, an enormous Sunday school and a handsome town hall, a lot of the work continued to be done by family labour and apprentices on the well-lit upper floors of the neat Georgian weavers' houses near the town centre.

Macclesfield's Georgian characteristics remained predominant because its economy suffered from the travails of the silk industry in the face of overseas competition, especially after 1860. Its population stagnated and declined while late Victorian Oldham surged onwards. Increasingly it became the industrial fiefdom of a single firm, the Brocklehursts, powerful paternalists who could afford to show benevolence when it suited them. As in Oldham, a lively working-class political radicalism in the early nineteenth century gave way to acceptance of the late Victorian *status quo*, but under very different circumstances. Indeed, Macclesfield's Victorian stagnation has affinities with the older woollen centres of the West of England and mid-Wales rather than with the northern textile towns: with Bradford-on-Avon in Wiltshire rather than with the larger Bradford on the Aire in Yorkshire.

As Macclesfield passed its peak, Widnes, in Cheshire, began a period of explosive growth from small beginnings. The most cursory comparison will dispel any idea that later developments were automatically better ones. Widnes was a chemical town: it produced soda ash, soda crystals, bicarbonate of soda, chlorine and bleaching powder, as well as household soap. It also had a foundry which made, among other things, prefabricated seaside piers. The ingredients for these industries were brought together most cheaply and conveniently at this point on the Mersey estuary by the transport developments of the 1830s and 1840s. Widnes's population grew from just over 3000 in 1851 to about 30,000 in 1891; but it grew under the grimmest of conditions. Chemicals meant pollution. In the early years, the fumes of the soda industry were discharged into the air, returning to earth as dilute hydrochloric acid, with dire consequences for the local vegetation. From 1863 onwards pollution legislation encouraged the transfer of this noxious by-product into the watercourses. Meanwhile, acres of land were being piled high with solid chemical waste, which seeped into the rivers and perfumed the air with the 'rotten

eggs' smell of hydrogen sulphide.

The work-force lived in the midst of all this, in mean streets of speculators' housing huddled around the works. Some of the houses had their foundations dug into chemical waste, and at one point the town's water supply was polluted with caustic soda. Chemical workers, whose jobs required strength and endurance rather than skill, worked very long hours in appalling conditions of lung-tearing gas, dust and heat. Many were Irish refugees from the famine of the mid 1840s, who coped with these new privations as best they could. Under the circumstances, Widnes's reputation for violence and hard drinking was not surprising; and by the late nineteenth century the rise of new technologies in new places was threatening the livelihood of a population who had come to equate smoke with what passed for prosperity. Even at the turn of the century, Widnes had no proper sewerage, and its employers and managers fled to a safe distance at the end of their working day. Widnes was a tellingly late, extreme example of the results of unplanned growth based on noxious industries with a minimum of regulation, and its circumstances horrified contemporaries. Here, and in neighbouring Runcorn and St Helens, was the industrial town at its ugliest and most forbidding. Here civic pride was most difficult to sustain: though some tried, heroically, even here, arguing that the fumes cured whooping cough, and pointing hopefully to the new churches and public buildings of the turn of the century.

At the other end of the scale came those industrial towns which sustained their growth over long periods, diversified their sources of employment, adapted to changing circumstances, kept the loyalty of their middle-class citizens, and sustained a satisfying range of cultural institutions. These were the new capitals of the industrial regions.

Leeds was not the largest, but it illustrates the processes well. In the later eighteenth century it grew as a market town and transport centre, as a gateway between the contrasting economies of east and west Yorkshire, and above all as an organising centre for West Riding textiles. Georgian Leeds finished and marketed Yorkshire woollens, which were brought to its cloth markets from a hinterland of industrial villages, and passed through the warehouses of the town's wealthy 'gentlemen merchants' on the way to often distant consumers. As in neighbouring towns like Huddersfield and Halifax, elegant cloth halls expressed the importance and opulence of this trade. Leeds was also a centre of polite society, as merchants mixed with surrounding gentry families at assemblies, balls and concerts; and it had a multiplicity of lesser trades to dilute its specialisation in cloth. Importantly, too, its prospering middle classes attracted banking and professional services, and by the late eighteenth century it was more than just a 'woollen town'.

Halifax's Piece Hall, built as a cloth market for the surrounding rural manufacturers in 1775 and containing over three hundred rooms on the four sides of its sloping courtyard.

Leeds' accelerated growth between the 1790s and the 1840s was fuelled by new influences. Its merchants invested in large woollen mills, some of which employed a thousand or more people; and a flax-spinning industry also developed, as did cotton-spinning, briefly. Machine-making, iron-works, tanning, bootmaking, chemicals and dye-stuffs grew, partly in response to the needs of the textile industries, but increasingly showing a dynamism of their own. Meanwhile, mercantile aspirations to culture and civility expressed themselves in the sponsorship of art exhibitions and musical performances, and in the foundation of a Philosophical and Literary Society.

The second half of the nineteenth century saw the town's population more than double to nearly half a million, but with a changing basis for prosperity and employment. The flax industry collapsed and woollens expanded only slowly, but locomotive building and other kinds of engineering, leather working, colour printing and, above all, the manufacture of ready-to-wear clothing took up the running, continuing to provide a range of work for skilled men, women and children, and opportunities for small entrepreneurs at the workshop level. The Jewish refugees from Eastern Europe who went into the clothing trades gave a novel and cosmopolitan air to the population, and the building of an opulent town hall, a corn exchange and a college which eventually flowered into a university helped to provide the buildings and institutions which marked Leeds out as a beacon of provincial culture. It shared problems of housing, sanitation, pollution and poverty with other industrial towns; but it also offered resources and experiences which only a regional capital could provide. It stands comparison with Manchester, Birmingham, Newcastle and, indeed, Liverpool and Bristol, as a great industrial and commercial centre whose wealthiest citizens were numerous and influential enough to transform it into more than just a place where money was made.

Scotland had contrasting and distinctive provincial capitals of its own. Edinburgh was, of course, a national capital, despite the loss of its parliament to Westminster; and its social structure reflected this, with large numbers of lawyers and administrators, and a swelling population of genteel residents in the politely-planned New Town. It never acquired factories or heavy industry, and its trades were workshop-based and oriented towards consumer goods. Its legal, administrative and intellectual importance ensured that printing would become a major employer.

The contrast with Glasgow could hardly have been more extreme, despite the two cities' shared medieval origins and important universities. Glasgow's rise to commercial and industrial pre-eminence began with its engrossment of the tobacco trade in the mid eighteenth century, when its merchants acquired resources and contacts which enabled it to become the greatest centre of the cotton industry outside Lancashire. As in Leeds, textiles attracted chemical and engineering industries; but Glasgow's assets were more numerous and more potent. Not only did its engineering industry branch out into steam locomotive manufacture on a scale unchallenged

elsewhere: the Clyde estuary, and the port's nodal position in the Atlantic trade, enabled Glasgow to become the world's leading manufacturer of giant ocean-going steamships in the late nineteenth century. The skills of the Clydeside shipbuilding workers and the sophistication of their technology became legendary. A numerous and prosperous middle class burgeoned, and the teeming tenements of the city centre and the adjoining industrial suburbs made for a uniquely boisterous and lively working-class social life. Textiles were declining in the late nineteenth century, and the dependence on heavy engineering was becoming a potential source of difficulty in a changing world; but before 1914 this was one of the great sustained success stories of industrial Britain. It was not without blemishes, especially in housing; but it was an astonishing human achievement.

Even more striking was the continuing growth of London. The most fascinating aspect was the concentration of wealth in the capital. London's financiers consistently left the biggest fortunes in the largest number, and in mid Victorian times London's income-tax payers (who by definition at this time had comfortable incomes) far outweighed the most prosperous areas of the provinces. The great industrialists in the north of England and the Midlands exerted more direct and visible influence over their work-forces and in local politics, but in sheer accumulative power the manipulators of money were much more effective than the manufacturers of goods. The spread of opulent housing westwards, from Bloomsbury to Regent's Park and Mayfair, was also stimulated by London's powerful attraction for the growing band of wealthy annuitants who lived leisured lives supported by rents and investments; and of course the aristocracy and many of the gentry kept their town houses for the London season. The French professor Hippolyte Taine was astounded by the enormity of it all:

Paris is mediocre by comparison with these 'squares', 'crescents', 'circuses', and the endless rows of monumental houses built of massive stone, with porticos and carved fronts, lining the very wide streets. . . . From London Bridge to Hampton Court there are eight miles . . . of buildings. After those streets and quarters built all of a piece . . . come innumerable houses, built for their owners' enjoyment, cottages set in lawn and trees, and in every style, Gothic, Greek, Byzantine, Medieval or Renaissance Italian, or in a mixture of every variation on these styles. . . . They turn out houses as we turn out Paris fancy-goods. What a multitude of easy, comfortable, of wealthy households.

Other Londons were also spreading and swelling. There was the Victorian suburban London of the endearingly absurd Mr Pooter and others like him: City clerks travelling to work by horse omnibus from Holloway or Camberwell, and later by underground railway or tram from more distant outposts. The suburban frontier was forever expanding, as smaller, mass-produced houses for the middle and lower levels of the middle class invaded the sanctuaries of the opulent pioneers in what had been rural retreats. In the inner suburbs, meanwhile, the middle-class rearguard watched anxiously for evidence of working-class intrusion, as expressed in informal dress and unsupervised children's play in the street. An immense square mileage of terraces and small semi-detached houses spread across north and south London, and leap-frogged into Essex. They varied subtly in detail and embellishment, in ways which mattered immensely to many of their occupants. The scale and complexity of this petty bourgeois suburbia was novel and unique.

And then there was working-class London: not just the East End of docks and sweatshops, but also the Kentish London of skilled craftsmen and transport and munitions workers in maritime Deptford and Woolwich. The older residential areas had working-class enclaves to house and sustain the providers of essential services, and for much of the nineteenth century there were 'rookeries' of the poorest and most dangerous classes in threatening proximity to the opulent shops and houses of the West End. But it was the East End, seen as a seething mass of poverty and potential unrest, which brought intermittent terror of disease and revolution to the rich families of the West End, whenever there were strikes, riots, epidemics, or exposés of living conditions in the press. Such panics were short-lived, and the contrasts between poverty and opulence were smoothed over by the physical as well as social distance between the extremes. Even the East End had its scattering of the respectable and the affluent; colourful costermongers and necessitous needlewomen formed only a small, though much-publicised, part of its Victorian population.

The Victorian years, especially, saw the development of other Londons: the theatrical and high-class shopping districts of the West End, the London of the gentlemen's clubs, and even that part of St John's Wood in which quiet respectability lived cheek by jowl, in leafy privacy, with a colony of artists and the kept women of the wealthy. Different suburbs acquired distinctive

Bed-sit industry: an artist's impression of Jewish cigarette makers in London's East End in 1903.

social characteristics and reputations: stockbrokers and commercial agents in the Bayswater and Clapham of the 1860s, clerks in Edwardian New Cross and Forest Hill. Within the expanding sprawl of this world metropolis, most of its inhabitants lived at the level of home, street, neighbourhood and, in effect, village, with little conception of the city as a whole.

The other great towns, as they grew, became similarly separated out into distinctive social areas. The provincial capitals, especially, developed their downtown shopping areas, in which the new multiples and department stores presented ambitious new façades in the late nineteenth century. Adjacent streets were given over, at about the same time, to the professional services of an increasingly complex commercial system: solicitors, insurance offices, and so on. Every large town came to support a West End of its own. Birmingham's Edgbaston, Nottingham's Park Estate and Leeds' Headingley provided protected settings for middle-class family life at a safe distance from the noise, traffic and pollution of the city centre and the contaminating proximity of the working class.

Beyond the ever-extending frontier of outer suburbia, where outposts of development awaited the supporting services of tramways and drainage systems, Victorian transport improvements enabled wealthy employers and professionals with short or flexible working hours to live beyond the towns in which their wealth was created. London was especially prolific in spawning these commuterlands. Old market towns like Croydon or Bromley were expanded beyond all recognition by new estates of villa residences. Their inhabitants altered the social structure (and, by importing servants, the balance between the sexes), the trading patterns and even the politics of what had been sleepy backwaters. The larger provincial towns were creating similar effects on a smaller scale by the 1840s and 1850s. Manchester businessmen took root in the Cheshire countryside at Altrincham, Alderley Edge and Disley, while Glasgow sowed similar seeds along the Clyde coast.

These residential outer suburbs were prominent features of the fastest-expanding British towns of the late nineteenth and early twentieth century, providing an impressive illustration of the growth of the prosperous middle classes and their spending power. These people also fuelled the explosive increase in health and pleasure resorts, novel, specialised towns which drew their sustenance from holiday-makers and those who could afford to retire to them: they also acted as outer suburbs in their own right, providing healthy habitats for commuters and their families.

Not all resorts developed this role, admittedly. Bath, the first and best known of the spa towns, did not maintain the popularity it had achieved by the mid eighteenth century, when the nobility, gentry and socially aspiring crowded here in search of a characteristic combination of medical services, the social round of dancing, assemblies and marriage-making, and the neighbouring delights of fresh air and countryside. By the late eighteenth century its imposing Georgian terraces and crescents had become places of retirement for wealthy invalids and annuitants, as high society took its pleasure elsewhere. The 1771 Assembly Rooms (see p. 233) were not deserted, but their palmiest days were already over by the turn of the century. Commuters did not become a prominent part of Bath society, as they did in other spa resorts which followed a similar trajectory later. Clifton (an appendage of Bristol), Cheltenham, Leamington Spa and Harrogate also had their brief whirl of fashionable gaiety, on the national or provincial stage, and then settled back into genteel and sedate retirement. But here, and wherever concentrations of business and commercial wealth were within reach, Victorian spas became dormitory towns as well as retirement centres.

By the early nineteenth century the main focus of resort development was shifting to the seaside. Sea-bathing and sea air offered a more palatable and sociable alternative to the curative regime of the spa, and a wider range of tastes and needs could be catered for on beach and promenade. Proximity to London and the patronage of the Prince Regent helped to transform Georgian Brighton from a decaying fishing village to the height of metropolitan fashion, a haven of delight, dalliance and dissipation. On the eve of the railway age its seaside competitors paled into comparative insignificance. The second half of the nineteenth century, however, saw Brighton becoming more plebeian, while new rivals emerged to entice the moneyed and the fashionable. Prominent among these were Eastbourne, under the patronage of the Duke of Devonshire, and Bournemouth, where early Victorian villas for consumptives, set among quiet pine woods, gave way to the piers, promenades, music and bustling shops of the sophisticated Edwardian middle-class family seaside holiday.

In a completely different idiom, the fiery red-brick terraces of Blackpool proclaimed its status as the world's first working-class seaside resort, catering for families from the Midlands and Yorkshire as well as for the Lancashire millworkers who created its distinctive character. Even here, however, the more populist, assertive kind of Lancashire millowner took his house on the select North Shore, and commuters to mercantile Manchester and the cotton towns reached down the Edwardian social scale as far as commission agents and senior clerks. Southend grew just as rapidly, similarly combining a whiff of the sea for day-tripping East Enders with houses for City clerks to rent for their families while they commuted by train to London. There were many other variations, and the Clyde estuary likewise provided a range of holiday habitats for Victorian Glasgwegians who could afford a day-trip or a few days by rail and steamer to Dunoon or Rothesay.

RIGHT *Quarry Bank Mill, Styal, nestling in its attractive wooded Cheshire valley : a typical setting for an early water-powered cotton mill. The bell-turret and clock indicate the new importance attached to punctuality and labour discipline.*

BELOW *Oak Cottages, Styal : a particularly appealing example of housing provided by employers for their workpeople. The cellars were suitable for cotton hand-loom weaving, but in the event they were not used for this purpose.*

ABOVE LEFT *The woollen industries of Yorkshire's West Riding adopted the factory system later and more slowly than Lancashire cotton concerns. This is the stone-built Triangle Mill at Sowerby, between Halifax and Todmorden.*

BELOW LEFT *Philip James de Loutherbourg, an expert in lighting effects for the stage, produced this dramatic infernal vision of a Coalbrookdale ironworks by night at the end of the eighteenth century.*

The thatched cottage in Cromarty in which Hugh Miller was born in 1802. Miller began his working life as a stonemason, but became an eminent geologist and a widely-read commentator on Scottish society in his time.

LEFT *Cheltenham took over from Bath as the most fashionable inland resort of the early nineteenth century. In emulation of Bath it acquired its own Royal Crescent, but in the brick, stucco and ornamental ironwork of the Regency, as this detailed view of one of the balconies shows.*

BELOW LEFT *Llangelynin Church, Gwynedd : a typically isolated site for a Welsh upland church, in the sort of countryside which was readily colonised by Methodism and other brands of Nonconformity from the later eighteenth century.*

BELOW *The sanctuary ceiling of William Burges' High Victorian masterpiece, the richly-embellished church of St Mary at Studley Royal in North Yorkshire. Gorgeously-attired angels swirl dizzily upwards to a starry firmament.*

ABOVE *Customers are served in the seductively ornate late Victorian setting of the Crown Liquor Saloon, Belfast.*

LEFT *The washstand in the main bedroom at The Hill House, Helensburgh : a representative example of Charles Rennie Mackintosh's unremitting but endlessly fertile attention to every domestic detail in his work as architect and designer.*

RIGHT *Troutbeck Park Farm, Cumbria, with The Tongue behind it, seen from the Kirkstone Pass road, which was already busy with tourist traffic in the late nineteenth century. The farm is owned by the National Trust, and the picture encapsulates the Trust's concern to sustain established farming methods as part of the process of protecting landscape in an area where pressures for intrusive change are particularly powerful.*

The Giant's Causeway, now in the care of the National Trust. The hexagonal basalt rock formations and unique scenery were already attracting tourists to this part of the Antrim coast by the 1880s, when an access route was successfully defended against a closure threat.

By the turn of the century the number of British seaside resorts was well into three figures; and there were also spas, and inland resorts like Ambleside in the Lake District or Church Stretton on the edge of the Shropshire Long Mynd whose stock in trade was scenery and fresh air. But to concentrate on the great urban success stories, the Blackpools and the Bournemouths, is to distort: many resorts were mere villages, or little more. Long tracts of coastline were too far from population centres to attract more than a select, professional middle-class clientele seeking seclusion. The impressive scale of resort growth, especially in England, deserves to be highlighted; and so do the conflicts which arose from the clashing interests of noisy excursionists and sedate middle-class families, of entertainment caterers and retired residents in search of seclusion. But many towns which slumbered, or failed to fulfil their promise, can be listed alongside the household names; and, more generally, due emphasis on the importance of urban growth and change in this dynamic period should not blind us to the fact that it was far from universal.

Towns stagnated or declined through all or part of this period for a variety of reasons. Some were bypassed by transport improvements, and languished while their competitors benefited. Falmouth lost much of its maritime trade; Stamford suffered from the loss of its Great North Road coaching traffic, and failed to attract the main-line railway in compensation. Many failed to generate new industries, and remained mere market centres for a rural hinterland. Some lost existing industries: Whitby found jet-working and tourism no substitute for the decline in whaling. And a large number of country towns, and indeed cathedral cities like Hereford or Wells, jogged gently along at their established tempo, with a few innovations and a gentle upward curve of population, while falling into insignificance when compared with the dramatic developments elsewhere. Places which happened not to have workable mineral resources, or industries whose products were in immense demand, or key positions on the transport system, or remarkably successful entrepreneurs, accounted for a large and important proportion of British towns and the urban population as a whole. Their failure to grow dramatically, or at all, in this disruptive period has made little towns like Ludlow, Lewes and Lavenham all the more attractive to later generations. They may have acquired clock towers, railway stations, new brickwork and Victorian shop-fronts, but they show a sense of continuity with more distant pasts which provides a measure of reassurance as well as interest and pleasure to the eye.

The rapid growth of the more dynamic towns of this period was not only disruptive visually, as new streets proliferated, old landmarks disappeared and buildings and their settings were changed beyond recognition. More fundamentally, it was disruptive to the lives of those who lived in the towns: and especially to that majority, as it was for most of the period, who were first-generation town-dwellers, having migrated in from the countryside. Much migration was short-distance, admittedly, and this made it easier to cope with. Nevertheless migrants, usually in their teens and twenties, still had to adjust to a new scale of living and new patterns of working, to new temptations and opportunities. The legions of domestic servants uprooted from their villages must have found town life particularly perplexing and demanding. Significant numbers moved long distances, especially to London, the provincial capitals and the new towns of the railway age, although they often used industrial villages and small towns close to home as 'stepping stones' along the way. London's recruitment area was truly national: building workers from the West Country, domestic servants from Shropshire, and enough Cumbrians to form a flourishing society of exiles in the capital. But it, and many of the larger towns, also attracted migrants from more distant places, both geographically and culturally. The most numerous of these were the Irish.

A steady flow of Irish seasonal workers had long been settling in English towns, especially in the north-west; but the great famine of the mid 1840s pushed out an enormous number of half-starved refugees, many of whom settled in Liverpool, Manchester and the lesser Lancashire towns. Many also found their way to London, and the Irish became very numerous in urban Scotland, especially in Glasgow. The poverty of these migrants gave them a limited choice of housing, and they clustered in the most crowded and unhealthy areas. They were readily identifiable by accent (and sometimes by the Gaelic language), distinctive in religion (usually Roman Catholic), and, so their critics claimed, distinguished for their propensity to crime, violence and immorality.

Whatever the truth of this, the poor Irish in general were perhaps the most indigestible element in the urban populations of the mid nineteenth century. There were also other distinctive migrant populations, some of whom were singled out and

stigmatised by neighbours and social reformers. Glasgow, especially, acquired a numerous population of Highlanders, fleeing from conditions which had some similarity with those in Ireland. Liverpool, as well as its Irish and Scots, had a Welsh-speaking contingent with its own chapels and newspapers: but the Liverpool Welsh were concentrated in the building trades, and had a relatively respectable image. London, Manchester and other cities attracted not only wealthy Jewish merchants and financiers, but also shopkeepers and poor clothing workers, especially after the East European persecutions of the late nineteenth century. Italians, too, were becoming a conspicuous minority, especially as hawkers and street musicians, by the turn of the century.

Despite the presence of exotic and sometimes unpopular minorities, however, most of the urban population growth of the period was supplied from local sources, as the towns soaked up the surplus population of the surrounding countryside. Even the long-distance migrants were rarely socially isolated: they could generally find lodging and company with relatives or people with similar roots. And by the late nineteenth century many towns were deriving most of their growth from the natural increase of their own inhabitants: they were developing stable populations of second- or third-generation urbanites. Where this stability was rooted in inner-city slums, it could be a problem rather than an asset; but it probably offered more security, if narrower horizons, for an increasingly streetwise urban working class.

How were the new urban dwellers of this period housed? The most difficult problems involved the building of enough cheap housing for the working classes, at rents they could afford without overcrowding. Without housing subsidies from central or local government, this was impossible; and the idea of subsidised housing was only just becoming thinkable in the late nineteenth century. It was still highly controversial in 1914. So houses were built for profit, the vast majority by small firms who were perennially in debt, living from hand to mouth and trying to complete each job as quickly as possible in order to stave off their creditors. Detailed variations between houses in

seemingly uniform terraces often show that they were actually built a few at a time, by many different people. From the 1840s onwards, local government by-laws increasingly prescribed minimum standards of space, construction and sanitation; but the legacy of crumbling, subdivided older houses and tightly-packed slums from the first great period of urban expansion remained to perpetuate squalor and disease.

Builders in different cities and areas devised various ways of cramming as many houses as possible on to a plot of land. Between the 1780s and 1840s Liverpool became a centre of courts (hollow squares of back-to-back houses enclosing a central yard) and cellar dwellings. Leeds and the adjoining West Riding towns became particularly attached to the back-to-back, which continued to appear with increasing elaboration until the 1930s. Early examples offered only two rooms and no sanitation; but by the late nineteenth century four-storey houses with cellar lavatories and a scullery might be embellished with barge-boards and ornamental porches, stained-glass windows and little garden plots. Only the best examples, of course, survive.

The same applies to the multi-storey tenements in which most of the Scottish urban working class lived. Scottish land law encouraged developers to build upwards, and the severe stone tenements were subdivided into tiny flats reached by intricate and often fetid systems of stairways and landings. In the 'single end' families achieved miracles by packing children into tiny beds in cupboards and wall recesses; but this merely palliated the reality of gross overcrowding, for which Scottish cities had a much worse record than anywhere else in Britain. A half-way house between English and Scottish practice was the Tyneside 'flat', with one family on each floor and completely separate arrangements. This system, too, was accompanied by high levels of overcrowding, with perhaps one-third of the population living at more than two to a room in the late nineteenth century. The standard working-class housing type in most of England, Wales and Northern Ireland came to be the through terrace with rear yard, which was encouraged by legislation; but there were many minor variations in internal arrangements and building materials.

LEFT *Lewes High Street in the mid nineteenth century. Most of the houses in the centre of this quiet traditional county town would still be recognisable today.*

OVERLEAF *A solidly-built street of Leeds back-to-backs, of a type still common in the West Riding of Yorkshire. The stone facings, bay windows and neat curtains are emblems of working-class respectability.*

Whatever the deficiencies of urban working-class housing, it was always well above the level of the shanty town and it was often an improvement on the rural housing from which migrants came. This was even true of Highlanders moving to Glasgow tenements. Most of the houses themselves were owned not by industrialists or large landlords, but by shopkeepers, small tradesmen, skilled workers and their widows. They provided security and a basic income (when the rent could be collected), rather than vast profits. The problems of working-class housing were due less to the misdeeds of owners and builders, than to the economic conditions under which the houses were built.

Patchily from the late eighteenth century, and with gathering momentum from the 1830s and 1840s, local government began to improve urban amenities. Sanitary conditions attracted particular attention after the great cholera epidemic of 1832, and awareness of the high social cost of avoidable illness and premature death, and of the risks to middle-class as well as working-class families, spread rapidly thereafter. Local government intervention began with drains and sewers, and soon extended to water supplies and minimum housing standards. Even the municipal parks which were pioneered at this time were largely public health measures – the 'lungs' of the cities – as well as offering morally acceptable, 'improving' environments to be enjoyed by working-class families. Local government increasingly took over the administration and supply of basic amenities on the widely-accepted Victorian principle that these were 'natural monopolies' which ought to be run for the benefit of ratepayers and consumers rather than for a small number of often non-resident shareholders. Gas, electricity, tramways and water all gradually fell into the local authority net. Eventually, this meant that basic amenities became available to slum-dwellers who could not have obtained them without municipal intervention.

Such improvements took a long time to become general and effective. Their spread was delayed by disputes over rival technologies, best practice, and the competing claims of private and municipal enterprise, as well as by battles between rival local government bodies. Above all they were obstructed by political campaigns by ratepayers and industrialists who urged that 'the minimum of rates was the maximum of happiness' and formed 'dirty parties' to block or reduce improvement spending in many towns and cities. But by the 1870s these municipal ventures were being reflected in falling rates of death and disease, even in the grimmest places.

These developments affected all town-dwellers, but they mattered rather less to the substantial middle classes, because for them private enterprise was able to deliver a much better standard of housing and living conditions. In the later eighteenth century appendages of neat Georgian terraces appeared on the fringes of all towns of any size; and where there was enough money about, as in Bath, London or Edinburgh, the results could be very impressive. Edinburgh is especially interesting, because the building of its planned New Town was part of a deliberate campaign to turn the old, cramped city into a worthy capital for a European nation, and to make the city attractive to the aristocracy. The New Town's early layout was not strikingly innovatory, but its spacious squares and shared architectural idioms were in sharp contrast with the medieval squalor of some of the tenements in the Old Town, where the 'better classes' still lived in uncomfortable proximity to the poor and disreputable. To enhance the New Town still further, Robert Adam was commissioned in 1791 to design the flagship of the scheme, Charlotte Square, where the National Trust for Scotland now owns nos. 5, 6 and 7 on the north side. This secured the New Town's reputation, and the result has reaped high praise from recent architectural historians:

The frontages, monumental, yet elegant and human in their proportions, are completely unified in treatment, and the north side is a replica of the south. Every side is three stories high, plus attics and basement, and the splendid north and south sides are centred on a pediment mounted on four Corinthian pillars. The appearance is enriched by restrained use of balustrades, festoons, and circular panels. . . . Charlotte Square is a marvellous achievement. Spacious; elegant; symmetrical without needless duplication; full of variety yet harmonious and devoid of fussiness. . . .

The New Town provided the privacy and status of single-family dwellings, while offering sociability and space in its squares and gardens. In these respects it was very much in keeping with contemporary developments elsewhere. It was unusual in being planned as a whole by the city corporation, rather than arising from a mosaic of private developments or being laid out at the behest of an aristocratic landowner. At Bath, for example, although some of the Georgian townscape was built on corporation land and under municipal supervision, the town's character was derived from

The architectural climax of Georgian elegance in Edinburgh's New Town: nos. 5, 6 and 7 Charlotte Square, owned by the National Trust for Scotland.

the speculations of individuals, most remarkably the Woods, who successfully interpreted the demands of the market. But this kind of development took time and required extensive reserves of capital and borrowing power; and, as in the case of Charlotte Square, what we now see as a superb whole was full of gaps and blank spaces, and subject to building operations, for the many years that it took to complete the scheme.

Glasgow offers an instructive contrast. When its merchants began to seek escape from an increasingly crowded town centre in the late eighteenth century, they moved at first in all directions. Then new houses for the middle classes began to be concentrated in Blythswood, to the west of the town centre: Glasgow's answer to Edinburgh's

New Town, but less carefully planned and protected. By 1830, there was a growing demand for housing further west, and the woods, ravines and little hills of the Kelvin valley and its environs, opened out by the new Great Western Road, were gradually covered with terraces, crescents and villas. Here again, the corporation became involved, laying out a park and building magnificent terraces on the skyline above it. The University and the Botanical Gardens became added attractions. Most of the West End houses had between six and ten bedrooms, and they are a further impressive testimony to the numbers and prosperity of the Victorian middle classes.

But the West End also offered apartments in tenement blocks; and this is a reminder that apartment life spanned the classes in Glasgow. A suite of six or eight rooms, with kitchen and bathroom and its own separate entrance at street level, and tiles instead of painted plaster, was very different from a Gorbals 'single end'. There were many levels in between. Miss Agnes Toward's compact four-room apartment in Buccleuch Street, with its solid furniture, cosy kitchen and neat parlour which could be reserved for Sunday entertaining, illustrates the middle range: it was home in the early twentieth century to a widowed dressmaker who took in lodgers, and her daughter who became a shorthand typist. They were pillars of respectability, despite their cramped accommodation; and every inch of space was utilised to the full. The survival of their home as the Tenement House in the hands of the National Trust for Scotland gives an unexpected insight into a way of life which would otherwise have been almost completely lost.

By the 1880s, the wealthiest of Glasgow's middle classes were beginning to look beyond the West End, which was now becoming heavily built up, and to seek romantic seclusion along the railway routes following the Clyde estuary. Much of the resulting outer suburbia was fairly humdrum. But at Helensburgh, in 1902, the Glasgow publisher Walter Blackie commissioned Charles Rennie Mackintosh to design The Hill House (NTS) for him; and on this windswept site, with its dramatic views down the Clyde, something completely different was created. Externally, Mackintosh and his client sought to adapt the vernacular styles of traditional Scottish building to new needs and a new setting; but Mackintosh also insisted on designing the interiors first, and building the house around them. The rooms he devised were strikingly original in colour, lighting, arrangement, decoration, and the shapes and arrangement of furnishings, even down to details like drawer-handles and window-catches; and the remarkable qualities of the house stand out even more when it is compared with the mock Tudor and derivative gothic villas which surround it, forming as they do the small change of everyday suburban architecture.

Sadly, The Hill House was a one-off. Most suburbanites chose to stay within the conventions;

Miss Toward's kitchen in the National Trust for Scotland's Glasgow Tenement House. The servant's box bed, the gleaming coal-fired kitchen range, and the evidence of a multitude of activities going on in a confined space, are all characteristic of this kind of housing at the turn of the century. It is difficult to imagine life in this environment with two or three small children; but there were plenty of complete family dwellings in Victorian urban Scotland which were no bigger than Miss Toward's kitchen.

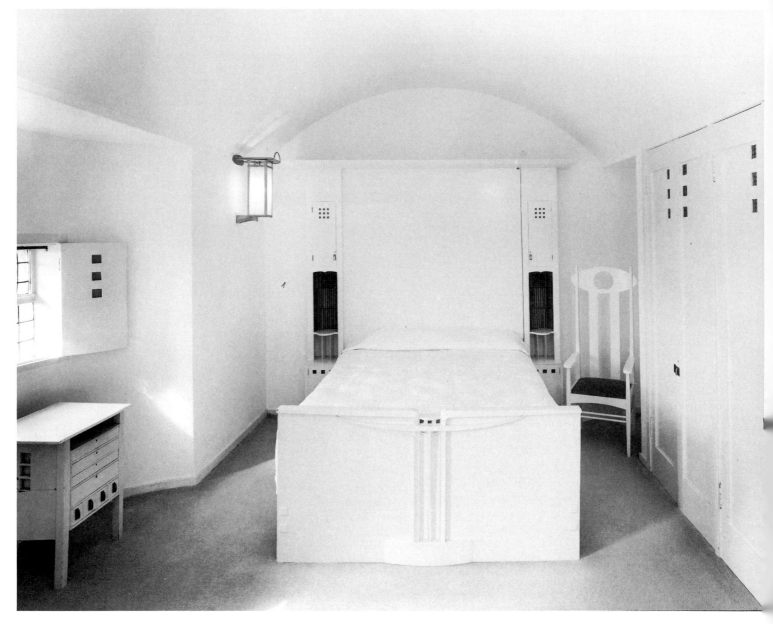

The main bedroom at The Hill House, with characteristic furnishings, décor and details by Charles Rennie Mackintosh.

and most speculative builders could not afford to flout them. This was true of Britain as a whole. There were outposts and islands of the innovative and original: Norman Shaw's essays in the Queen Anne style at Bedford Park, London, from the late 1870s, or C. F. A. Voysey's 'long, low roofs, low-toned materials – slate and roughcast, usually – and ground-hugging outlines' built around the turn of the century in Surrey and elsewhere. As Ian Nairn points out, this style suffered the fate of 'becoming in a debased form the ideal of speculative house-builders of the 1920s and 1930s', engulfing Surrey itself and proliferating along every bypass. The

essence of mass-produced suburbia was safety and conformity, and this invariably outweighed the less pressing suburban aspiration to rusticity and communion with nature.

The rise of suburbia also condemned its female inhabitants to a life of almost unrelieved domesticity. Whereas in the late eighteenth century the wives of tradesmen and professionals living 'over the shop' in the centres of towns as different as Birmingham and Colchester might expect to take an active and valued part in the running of the business, the move to the suburbs wrought a transformation. A woman's role was limited to household management, supervising the servants and sustaining the fires of domestic comfort. Otherwise, she was a discreet consumer of her husband's income, a living advertisement for his spending power, and an exchanger of conventional social visits which were governed by strict rules of etiquette and precedent which had to be learned thoroughly. For the solid middle and upper middle classes, this important change in attitudes, values and expectations, and in the balance of power within families, was practically complete by 1850. Its effects were still being felt in Edwardian times and long afterwards, even though in later years women could pass the long suburban summer afternoons in extended games of golf and tennis. Katherine Chorley, in her brilliant evocation of the wealthy Manchester suburb of Alderley Edge in the early twentieth century, captures the essence of this aspect of suburban values:

After the 9.18 train pulled out of the station the Edge became exclusively female. You never saw a man on the hill roads unless it were the doctor or the plumber, and you never saw a man in anyone's home except the gardener or the coachman. And yet it was a man-made and a man-lorded society. . . . For the men were the money-lords, and since for almost every family the community values were fundamentally economic, it followed that their women were dependents. They existed for their husbands' and fathers' sake and their lives were shaped to please masculine vanity.

The men were losers too. They became detached from the vital concerns of the cities in which they had their work and made their money. It became more difficult to stay behind for council meetings or charitable work, and fewer of them did it. The suburban life of privatised detachment, whose development was one of the key changes associated with nineteenth-century urban change and growth, thus widened the distance between the substantial middle class and the working class. The implications of this may have been profound, although they are difficult to assess. A fuller study of urban working-class life in this period will set these issues more firmly in their context. It is also very important indeed in its own right.

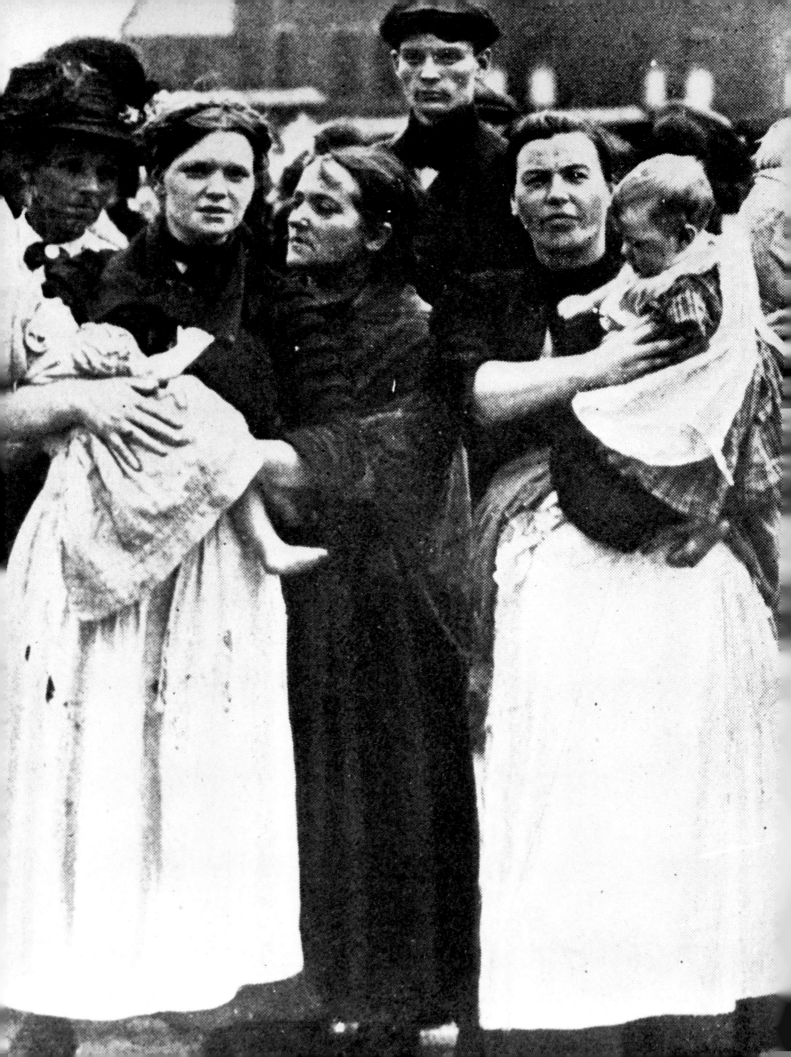

CHAPTER EIGHT

The Urban Working Class

A sympathetic and well-informed observer of working-class life in the iron and steel town of Middlesbrough had this to say in 1907 about the families whose homes she visited:

The dire need of the people who cannot find employment has been so ever-present to our minds in recent days that we are apt to believe that once employment is secured . . . all must be well, so long as the workman is steady and knows how to manage his money. But when we take this rosy view . . . we forget how terribly near the margin of disaster the man, even the thrifty man, walks, who has, in ordinary normal conditions, but just enough to keep himself on. The spectre of illness and disability is always confronting the working-man; the possibility of being from one day to the other plunged into actual want is always confronting his family.

Lady Bell, an ironmaster's wife who made it her business to counsel and befriend the crowded denizens of Middlesbrough's four-roomed cottages, made this insecurity the central theme of her social survey of the town. Her emphasis is more striking because this was a place of regular work and high wages. Moreover these comments come after a long period of falling food prices and rising working-class spending power, and a much longer period in which ways had been developed to mitigate the stresses and threatening unpredictability of wage-earning life.

At the other end of England, Robert Tressell's famous socialist novel about building workers in Edwardian Hastings, *The Ragged-Trousered Philanthropists*, developed similar themes, with an added emphasis on the duplicity and hypocrisy of employers and their lackeys among the work-force. Tressell was building on his own experiences to write heartfelt propaganda. By comparison, Lady Bell's portrayal of Middlesbrough is all the more compelling because she does not challenge the social system: she reports, with compassion, understanding and vivid illustration, on the lives of her husband's workers. From Hastings to Middlesbrough and beyond, the dominant theme in working-class life, throughout the period, was indeed insecurity. Much effort was devoted to the day-to-day struggle to keep it at bay, and to sustain self-respect and find room for enjoyment in the process.

Insecurity was built into the life cycle of wage-earning families. The problems arising when too many children arrived too quickly were predictable in principle but impossible to budget for properly. The same applied to the declining earning powers and heightened physical vulnerability of old age. The great social investigator Charles Booth found in the early 1890s that

. . . in town and country alike the large majority of the aged when past work are dependent on someone; either on their children, or on the (Poor Law) Guardians, or on the charitable, or on all three. They very often lead very hard lives, and one of the most striking features throughout is the extreme smallness of their means even when their condition is said to be satisfactory.

In the competitive labour markets and unhealthy living conditions of the towns, men might be old in their fifties or even their forties. There was little time to enjoy the brief spell of family prosperity when teenage children brought their wages into the home. And Booth's findings echo those of Sir Francis Eden at the end of the eighteenth century. Life ended sadly and uncomfortably for most poor wage-earners and their spouses. Always, too, there was the fear of a pauper funeral, or at least an inadequate send-off. At the very end of the period, the new old-age pensions eased the lot of half a million people over 70, who began to receive a maximum of five shillings a week in 1909; but even this was hedged about with restrictions, though more in theory than practice. As Pat Thane says, 'It was a pension for the very old, the very poor and the very respectable.'

The long road to the grave was also punctuated by less predictable adversities. Recurrent unemployment was a general hazard. Trade depressions could put thousands out of work at a time in industrial towns, as the demand for their products went into temporary eclipse. Many trades, like building, fluctuated according to the season or the weather. Others, like dock work, varied day by day, so that there was scant possibility for budgeting from one week to the next. And new inventions were always threatening to make established skills irrelevant and established jobs redundant. The bankruptcy, retirement or death of a small employer might also threaten the livelihood of his workpeople. In the absence of state or other benefits, a few weeks' unemployment could undermine the finances of the thriftiest household.

PREVIOUS PAGES *Wives waiting for news of husbands and other relatives after the pit disaster at Cadley in July 1912, in which 75 mine-workers were killed.*

Sheffield grinders working at their water-powered wheels in 1866. This was a trade of small workshops and sturdy independence. Skills and wage-rates were fiercely and sometimes violently protected by small, close-knit trade unions which in many ways resembled medieval guilds.

The threat of illness was ever-present, as was that of accident. Some industries entailed particular health hazards, like the 'grinder's lung' which brought most Sheffield toolmakers to an early grave, or the mercury poisoning which explains the legendary 'madness' of hatters. Others exposed their workers to extremes of heat, cold, damp and dust, helping to incubate tuberculosis and other classic chronic diseases of industrial society. Atmospheric pollution, bad water and over-crowded housing spread the dangers through the population at large. The great epidemics which attacked London and the manufacturing towns, reaching a terrifying climax with the visitations of cholera in 1832 and 1848, became less threatening in the late nineteenth century; but infant mortality levels continued to be inflated by such complaints as measles and 'infantile diarrhoea', which could still be mass killers in Edwardian times. Among the working population the need to keep a wage coming in, or to maintain the demanding routines of the conscientious housewife, led to illnesses being neglected until they became serious; and then the cost of medical treatment had to be met out of diminished resources.

The great disasters, especially in mining, which might kill hundreds at a time and devastate whole communities, stand out luridly in the industrial history of this period; but the regular toll of individual deaths and crippling injuries at the workplace added up to a great deal more. The hazards of the textile factories, especially in the early days of very long hours and unfenced machinery, are well known, and so are the obvious perils of work involving molten metals and noxious chemicals. As late as 1895 a Bolton journalist could gather the following information from the national official statistics for October:

In factory and workshop . . . 49 persons were killed; there were 174 amputations, 65 fractures, 4 loss of eye or eyes, 71 persons injured on head or face, and 654 other injuries. . . . Add to these figures 89 killed and 731 injured in mines, and 45 workers killed and 566 injured on railways . . . and we get an appalling total of victims annually slain in the interests of trade and commerce.

This was an ordinary month. The safety of the breadwinner, or of any member of the family working outside the home, could never be assumed from one day to the next.

Personal disasters of this kind were not peculiar to this period or this culture. But their overall importance was greatly increased by population growth and concentration, by the social problems associated with the new industrial and commercial towns, by the increasing scale of industrial processes and the new kinds of danger they engendered, and by the limited extent of assistance to victims and families from employers and the State. The dominant attitude among those in authority was that individuals should take responsibility for their own circumstances. So it was the business of individuals to save for a rainy day and insure themselves against accidents and illness. To this end they should abstain from expensive and dangerous vices like drink and tobacco, and from frivolities which diverted spending away from basic needs. If they neglected this advice, they had only themselves to blame.

These were not realistic expectations. For millions of families, wages were too low, and often too irregular, to allow for savings and adequate insurance. Mrs Pember Reeves' survey of families living in one or two rooms in Edwardian Lambeth, headed by respectable labourers in steady 'unskilled' employment, led her to conclude that the root of the problems she identified lay in low wages rather than domestic mismanagement:

That the diet of the poorer London children is insufficient, unscientific and utterly unsatisfactory is horribly true. But that the real cause of this state of things is the ignorance and indifference of their mothers is untrue. What person or body of people, however educated and expert, could maintain a working man in physical efficiency and rear healthy children on the amount of money which is all these same mothers have to deal with? It would be an impossible problem if set to trained and expert people. How much more an impossible problem when set to the saddened, weakened, overburdened wives of London labourers?

Admittedly, working-class budgeting was often made more difficult by expenditure on drink, tobacco, gambling and entertainment. But throughout the period drinking customs were so pervasive as to be almost inescapable among working-class men, despite the rise of the temperance movement from the 1830s. Beer was frequently smuggled into factories and workshops, and rituals of conviviality embraced everything from the completion of an apprenticeship to marriage and parenthood. These customs were in decline by the 1870s, but the warmth and comradeship of the pub, such as it was, remained a powerful lure.

As drink consumption fell steadily from its mid 1870s peak, betting became more visible as a social problem, especially betting on horse-racing which was assiduously promoted by illegal but ubiquitous street and workplace bookmakers and their 'runners'. To abstain from these pleasures was to become isolated from the interests and concerns of workmates and neighbours. Understandably, most people found this difficult. So wages which were already inadequate were diverted into the pockets of the publican or bookmaker. Those who suffered most were the women whose housekeeping allowances were cut, and who all too often bore the brunt of their husbands' violence, as well as skimping on their own and their children's food in order to sustain the wage-earner on whom the family's survival depended. The chronic insecurity which made it impossible to look to the long-term future, and which gave gambling a kind of rationality as the only chance of obtaining a substantial lump sum of money, makes it more understandable that men (and sometimes women) took whatever opportunities were available to seek enjoyment and temporary escape from monotony and care.

These comments apply most forcibly to poor families of the sort who in Edwardian times received the classic 'round about a pound a week' of the unskilled, when in work. Higher up the scale, by the later nineteenth century skilled workers in regular employment could afford to enjoy a drink, a flutter and a few creature comforts, in moderation, as well as insuring against a rainy day. This was precarious prosperity: the insurance might cover a short period of illness or unemployment, the savings might last for a few weeks, but they were no safeguard against the kind of severe or sustained misfortune which was all too common. Insurance

Fleet Street's pavement bookmakers helped to bring 'low life' into the centre of the capital, and into close proximity to respectable citizens like the couple on the left. They were a source of much complaint; but the array of top hats and fashionable attire among the punters suggests that many of the bookies' clients were raffish, aristocratic 'men about town' rather than the labouring poor.

rarely covered the illness of wives, who were terribly vulnerable to desertion as well as widowhood. On the other hand, even the poorest had *some* defences against starvation and destitution.

Relief through the Poor Law was the last resort of the desperate. In England, this was not the case everywhere in the eighteenth century, but it became so very rapidly in Victorian times. Until 1834, the Elizabethan Poor Law provided relief through the parish, paid for by rates levied on land and buildings. Most paupers were supported at home, with doles, food or the payment of rent, but increasingly parishes were joining forces to build workhouses, which were generally used as refuges for the sick and aged poor, and for unsupported children. From time to time attempts were made to test the severity of the circumstances of other categories of the poor, especially the able-bodied unemployed, by making relief conditional on entering the workhouse; but such a policy was rarely sustained for very long. Some applicants were deterred by the conditions of relief, and migrants over long distances often found it difficult to obtain help when a distant parish was legally responsible for them; but there seems to have been a widespread belief that poor relief was a right to which the industrious and well-behaved were entitled when times were hard. Some towns, such as Liverpool, were becoming increasingly tight-fisted by the 1820s; but the major changes came as a result of the new law of 1834.

This legislation was aimed at cutting spending on poor relief, in response to a very sharp rise in the early nineteenth century. All recipients were to enter a new kind of workhouse, in which men, women and children would be separated and conditions would be 'less eligible' than those endured by the poorest wage-earning families outside. In practice, conditions were never as severe as this. 'Outdoor relief' continued to be granted in many cases, especially during trade depressions. In many industrial areas, especially, the newly elected Boards of Guardians who were now responsible for relief in the localities, successfully resisted the building of the new workhouses for up to thirty years on grounds mainly of expense, but sometimes of humanitarianism. The 1870s saw a further drive to end outdoor relief and tighten up the system, but it was never completely successful: the 'deserving' elderly, especially, continued to be relieved at home.

But by this time the new regime had done its work. Its introduction had been controversial, and horror stories had been circulated about the new workhouses. Some of them were largely true; and they helped to reinforce the stigma which rapidly became attached to receipt of poor relief. Needy potential applicants were deterred by shame, and by fear of the grim monotony and discipline of workhouse life. Charles Shaw, who became a Methodist minister and journalist, gave retrospective substance to such fears when he described a boyhood stint in Chell workhouse, in the Potteries, in 1842. He remembered the unbending sternness of the officials, the harsh feel of workhouse clothing, the pain of separation from his family, the vileness of workhouse skilly, even to the hungriest child ('It might have been boiled in old clothes, which had been worn upon sweating bodies for three-score years and ten'), and the flogging which was handed out to a recaptured escapee. The workhouse did keep body and soul together; but some preferred to starve outside it. The Poor Law did not prevent the death by starvation of the unemployed porter Joseph West, surrounded by the opulence of Bath, in 1841. A local newspaper described the scene:

(His body) . . . was reduced by emaciation to a very skeleton (and) lay on the bare floor, its only covering being a threadbare blanket. There was not an article of furniture in the apartment, which was shared by the deceased, his wife, and four children; a heap of shavings in the corner . . . seeming to point out the sleeping place of the family. . . . Day after day their only food was two meals of dry bread, and tea. . . .

Deaths from starvation still occurred regularly in the London of the 1860s, where many women found the shame of prostitution less unbearable than the prospect of the workhouse. Workhouse conditions improved in the late nineteenth and early twentieth century, especially in the diet offered and the little treats for the 'deserving', but the dread of the workhouse remained overwhelming in the popular mind.

Scottish and Irish arrangements were different, but here, too, the Poor Law was the ultimate source of relief. In Ireland there was no Poor Law at all until 1838, and relief was then conditional upon entering the workhouse until the starving millions of the potato famine made this restriction untenable. In Scotland the poor were assisted out of the proceeds of collections taken at church, and other church revenues, and applicants had to satisfy comfortably-off lay representatives of the church that they were needy and deserving. Rates were not always levied although they were increasingly resorted to, especially in the towns, by the late 1840s. Relief was not supposed to be granted to the able-bodied, though in practice it sometimes was. The system was harsher than the English Poor Law, and depended more heavily on unreliable voluntary contributions; this remained so even after the passing of a new Scottish Poor Law Act in 1845.

Fortunately, the Poor Law was not the only protection against disaster. In times of crisis, town and city governments would administer relief funds for the unemployed and their families, providing employment on public works, soup kitchens and children's clothing. Such short-term palliatives were normally paid for by public subscription rather than the rates; but pride kept many workers aloof, pawning and selling possessions rather than taking charity. During the great Glasgow frost of 1895, very few of the hard-hit building workers applied to the Lord Provost's fund for support: as the Trades Council secretary said, 'They are not men who do that sort of thing.' When in 1906 local authorities were empowered to provide free school meals for undernourished children, such attitudes reduced the take-up rate. Even so, by 1914 310,000 children were being fed by those authorities which had chosen to adopt the new legislation.

But charity was one of the great growth industries of the period, providing everything from hospitals and orphanages to blankets and Bibles. Industrial Britain had inherited charitable endowments in profusion from earlier centuries;

but those which had not been devalued by inflation or swallowed up by corrupt administrators were concentrated into smaller or older settlements, and were in any case swamped by the growth of the urban working-class population. In London, for example, small City parishes were embarrassingly well-endowed while the East End in general inherited very little. There were plenty of gaps for the charitable to fill; and they acted from a mixture of motives. There was genuine humanitarian concern among the well-off for the circumstances of the poor. Usually this was mingled with an evangelical enthusiasm for saving souls, which was extending rapidly among all religious denominations in the later eighteenth and early nineteenth centuries, and sustained its momentum thereafter. In alleviating the poverty of the poor,

the charitable hoped to bring them closer to God; and if the influence of religion encouraged them to be thrifty and give up their evil ways, this in turn would improve their living conditions. Such developments would also make the poor more tractable; and this political dimension to charity should not be ignored, because the fear of riot and revolution was a powerful motive for almsgiving. So personal charity, especially when it involved face-to-face contact, upheld the social order, assuaged the consciences of the better-off, and, it was hoped, disseminated the values of self-help, thrift and respectability. It also provided a valuable outlet for the frustrated energies of middle-class women, who were barred by the social conventions of the time from taking paid employment.

From the late eighteenth century onwards, the most prominent form of charity was the visiting society. Often associated with churches and chapels, and with women doing most of the work, these societies tried to provide a visitor for every working-class street. As F. K. Prochaska puts it, 'Armed with the paraphernalia of their calling – Bibles, tracts, blankets, food and coal tickets, and

Women sitting out the evening of their lives in the workhouse, with a little plain sewing for occupation and a few plants on the window-sill for beauty and variety. The photograph was taken in 1911.

love – these foot-soldiers of the charitable army went from door to door to combat the evils of poverty, disease and irreligion.' Women also organised themselves to visit prisons, workhouses and even brothels in their work of reformation. Enormous numbers were involved: the London City Mission alone carried out two million visits a year in 1870.

By this time, however, worries were growing about the effectiveness of all this activity. The Charity Organisation Society feared that too many hand-outs were being given to 'undeserving' families whose life-styles were not being properly investigated, and who might be making a handsome income from charities and Poor Law relief combined. They sought to co-ordinate efforts to ensure that only the 'respectable' were helped, while those who continued to drink and misbehave were left to the tender mercies of the Poor Law. This frame of mind became increasingly influential in the later nineteenth century; but the importance of charity in keeping the poor from destitution remained absolutely vital, especially when trade depressions and unemployment in hard winters tore at the heart-strings and the purse-strings and stimulated spontaneous giving to relief funds.

Octavia Hill, a leading light of the Charity Organisation Society, was also involved in schemes for so-called 'five per cent philanthropy', which aimed to show that decent housing could be provided and managed for the well-behaved poor while generating a reasonable profit for its owners: and this is a reminder of the way in which much organised charity not only worked within the economic orthodoxies of the time, but sought explicitly to uphold them. A great deal of charitable giving was channelled overseas, too: missionary work was a particularly popular 'cause' for the promoters of charity bazaars, and it was here, above all, that children were enlisted as collectors. Charity might begin at home, but it certainly did not end there.

Even more important than this immense volume of assistance from above was the day-by-day assistance given by the poor to each other. In the nature of things, this cannot be counted or weighed; but contemporaries were well aware of its extent. Joseph Lawson, writing about the hand-

Octavia Hill, housing reformer and campaigner for the preservation of open spaces, as painted by John Sargent.

loom weaving settlement of Pudsey, in the West Riding of Yorkshire, in the 1820s, remembered that, 'They watch and nurse each other's families when sick, and borrow and lend almost anything in the house.' Such mutual help was not confined to this kind of setting: it soon grew up in the industrial neighbourhoods of the rapidly-growing towns, such as Preston, and expectations of mutual aid in times of crisis were strong in London's East End in late Victorian times. Women, especially, would make small loans to neighbours to tide them over temporary cash shortages, and would mind and discipline each other's children. Migration away from where a family was known, and really abject poverty, might remove or undermine these resources: one man brought up in an impoverished working-class enclave in Paddington remembered that neighbours did not look after his brothers and sisters, because, 'They was all busy looking after theirselves.' Families who sought the kind of respectability which held them aloof from neighbourly exchanges also made themselves vulnerable in hard times. In the newer working-class areas of the late nineteenth and early twentieth century, 'keeping oneself to oneself' became more widely regarded as a virtue; but these were the more prosperous working-class families, who needed each other less. There was, of course, another side to the importance of neighbourhood solidarities and communal living: they could breed grudges, spite and intolerance of behaviour that was 'different'; but without the willingness of neighbours to help each other through hard times, the lot of the poorer working-class household would have been even more precarious.

Help in hard times also came from family and workplace. Children were often looked after, and sometimes taken in permanently, by grandparents, uncles and aunts. Relatives found work and accommodation for each other: thus the novelist Bill Naughton's uncle found his father a coal-mining job in Edwardian Bolton, and helped him to set up house before bringing his wife and children across from Ireland. Migrants within England behaved in just the same way, and when the family was established fathers found work for sons and, where appropriate, daughters. Children, in turn, often supported their parents in old age, although little was expected of them when they started families of their own. No stigma was attached to elderly parents receiving poor relief at home, but when the workhouse beckoned it was often a different matter: families would economise on space to find room for the person under threat.

Mothers were easier to accommodate: they might be expected to help more with housework and child-minding. But room could be found for father, too. A popular story, almost certainly apocryphal, tells of the man who lived in a one-up-and-one-down house with his wife and four children, and set off to carry his crippled father, who could no longer live alone, to the workhouse:

When they got to near Scotland Bridge he paused to rest. He said, 'I'll have to put thee down here a bit, Dad.' His dad said, 'Coming along road I were just thinking, this is where I had to put my dad down. I just got to same bridge.' His son said, 'Bugger it. Tha's coming home with us. Tha sleeps downstairs in kitchen'.

This version of the tale comes from Ashton-under-Lyne; but it is widespread in northern England. It

A typical late Victorian trade-union membership certificate. The historical allusions to great inventors in the trade, and the emphasis on accident insurance and superannuation, are representative concerns of skilled trade unions at this time.

shows both an appreciation of what was expected of close family under these circumstances, and a sympathetic awareness of how difficult it was. Its popularity is very revealing.

Workmates also helped each other, especially with collections or 'gatherings' at the workplace to help families cope with illness or the aftermath of an accident. But families and neighbours, and especially women, provided the most reliable and effective help in hard times.

There were also more formal ways of guarding against misfortune. The most ubiquitous was the friendly society, which insured against illness, funeral costs and sometimes unemployment, in return for a weekly payment. Such societies were run by members of the working class, though they sometimes had eminent patrons to confirm their respectability; and they offered ambitious members the status that went with responsibility, power and high-sounding titles. Most also provided outlets for conviviality at their meetings, which were generally held in pubs, although some societies were offshoots of the temperance movement. Friendly societies were already multiplying in the later eighteenth century, and their numbers and importance grew enormously in the early decades of the nineteenth, when large, financially-secure bodies with hundreds of branches or 'lodges' merged. The Oddfellows, Foresters and the like, with their impressive funds and access to professional expertise, provided a real measure of security to their members.

In many industrial areas membership of friendly societies had almost reached saturation point by the 1860s and 1870s, although the largest and soundest organisations tended to recruit more from the skilled and the better-paid, while many of the poor had only enough insurance to cover a decent funeral. Also, as Thomas Wright, an astute observer from within the working class, commented in 1867, the societies' funds were sometimes put to dubious uses. He cited the annual procession and celebration of his own society, which involved a ragged parade, an incompetent band and a drunken banquet, after which:

Later in the evening a number of the brethren got up a supplementary 'demonstration', the chief features of which were a bacchanalian dance, accompanied by an appropriate chorus, performed in the high street of the town at the witching hour of night; and the carrying away of a number of . . . trade signs, such as barbers' poles and wooden cheeses.

The resulting encounter with the police was bad for

the society's image. But the societies provided access to medical treatment and a measure of income support during illness for millions who might otherwise have been left destitute and devoid of care; and for this Wright gives them due credit.

Wright had much more enthusiastic praise for his trade union, the Amalgamated Society of Engineers, one of the unions of craftsmen and skilled factory workers that offered many of the same insurance benefits as the friendly societies. During the first quarter of the nineteenth century, when combinations of workers were formally illegal, many unions had eased their survival by adopting this less provocative disguise. Despite a hostile legal climate, unions had been developing in many trades from at least the mid eighteenth century, and at times in the 1830s and 1840s they showed themselves capable of federating beyond the local level and even, occasionally, of combining beyond a single trade or craft. What made unions controversial was their challenge to the authority and control of employers as much as their potential for striking in pursuit of better wages and conditions or (more usually) in defence of existing ones. The very existence of unions challenged the economic orthodoxy that the correct level of wages would be reached by the sum of the individual bargains between masters and workpeople: so to much established opinion they were heretical, subversive and damaging to the interests of their members.

In practice, however, trade-union membership was dominated by skilled and supervisory workers, and much of their energy was directed to maintaining their privileged position, by resisting the dilution of their skills and the introduction of unskilled and especially female labour to compete with them and drive their wages down. From the 1850s onwards they were increasingly conciliatory in their demeanour, seeking the recognition of their right to bargain and seeing the strike as a weapon of last resort. If lightly resorted to, strike action would eat into the accumulated emergency funds of which the unions were becoming both proud and protective.

The 'new unions' of the unskilled which developed from the 1880s onwards lacked the bargaining power and financial stability of the older societies, and tended to be more combative. All unions were terribly vulnerable when they struck against wage cuts at the beginning of a trade depression, when work was in short supply, blackleg labour was abundant and the masters held all the cards. Even the Penrhyn quarrymen in

North Wales, whose union unusually embraced all grades within the quarries, whose skills were highly specific and had to be learned on the job, and who were pulled together by a strong village culture of Welshness and chapel-going, were defeated by the employers after a famous three-year confrontation at the beginning of the twentieth century. Nevertheless, it seems clear that without the protective power of the unions the lot of many workers in Victorian and Edwardian Britain would have been much worse than it actually was; and the unions fostered pride in craft and sometimes community, as expressed in the colourful banners and processions of events like the Durham miners' gala.

Trade unions were almost entirely a male preserve: even the unions in cotton, which had a lot of female members by the end of the nineteenth century, were run almost entirely by male officials. Women jute-workers in Dundee were able to organise quite effectively in informal ways, with strikes and often ribald demonstrations against their employers, and this may have been true elsewhere; but the female contribution to formal working-class organisations came most obviously through Co-op membership.

The Co-operative movement had its origins in the radical 1820s and 1830s, when followers of Robert Owen sought to build self-supporting alternative communities whose members would be paid according to the labour they put in. Efforts of this kind failed to take root, and the development of Co-operation as a mass movement was based on the Rochdale Pioneers' decision in 1844 to distribute profits among its members as dividends according to the amount of goods they had bought. This method of saving while spending proved immensely popular, especially when customers became accustomed to the unfamiliar unadulterated foodstuffs which the Co-ops sold, and Co-operatives on the Rochdale model proliferated, most notably in the textile districts of Lancashire and the West Riding of Yorkshire. By the late nineteenth century membership in some large towns had almost reached saturation point, and palatial new central department stores were appearing, while branches ramified in working-class neighbourhoods. Increasingly, the Co-op manufactured its own products, and it joined the older building society movement as an important provider of owner-occupier housing for the working classes. The Co-operative movement never entirely lost its commitment to building an alternative, uncompetitive, sharing society, and it provided libraries and evening classes to promote these ideals. The Women's Guilds, in particular, became doughty campaigners on issues relating to living standards, housing and women's rights. But most members used the Co-op to save as individuals, without subscribing fully to its values.

The Co-operative movement remained on the fringes of the formal politics of parliament and local government; and here working-class pressure for democratic reforms and greater influence on policy ebbed and flowed with the economy. Campaigners for manhood suffrage, some of whom envisaged votes for women, attracted mass support at various times in the 1790s, at the end of the Napoleonic Wars, at the time of the passing of the First Reform Act in 1831–2, and above all in the Chartist campaign for a democratic parliament with fair and open elections, which was sustained for more than a decade after 1838. These agitations drew support from small shopkeepers as well as wage-earners. They were fuelled by mass unemployment and wage cuts, and by resentment at government corruption and legislation directed against working-class interests, most obviously the New Poor Law of 1834.

Chartist activists included many high-principled advocates of democratic rights; but the pursuit even of manhood suffrage was not to come to fruition until 1918, despite many partial reforms on the way. The women's suffrage campaigns, which began in earnest in the 1860s and reached a climax in the early twentieth century, bore further witness to the persisting limitations on parliamentary, democracy in Britain. The Edwardian suffragists included many Lancashire cotton workers who felt that their contribution as wage-earners entitled them to a vote, at a time when women were becoming active and visible in local government. By the 1870s enough working-class men had the vote to make it worthwhile to seek the election of labour representatives to parliament; and socialist parties began to develop in the 1880s. At the start of the new century these trade union and socialist groupings came into uneasy alliance to form the Labour Party; but parliament remained dominated by Liberals and Conservatives. The Conservative Primrose League, designed to appeal to working-class people through patriotism and imperialism, had far more members than the parties of the Left. But despite their limited success in electoral politics, these campaigns and organisations made major contributions to working-class well-being. Their existence, and the threat it seemed to pose to the established order, compelled governments to

George Cruikshank's The Pawnbroker's Shop. *The tools and working clothes in the foreground are particularly expressive of personal tragedy: such things were only pawned in dire emergency.*

consider working-class interests, and to put forward reform programmes accordingly. Without such 'pressure from without', what improvement there was in rights and conditions would have come even more slowly and patchily.

Only a small minority of wage-earners sustained a more than ephemeral involvement in politics, although late Victorian election campaigns were hard-fought gladiatorial contests while they lasted. And the actual impact of the politics of labour on people's lives was too abstract and indirect to be visible to them at the time: it is hard enough for the historian to analyse. Most people's solutions to practical problems were couched at the level of the individual and the family.

In hard times, people could economise on space, by taking in relatives or lodgers and reducing the rent per person; or they could 'do a moonlight flit', a common expedient for evading the rent altogether when possessions were few. They could increase the family income by sending children out to work as early as possible. Women could take in washing, or go charring, or take waged work outside the home where opportunities were available: although in cotton Lancashire many married women chose to continue with factory work to boost an already tolerable standard of living. Credit from the corner shop, or even loans at high interest from local moneylenders, helped to tide families over difficult spells. So did the ubiquitous pawnbroker, who provided a useful service by loaning money on the security of prized possessions which were only wanted on special occasions, and for which there was limited storage space in small houses. Increasingly from the later nineteenth century, first in textile areas, last of all in mining villages, smaller families were becoming the norm, as ideas about contraception and abortion spread. Small businesses could be opened on the side, and sometimes became a route out of the working class altogether, as a greengrocery or fish-and-chip shop grew to dominate the family economy. And, of course, petty crime and prostitution were extreme, but far from uncommon, solutions for the desperate or the not too particular. A full list of possible expedients would be interminable; but the point is that there were many ways in which individuals could strive to reduce or postpone the impact of really difficult times. What most of them were unable to do was escape altogether from the clutches, or the threat, of poverty.

All these expedients had costs, of course. They traded comfort, or space, or time, or quality of family relationships, or self-respect, against the even more pressing need for food, warmth and shelter. The great mutual assistance organisations, the friendly societies, the trade unions, the Co-op and the rest, offered more security at lower cost. But the trouble was that they did not reach the people who needed their resources most. The friendly societies only provided adequate support in the short- and medium-term, to those who were fit enough to pass a 'medical' and could budget for the regular payment of substantial contributions, which might come to one shilling in the pound of the weekly wage. The Co-op generally refused to give the credit which its poorer members often needed, and only a minority of its members were able to reap the full benefits of the 'divi'. The trade unions, again, offered much more to the skilled than to the vulnerable and poorly-paid labourers. To those who had some resources, these organisations provided a little more security. The same applied to savings banks and commercial insurance schemes like those of the Prudential. Significantly, it was in cities with a predominance of casual labour and low, unreliable wages that these institutions were weakest: Liverpool is a case in point. Thrift and membership of voluntary organisations reduced the risks of working-class life for a growing minority, but not for the most vulnerable and disadvantaged groups.

This chapter has dealt with the material conditions of working-class life. It has touched on matters of the mind and the soul only in passing. But these were, of course, vitally important to contemporaries; and the next chapter deals with the role of religion and education at all levels of society in this period.

CHAPTER NINE

Church, Chapel and People

The first and only census of religious worship in Britain was taken on Mothering Sunday, 1851. Clergy and ministers were asked to count the congregation at each service, and to answer additional queries about such matters as Sunday school attendance. The imperfections of the census, and of the ensuing report, were much debated. We do not know how many people actually attended a place of worship on the day: figures exist for morning, afternoon and evening services, but an unknown number of people went, and were counted, more than once. Some worshipped at their parish church in the morning, and at a Nonconformist chapel in the afternoon or evening: a pattern which seems to have been quite widespread, and is a warning not to put Church and Chapel too simply into separate boxes. Their spokesmen saw them in that way, but some of their hearers thought differently. Despite the complexities and problems, the census forms a useful vantage point from which to view the changing importance of religion in Britain.

What really upset contemporaries was the evidence that up to half the population of England and Wales chose not to attend worship on census Sunday. Of those who did attend, moreover, fewer than half adhered to the Church of England: a point which was not lost on those who agitated for the ending of the special relationship between the Church of England and the State, at a time when such disestablishment was a live political issue. Attendances were highest in the south and south-west, lowest in the far north; and they were higher in country than in town, with the industrial towns and great cities presenting a particularly godless profile. The larger the town, the weaker the Church of England's attendance figures, while Nonconformity of various kinds flourished in a wide variety of settings, rural as well as urban. Above all, the absentees, especially from Church of England services, were overwhelmingly working class; and religion of any kind seemed to be alien to most of the urban industrial wage-earners. This is not the only way to look at the figures. From today's vantage point, what may seem remarkable is how *many* worshippers turned out, especially where the

weather was bad. Moreover, many occasional worshippers would not be picked up by a one-off census of this sort. The early Victorians had high expectations. How realistic they were, in the light of England's religious past and the magnitude of recent social changes, is another matter.

England contained many varieties of Christianity. By 1851 the Church of England itself embraced, at one extreme, clergy who were Roman Catholic in everything but their allegiance to Queen rather than Pope. On the opposite flank were Low Church zealots whose dislike of surplices and ceremonial were symptoms of a frame of mind which had much in common with many of the Nonconformists. There was a significant Roman Catholic presence, above all in parts of northern England where Catholic survival from pre-Reformation times was reinforced by Irish immigrants whose social status and style of observance were very different. Much more numerous in England as a whole were adherents of various Protestant Nonconformist sects which had been formed in the religious controversies of the seventeenth century: Baptists, Congregationalists, Presbyterians and other smaller groups. Where the Church of England recruited most of its support from the gentry, the substantial middle classes and their dependants, the older branches of Nonconformity attracted urban manufacturers, shopkeepers and the more independent of the skilled craft workers.

All these bodies had been caught up in the Evangelical Revival which had gathered momentum from the later eighteenth century, propagating the view that all could be saved by faith and right living, and giving rise to earnest and sustained campaigns to bring the poor to God. But it was the Methodists, the fastest-growing religious grouping of the later eighteenth and early nineteenth century, who expressed this trend most faithfully. They had begun under John Wesley as a ginger group within the Church of England, campaigning against its complacent laxity and trying to evade the inflexibility of its parish system by introducing itinerant preachers. They did not formally secede from the Church until the 1790s, after which they themselves split into several distinct groupings, even as Methodism as a whole continued to grow rapidly between the 1790s and the 1840s. Methodist simplicity of worship and early emphasis on spontaneity attracted support from the working class as well as the middle ranks, and they did especially well in areas of rural industry or developing agriculture which lay beyond the reach

PREVIOUS PAGES *Church and countryside at Morwenstow, on the north Cornish coast: the parish of Robert Hawker, one of the great Victorian clerical eccentrics.*

of the ancient parish structure of the Church of England. In the second quarter of the nineteenth century the Primitive Methodists, especially, gained the emotional loyalty of large numbers of mining and labouring families in parts of rural Lincolnshire, the Potteries and other areas which had been isolated from more orthodox religious influences.

At the other extreme of Nonconformity stood the Quakers and Unitarians, old-established sects which by this time appealed more to the intellect than the emotions. They were highly unorthodox: the Quakers were distinctive in manners, behaviour and form of worship, and the Unitarians denied the divinity of Christ. These sects had few adherents, but their influence was disproportionately great: they included large employers, merchants and professionals who formed prosperous, much intermarried leadership groups in major cities like Manchester, Liverpool and Birmingham. And there were even smaller or more localised sects. Some were survivors from the millenarian days of the early nineteenth century when prophets like Joanna Southcott could surround themselves with believers in an imminent second coming. Or there were new imports like the Mormons, still on the crest of a wave of conversions in 1851, but soon to be subdued by their leader Brigham Young's embarrassing adoption of polygamy in the following year.

The census found the Church of England in the early stages of a substantial recovery from a serious and highly visible decline in its influence, which was already marked in the mid eighteenth century and continued into the nineteenth. Population growth had been concentrated in areas where the Church was historically weak, with large parishes, underpaid and often absentee clergy and inconveniently sited churches. Over much of northern England Church influence on the daily lives and attitudes of the people at large had always been very limited: belief in witches, ghosts, boggarts and magical practices remained widespread even in the industrial areas in the 1830s and 1840s. Even if a church was close at hand and acceptable in principle, it was often inhospitable to the lower orders. The best pews were reserved for those who paid rent for them, and even in the free seats (which were often a minority) standards of dress were expected which working-class people found it difficult to meet. Services, and especially sermons, were usually directed at the propertied and formally-educated members of the congregation. The Church of England expressed the culture, the

preoccupations and even the politics of the landed and prosperous ruling groups in English society.

Signs of important changes became apparent in the 1820s and 1830s. A new generation of earnest Evangelical clergy began to concern themselves with the spiritual, and sometimes the physical, well-being of the poor. A church-building programme began, especially in neglected areas of towns, cities and industrial settlements. Day school and Sunday school provision was greatly increased. Worrying as the Church of England's position might appear to some of its supporters in 1851, it reflected a considerable recovery over the past generation.

Most branches of Nonconformity fared little better than the Church in attracting and keeping the working classes, especially in the large towns. The Methodists were most successful: especially the Primitive Methodists. Methodism flourished in Cornwall, where it dominated village after village, eclipsing and outlawing the rumbustious old popular culture of beer, revelry and semi-paganism, and claiming two-thirds of the county's worshippers in 1851. In Lincolnshire, Durham and the whole of Yorkshire, Methodism accounted for nearly half the worshippers; and here, as in Cornwall, far more were reclaimed from apathy than were seduced from the Church of England. But in most of Lancashire, and the London area, Methodism remained comparatively weak; and the reasons for these differences are still far from clear.

The Old Dissent of Baptists and Congregationalists, tracing its descent from the seventeenth century, had been in general decline in 1750, but recovered convincingly in its old strongholds of East Anglia and the South Midlands, where the traditions of the Puritans and John Bunyan had left deep local roots. It was weak, on the other hand, in the far north and west of England, where the Methodists evangelised populations which had hitherto been largely free of religious influences. The Old Dissent had outposts everywhere, but in many rural areas it was a matter of quiet persistence rather than dynamic growth. The survival of the early eighteenth-century decor of the Baptist chapel at Loughwood (NT), in Devon, for example, bears witness to a more general lack of pressure for expansion or change during a period when many other denominations underwent remarkable transformations.

The most controversial development of the period was the rise of Roman Catholicism, fuelled by the Irish immigration which reached its peak in the late 1840s. Lancashire bore the brunt of this

ABOVE *The Baptist meeting house at Loughwood, Devon, which has hardly changed since the early eighteenth century.*

RIGHT *The Congregational chapel at Little Longstone, in the Derbyshire Peak District, expresses the mid and late Victorian retreat from Nonconformist austerity, with its turret, elaborate windows and heavy, ostentatious stone dressings.*

influx, and in 1851 Roman Catholics were the largest single worshipping group in Preston, while they ran the Church of England close in Liverpool and Wigan. They were also a significant minority presence in towns as scattered and diverse as Carlisle, Coventry, Walsall, Newcastle upon Tyne and even the ancient cathedral city and centre of Anglican high society, York. Roman Catholics had only been granted full civil rights as recently as 1829, and prejudice against them was fierce. Most

of their number had brought a superstitious, semi-pagan religious culture with them from Ireland, and priests and churches were in short supply. But the Catholics were also making converts among people of means and education, especially at Oxford University; and this deepened the worries of those who feared the ambitions of the Church of Rome as a threat to English Protestant institutions.

The picture that emerges shows an accelerating increase in religious influences on the people of England between the late eighteenth century and the religious census of 1851. The unassuming little boxlike Methodist chapels dotted the windswept uplands of the north and the far west, and in mining and sheep-farming districts like the northern Pennines around Alston Moor and Weardale their influence was hard to escape. The revival of Old Dissent, less spectacular but widely influential, and the explosive growth of Roman Catholicism in some urban settings, point in the same direction. In belated response to competition and challenge, and with a renewed sense of mission, the Church of England was also reaching out to new adherents after the Napoleonic Wars. Instead of wailing and gnashing their teeth at the results of the census, contemporary churchmen might reasonably have taken some modest comfort from them.

Efforts to consolidate and extend the influence of the churches continued energetically in the second half of the nineteenth century. Church- and chapel-building reached a peak in the 1860s and 1870s; and the results of this investment are still obvious, though often crumbling and neglected, in today's urban landscape. But many of these churches were never or hardly ever filled. The Church of England, especially, found that it was not enough just to provide accommodation in working-class areas: new buildings would not automatically be packed by eager congregations of the spiritually deprived. Something more was needed, and only a small minority of popular and sympathetic clergy had anything resembling an answer. The opening of mission churches of wood or corrugated iron in slum areas made church-going less socially daunting, but emphasised even more the gulf between rich and poor.

Nonconformity had different problems. It lacked the Church's universalist drive to offer worship to all, but many of its prospering mid Victorian urban congregations were tempted to build new chapels which challenged the Church of England in architectural opulence. This venture into stained-glass windows, gothic arches, spires and marble columns was particularly seductive to Wesleyan Methodists and Congregationalists. But the diversion of cash into turrets and tracery channelled energies into fund-raising and debt-financing rather than evangelism. Moreover, the new chapels of the cities tended to be sited in the suburbs, adding geographical distance to the social separation between comfortably-off chapel-goers and the working class at large. Meanwhile, the Roman Catholics were busily building churches and cathedrals, sometimes on the grand scale, for their expanding congregations.

For all denominations, it was becoming harder to recruit acceptable clergy and ministers, as expectations rose, vocations became fewer and the more worldly-minded were distracted by the growing array of lucrative opportunities in the newer professions. The Church of England was hampered by its continuing reluctance to recruit below the ranks of the classically-educated and gentlemanly levels of the middle classes. This further heightened the difficulty of bringing the Gospel to the urban wage-earners. From the 1880s onwards the Settlement movement sought to establish colonies of well-intentioned graduates to bring religion and high culture to London's East End and other working-class ghettoes, making up for the absence of an idealised squirearchy. Enthusiasm ran high, but conversions were few in relation to the sheer number of people living in the target areas.

Some branches of Nonconformity found it less difficult to bridge the gap between a less exalted ministry and the better-off levels of the working class. But chapels as well as churches had rented pews, and kept them into the new century; and some became more socially exclusive as their members climbed through the ranks of the middle classes. Those who coveted higher status still slipped quietly off to join the Church of England. But chapels did provide more scope for active lay involvement, including preaching; and in some cases this made their services more accessible and attractive to working-class people. This was particularly true of the Primitive Methodists and some of the smaller sects, and of new, vigorously evangelical bodies like the Salvation Army.

All religious organisations surrounded their central acts of worship with a 'penumbra' of clubs

All Saints, Margaret Street, Marylebone, London: William Butterfield's unremitting assault on the senses, an overwhelming variety of colours, textures and materials.

and social activities: Bible classes, sewing circles, temperance societies, savings banks. By the late nineteenth century they were diversifying into leisure pursuits of a less directly religious or 'improving' nature: football, cricket, even amateur dramatics. The aim was to provide a full and fulfilling social life within the secure setting of the church and its congregation. This was all the more necessary when the earnestly religious, who were made conspicuous by prudery and abstention from drink and swearing, often became the butts of the irreligious majority at the workplace. But the danger, as perceived at the time, was that these activities might become ends in themselves, and distract from the central commitment to worship and spiritual improvement. In a similar way, the popular late Victorian innovation of the 'Pleasant Sunday Afternoon' came under fire from earnest critics. Its mixture of hymns, music and a short address was felt by some to be morally lightweight, and to dilute the religious message too far. To expand, and even to hold their ground, churches were having to broaden their range of activities and tolerance, and conflict frequently ensued within their ranks.

Despite their efforts, churches and chapels in late Victorian and Edwardian England failed to keep pace with rising population and urban growth. The supply of buildings and ministers lagged behind, and so did attendance at services. Not that these are the only measures of religious influence: but they are highly significant. And religious attendance and church membership remained disproportionately upper- and middle-class activities. Thus a census taken during 1902–3 showed that about one in every five Londoners would attend a service on any given Sunday. But in wealthy suburban districts it was one in three, and in poor areas one in ten would be a better estimate. These were not negligible figures; but to the churches they represented failure and widespread spiritual dereliction.

Scotland, Wales and Northern Ireland had different denominational patterns from England,

but their churches shared similar problems. The Scottish established church was Presbyterian, governed by parish, district, provincial and national assemblies, in each of which the elders (godly and comfortably-off members of the congregation) had a major voice. The Episcopal Church, analogous to the established church in England, was a small, mainly rural remnant whose pockets of local influence were few and scattered.

In the later eighteenth century the Presbyterian Church of Scotland was dominated by a 'Moderate Party' which resembled the Church of England at that time: it emphasised 'reasonableness' and discouraged undue fervour, offering polished sermons and support for the established order. But from the 1760s a reaction against this produced large numbers of dissident Presbyterian congregations. Most joined the Secession and Relief Churches, which were more austere and cleaved more certainly to the Calvinist doctrine that only a pre-ordained elect was destined for salvation, while the rest were irrevocably consigned to hell. Late in the century such views were being challenged in turn by an Evangelical belief that Christ died for all and all might be saved. This viewpoint made most headway within the Church of Scotland, but its rise was an important influence on the splits which developed in the newer Presbyterian churches at this time. In 1843 it contributed to the Disruption of the Church of Scotland, when the Evangelical wing seceded to form the Free Church of Scotland, taking nearly two-fifths of the clergy and many of the congregations with it.

So a multiplicity of rival Presbyterian groups emerged. Small farmers, weavers and skilled labourers found their way into Presbyterian dissent, which largely filled the niche occupied by Methodists and Congregationalists in England. Over much of the Highlands and Islands the crofters' hostility to their landlords underpinned the strength of the most austere and restrictive of the Presbyterian splinter groups. The only other numerous denomination here was the Roman Catholics, whose survivors in parts of the Highlands were supplemented, as in England, by Irish immigration into the Lowland industrial areas.

Despite Scotland's reputation for religiosity, attendance levels were similar to England's, and the Scottish churches shared the problem of winning over the less respectable strata of the working class. And rival rural superstitions died hard. The Society of the Horseman's Word, which brought together most farm servants who worked

PREVIOUS PAGES *An unusually ornate chapel interior of the early nineteenth century, that of the Countess of Huntingdon's Connexion, a small Methodist sect, in Worcester. The emphasis on the pulpit as the focal point of the chapel is characteristic of most Nonconformity, but the elaborate organ and stained-glass windows, and the decorative ironwork, mark the building out as unusual and attractive.*

with horses, required its would-be initiates to abstain from church-going for three years and to read the Bible backwards three times; and the initiation ceremony was a parody of a church service, culminating in a symbolic shaking of the Devil's hand. This had English parallels. What distinguished Scotland, apart from denominational peculiarities, was the special emphasis on Sunday observance, along with the strength of the temperance movement and the careful policing of morals by religious bodies. But all this coexisted with Glasgow's notorious drunkenness problem and high levels of rural illegitimacy: a reminder that church expectations were often widely at variance with popular culture.

Lowland Scotland became a hotbed of vicious sectarian rivalry between Protestants and Catholics, whose only English parallel was in Liverpool. Much of it was imported from Northern Ireland. Unlike the rest of Ireland, the six counties had an almost even division between Catholics and Protestants in 1861, although the Protestants were divided between the Church of Ireland and various other groups. Throughout the period Ulster's Catholics were poorer than the Protestants, with worse jobs and housing. For most of the eighteenth century the Catholic Church had existed on sufferance, and Catholics were denied the vote until 1829, as in the rest of Britain. Sectarian disturbances were already endemic in the 1790s, and tensions mounted during trade depressions in the growing towns of the nineteenth century. Catholic church attendance was low until the 'devotional revolution' of the later nineteenth century, but loyalties ran strongly all the same. Belfast and Londonderry became particular foci of conflict, and the sectarian divisions expressed themselves in Belfast in the emergence of separate housing zones. By 1901 Belfast was already highly segregated, with many Catholic streets in which no Protestants lived at all. The witch's brew of hatred and mutual incomprehension was already simmering.

Wales was different again. The Principality had an impressive level of religious attendance in 1851, and this was still the case in Edwardian times. But the established Church was completely swamped by Nonconformity, especially the various Methodisms, some of which were peculiar to Wales. In many chapels the services were in Welsh, and religion became closely bound up with expressing a sense of national identity. Much Welsh Nonconformity had a puritanical and Calvinist streak, which issued forth in Sabbatarian and temperance campaigns. But, as in Scotland, this earnest desire for regulation and control coexisted uneasily with drink, superstition and extramarital sex, and these ambiguities suggest that it would be dangerous to stereotype the Welsh too readily. Nor should we forget the vibrant musical culture of the chapels and their *eistedfoddau*.

Changes in the religious climate are well illustrated by two themes in the Church of England: the character of the country parson, and the nature of the church-building programme. The rural clergy had more than their fair share of eccentrics, but even the most peculiar convey the flavour of their times. James Woodforde, Rector of Weston Longeville, Norfolk, in the last quarter of the eighteenth century, displays an overriding interest in food and drink, coursing, gambling and undemanding enjoyment. He is genially but unthinkingly generous to the poor at appropriate seasons, and his time at Oxford appears to have prompted no interest in theology, still less in spirituality. In the next generation, the diary of William Holland of Over Stowey, Somerset, reflects the developing social tensions at and beyond the turn of the century. Holland emerges as an irascible Tory patriot, with a short way with Methodists and political radicals: he described Coleridge's wife, during their sojourn in Nether Stowey (in a cottage which now belongs to the National Trust), as

that Democratic hoyden . . . who looked so like a friskey girl or something worse that I was not surprised that a Democratic Libertine should choose her for a wife.

Holland was proud, assertive, and protective of his rights and property. But he visited his parishioners, reflected on his services and sometimes confided thoughts on the state of his soul to his diary.

But the new evangelical seriousness, which Holland distrusted, really came to the fore in the 1830s and 1840s. It was writ large in men like William Andrew of Ketteringham, Norfolk, with his long sermons, sustained belief in the direct intervention of Providence in everyday life, and earnest disapproval of all deviations from rigid seriousness of conduct and demeanour. Alongside such men, the Church in this generation still found room for 'Parson Button' of Llanbedr, who used to get fighting drunk and denounce his adversaries from the pulpit the day after. It also embraced the wonderfully odd Revd. Robert Hawker of Morwenstow in Cornwall. Hawker loved his remote and beautiful parish extravagantly, and embroidered a famous array of songs and legends around it. He was an undoctrinaire High Churchman whose services were enlivened by the antics of his nine cats, and whose preferred style of vestment was a claret-coloured 'cassock coat' with long tails and matching hat. This distinctive figure was renowned for his hospitality, his crusades against wrecking, his concern for the underpaid agricultural labourers of his parish, his campaigns against the local Methodists, and his interest in folklore. Many of his traits were reproduced, less outrageously, in his brother clergy.

Hawker's biographer, Sabine Baring-Gould, is an example from the next generation. He began his career in the Anglo-Catholic Tractarian movement, rubbing shoulders with early Christian Socialists as he helped to reach out to the East End poor in the 1850s. Later he was a successful curate and teacher in a tough industrial area of Horbury, in the West Riding, where he wrote *Onward Christian Soldiers* and married a working-class girl from his congregation. But he spent the last 43

years of his long life as squire and parson on the family estate at Lew Trenchard, in Devon. Here he combined an active ministry with rebuilding the village, restoring its church, defending traditions and collecting folk-songs. Above all, he was a prolific writer, of novels as well as hymns.

These were larger-than-life figures, sometimes enveloped in controversy. But this indicated the seriousness with which religious issues were taken in a divided and effervescing Church of England, as well as beyond it. There were still timeservers in the late Victorian church; but it was not all Trollope's Barsetshire. The battles between Anglo-Catholics and Evangelicals, Broad Churchmen and Christian Socialists, were evidence of life and active concern.

This was also apparent in the growing seriousness with which church architecture was regarded. The nineteenth century was a golden age of church-building. At an early stage the classical Georgian fashions, the pediments and Venetian windows, were abandoned. Gothic, as analysed and classified by John Rickman, was recognised and revived as the only true religious architecture. At first, in the new churches after Waterloo, it was spindly, etiolated and unscholarly. By the 1840s, fuelled by the indignant industry of Pugin, well-informed reproductions of medieval idioms were appearing, as part of a more general quest for ancient certainties in a time of flux. Earnest Christian architects worked within, and sometimes beyond, the revived gothic forms, from the harsh but heartfelt polychromatic confections of Butterfield to the grandeur of Bodley, as expressed in his late Victorian chapel at Clumber (NT). By the new century some architects were marrying new methods to old idioms. Lethaby's innovative church at Brockhampton, in the Wye Valley, brought together concrete and thatch in unexpected harmony, and used novel patterns and dramatic effects in window tracery and vaulting. The theoretical influence of Ruskin, urging that art and morality were inescapably intermingled, and the practical activity of William Morris and his allies, helped to usher in renewed pride in traditional skills and crafts. It was not always thus: many church restorations were mechanically and unimaginatively done, as walls lost their mellow texture and old furnishings were thrown out in the name of progress and convenience. Even so, the new seriousness made a widespread and telling visual impact.

What did religion mean in people's lives? Church-going tells us little about this in itself.

BELOW *Bodley's elegant late Victorian estate chapel still stands in splendid isolation in Clumber Park, Nottinghamshire, having outlived the great house it was built to serve. The interior (RIGHT) is opulent but restrained.*

W. R. Lethaby's innovative Edwardian church, in an idyllic setting at Brockhampton by Ross, Hereford and Worcester. It combines traditional craftsmanship and a medieval atmosphere with modern materials and novel motifs.

The kirk at St Kilda, centre of the religious life of the archipelago, as restored by the National Trust for Scotland.

Attendance could be an empty convention or a worldly display of fashion, an affirmation of sociability or a bid for social acceptability and advancement. The emotional revivals which drew enormous crowds to the first meeting of the Primitive Methodists on Mow Cop (NT), in Cheshire, in the early nineteenth century, or set the Welsh Valleys aflame later on, made many temporary converts; but contemporaries alleged plausibly that some went for more secular motives which included curiosity and the pursuit of the opposite sex. On the other hand, absence from church did not necessarily mean the rejection of Christian doctrines in everyday life.

The difficulties are illustrated by the extreme case of St Kilda (NTS). On this remote group of islands in the North Atlantic, the inhabitants surrendered their songs, games and profanities at the behest of a missionary in the 1820s, and then fell in thrall to a succession of resident ministers after 1829. Church attendance bit deeply into their daily routines, and Sunday was completely given over to devotions. Even the imminent threat of starvation would not induce the islanders to land a cargo on a Sunday in 1877, and the distinctive local economy, which revolved around the collection of sea birds from the cliffs and stacks, was undermined by the exactions of religious observance. But to many, this commitment smacked more of superstition than of spirituality; and the St Kildans kept many older beliefs which affected their lives deeply. It seems likely that the infant tetanus which effectively prevented the population from recovering from the emigrations of 1856 was caused by traditional birth ceremonies. These were performed by the 'knee-woman' who attended births, and probably involved the application of a mixture of fulmar oil and dung to the severed umbilical cord. The St Kildans also had distinctive burial and mourning customs on to which Christian rites were grafted. Even here, the real influence of 'official' religion is hard to disentangle from other beliefs and practices.

Towards the opposite extreme, few of the urban working class appear to have been completely impervious to religious influences in the broadest sense, even if they did not choose to express them by attending services. Ruth Richardson points out that the urban poor in the 1830s, and after, were deeply attached to funeral rituals involving the washing and laying out of the body, taking leave of it, sitting up with it and even, in some areas, providing it with grave-goods. These rituals mixed Christian notions of heaven and judgement with a need to placate and control the soul of the departed during a dangerous period of transition. If the proper formalities were neglected, disaster might ensue. Hence the fear and humiliation associated with a pauper funeral, especially after the Anatomy Act of 1832 provided that 'unclaimed' paupers who died in the workhouse could be handed over for dissection in the teaching hospitals.

More generally, Hugh McLeod identifies a prevalent 'do-as-you-would-be-done-by' frame of mind, associated with an undoctrinaire and residual Christianity which believed in Heaven rather than Hell and had little patience with complications or making a parade of church-going. The poor were too busy making ends meet to spare time and energy for religious speculation. By the same logic, working-class secularists and atheists were few, though articulate and therefore conspicuous, as were the adherents of minority creeds like spiritualism. There was little outright rejection of religion, though humbug and hypocrisy were fiercely attacked; and many working-class people were occasional church attenders. In London, for example, the New Year Watch Night service was a favourite, often attended by men who had been celebrating beforehand. All this points to the complexity of religious influences and the difficulty of separating them from both surviving magical beliefs and common-sense secular morality.

Much working-class opinion saw religion as something suitable to be taught to children, while not expecting an active interest in it to be sustained in adulthood. This helps to explain the paradox whereby working-class Sunday school attendance became almost universal in many areas in the nineteenth century, without being translated into church- or chapel-going later in life. The rapid spread of Sunday schools from the 1780s reflected a variety of concerns. Alongside teaching the rudiments of religion, and the literacy skills necessary to read religious tracts and perhaps the Bible, the schools were promoted and given financial support because they would keep children off the streets and out of mischief and, it was hoped, teach order, discipline and the gospel of subordination and hard work. Initially at least, Sunday schools were also a response to the failure of day schools to expand and cope with the rising birth-rate, and in areas where child labour was becoming more important they provided practically the only formal education for most children in the early nineteenth century. Many Sunday schools taught writing as well as reading and religion under these circumstances, and the Wesleyan Methodists lost many pupils when they abandoned writing, ostensibly on the grounds that it was too secular an activity for the Sabbath. The expansion of day schools from the 1830s and 1840s onwards enabled the Sunday schools to retreat more completely into religious teaching, but it remained unusual for a working-class child not to go to Sunday school, whether or not the parents went to church or chapel. Attendance in proportion to population actually reached a peak in the 1880s, and included teenagers and young adults as well as children.

What was the impact of Sunday schools? There were limits to what amateur teachers could do in three to five hours a week, and many Sunday schools probably made little difference to the spread of the ability to write. Some would argue that they taught submission to authority in ways which inhibited the development of working-class radical politics, but the evidence on this is ambiguous. There were working-class radicals, Chartists and trade unionists among the teachers, and many socialists were to be nurtured on biblical precepts and allusions. What the schools did was to nurture reading skills and provide a ladder of advancement for keen students, while passing on the values of working-class respectability in a religious setting. Their power to brainwash into submission was strictly limited, as recurrent complaints about Sunday scholars frequenting fairgrounds and beerhouses bore witness.

Other agencies of part-time education, such as factory schools, were much less important than the Sunday schools; and when day school provision for the working class began to increase rapidly it was overwhelmingly under religious auspices, and especially those of the Church of England. Indeed, the older framework of schooling which had sustained a rise in basic literacy into the 1750s and 1760s was largely Church-dominated, both in England and Scotland. The parish schools were opened and maintained under Church auspices, and most of the grammar schools were presided over by the local vicar.

Nineteenth-century developments largely reinforced this position, although Nonconformists and Roman Catholics added schools of their own. In England the Church's resources enabled it to found large numbers of new schools in the aftermath of the 1870 Education Act. Even where elected School Boards were set up under this Act to provide extra accommodation of an unde-nominational kind, they were usually dominated by Church interests. The same applied to the elected boards which were introduced in Scotland in 1872. Meanwhile, the small working-class private schools, the so-called 'dame schools' which operated in the houses of widows and retired or incapacitated workpeople, remained important providers of cheap and accessible schooling for much of the nineteenth century. Until about mid century the standard of teaching in these establishments may not have been inferior to the religious

An idealised view of a Sunday-school class in 1889, showing an elegant young lady presiding tranquilly over a remarkably well-behaved group of small children.

day schools, in which older scholars taught the younger ones, in a necessarily mechanical way. After this, increasing government grants to 'efficient' schools, fortified by inspection, squeezed these little independent schools out, and growing numbers of teachers were being formally trained in the colleges which proliferated from the 1840s onwards. By the late nineteenth century the combined power of Church and State was being felt through the imposition of free, compulsory day schooling, most of which took place under religious auspices.

In one way, the impact of this is clearly measurable. We can assess changing levels of literacy by looking at the proportion of people marrying who made a mark rather than signing the marriage register. This is an imperfect measure – it tells us very little about *reading* ability or the *quality* of literacy – but it is useful even so. It is clear that the decline in basic literacy which accompanied the social changes of the late eighteenth and early nineteenth century was being reversed towards mid century. Mass literacy was well on the way to being achieved before the Education Acts of the early 1870s. It came last to miners and labourers, and only in the second half of the century did women catch up and overtake men; but it was pervasive enough to generate a lively market for cheap publications. Most of these were decidedly secular in tone: they dealt with crimes, romances and snippets of titillating information. And this in turn suggests that the religious influences imparted by all this schooling made little impact, except on a serious and respectable minority. The working-class day schools at the turn of the century were more effective politically, in conveying notions of national superiority and imperial glory, than in promoting loyalty to denominational religion. But the home, the neighbourhood and the workplace taught values more effectively than the school.

The schools did provide a basis on which some could build, especially in Scotland, where such luminaries as Thomas Carlyle and Hugh Miller rose from village artisan origins to literary eminence. Mutual improvement societies allowed working men to stimulate each other's thirst for knowledge and understanding. Some had a religious connection, but others were racily independent. Robert Burns and his friends were capable of inaugurating a debating club in a remote corner of Ayrshire in 1780, for example, and half a century later some Nottingham pubs had libraries for their customers. This tradition was not lost, and it resurfaced in the late Victorian socialist movement. Meanwhile, more formal provision came with the Mechanics' Institutes from the mid 1820s, although these soon lost most of their pretensions to supplying scientific education of practical value, and shifted into more recreational channels, appealing more to clerks and shop-keepers than to manual workers. As the institutes declined after mid century, the torch was taken up by university extension classes, and by evening classes under a variety of auspices. These developments affected a small but important minority within the working class. They were given further opportunities by the spread of the free public library movement from the 1840s, but the vast majority of the borrowings were popular fiction.

What was missing, outside Scotland, was a ladder of opportunity from the working-class elementary school to the university. Even in Scotland it was much more difficult than is often supposed; but the Scottish universities were much more accessible than the English ones. And Glasgow and Edinburgh were centres of intellectual ferment in the late eighteenth and early nineteenth century, when Oxford and Cambridge slept. The only routes to England's ancient universities lay through the public schools or the grammar schools, where the requisite classical education could be acquired. For much of the period, too, dissenters from the Church of England were barred from Oxford and Cambridge, and set up their own institutions of higher learning. Above all, money or patronage was essential if formal education was to be pursued beyond the level of elementary school or trade apprenticeship; and this stark fact remained as true in England at the end of the period as at the beginning. English education was stratified according to what parents could afford to pay. This was one of the most fundamental of social inequalities, mocking any notion of a society based on equality of opportunity. The rise of the new university colleges in the provinces in the second half of the nineteenth century, with their more practical and commercial curricula, did little to alter the position.

The Church of England retained a strong grip on English educational institutions, from the ancient universities downwards. The question of religious tests for university entrance became a hot political issue in the mid nineteenth century, and it was one of many ways in which religious questions entered politics. Indeed, by the 1830s religion was becoming the most important touchstone of political allegiance: almost all Tories were attached to the Church of England, while active Liberalism was dominated by Nonconformity, though its landed Whig leaders were Churchmen. The special privileges of the Church of England were debated, attacked and undermined. This reflected the importance of religious identification among the propertied classes who made up the political nation; but plenty of working-class voters after

Reform in 1867 identified politically with a Church of England whose services they hardly ever attended. The Toryism of 'Church and King' runs through the period from the anti-radical mobs of the 1790s. Anti-Catholicism was also a major ingredient of popular politics.

It has even been alleged that the rise of Methodism helped to prevent revolution in the late eighteenth and early nineteenth centuries, diverting working-class attention away from material ills in this world towards salvation in the next; but it is unlikely that there were enough Methodists to make a significant difference. Many people oscillated between Methodism and radical politics

The unpretentious building in Tarbolton, Ayrshire, in which Robert Burns and the other members of the local Bachelors' Club met regularly during the 1780s.

at this time, and there was no necessary incompatibility between the two until most kinds of Methodism moved towards uncritical endorsement of the established order in about 1820. Similarly, the notion that a Nonconformist 'Protestant Ethic' was an essential ingredient in industrialisation fails to convince. The idea is that Nonconformists, encouraged by their religion into a questing and enquiring frame of mind, and seeking advancement in this world to confirm their status in the next, were pulled into industry. Meanwhile, they were barred from the established educational, professional and social institutions of the landed ruling class of the eighteenth century, and this reinforced their entrepreneurial orientation. The example of the Quakers fits this scheme

well; but most industrialists came from the ranks of the Church of England, and many were related to established gentry families. The argument is tempting, but the case is not proved.

All this does show that religious issues and influences were of central importance during this period. They bulked large in the lives of the governing and propertied classes, who in their turn sought to extend religious influences to the lower orders, for a complex mixture of interested and disinterested motives. It is arguable that during the Victorian years organised religion made a greater impact on the lives of a larger proportion of Britain's population than ever before or since. This idea can be tested further by looking at the ways in which people spent their leisure time.

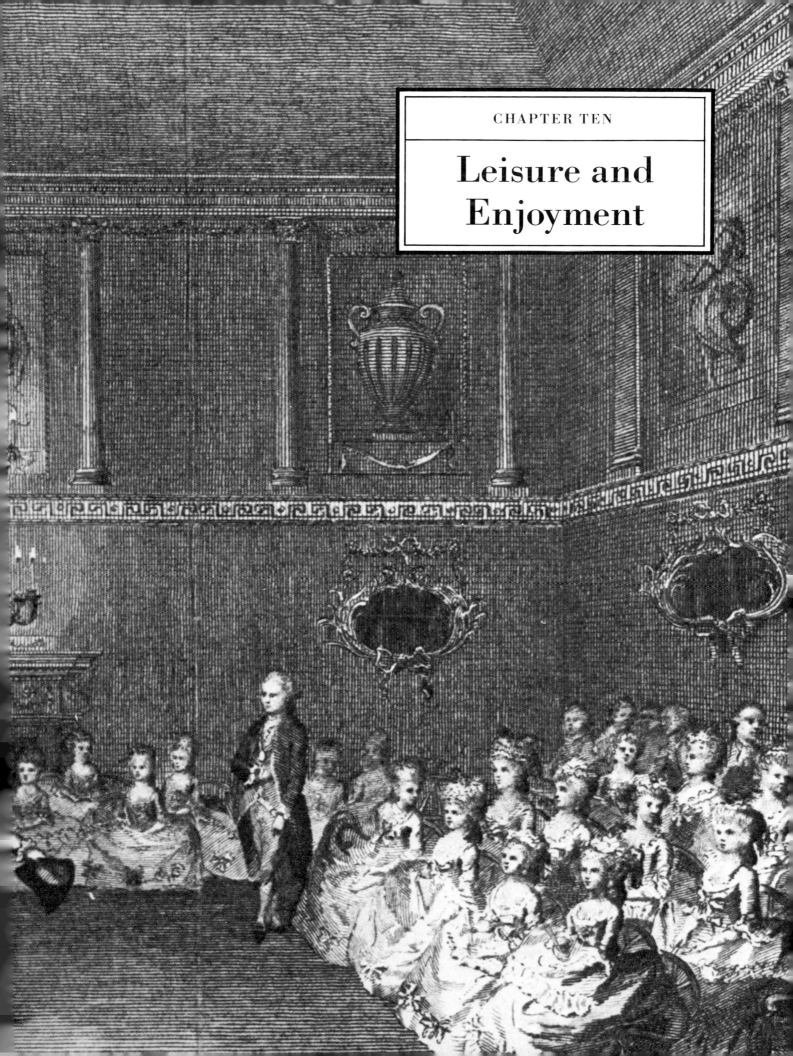

In the mid eighteenth century the amusements of the lower orders – wage-earners, smallholders and petty traders – were still governed largely by the seasons and the calendar. The activities which are most visible to historians were communal and convivial, with drink, dancing and mutual hospitality well to the fore. They might be rowdy and boisterous, and at times they might give rise to drunkenness and sexual dalliance. Often they involved violence and what some already identified as cruelty to animals. But they were supported by custom and popular attachment, and they were to prove remarkably resilient in the face of the economic and social changes of the next century.

The great festivals of the Church were generally observed as holidays. Christmas was not only a time for exchanging gifts and hospitality: it also involved mummers going in disguise from door to door with their rhymes and playlets, carol-singers, wassailers and sword-dancers, all expecting largesse. Mummers might also appear at Easter, when other customary pastimes included the rolling of decorated eggs (especially in Lancashire) and the 'lifting' of unwary men by bands of aggressive women on Easter Tuesday, when roles were reversed and working women temporarily asserted the upper hand. Whitsuntide, above all, was a great popular festival of drinking and dancing, with morris-dancing, races and traditional games such as stool-ball.

The details of the recreational calendar varied from place to place; but many observances were widespread. Shrove Tuesday was a day of pancakes and popular festivities. Mass football games were played in many villages and small towns, as still occurs at Ashbourne in Derbyshire and elsewhere, although the most spectacular survival is probably the Easter Tuesday game at Workington in Cumbria. Cock-fighting was also widespread, as was the custom of throwing stones at a cockerel tied to a stake until it was killed.

May Day was generally observed. It marked a seasonal transition, when the first flush of spring grass made milk and cream available in abundance after winter shortage. Gorging on cakes and cream formed an important part of the festivities for Londoners who went out to the villages surrounding the capital. More famously, the renewal of the vegetation was celebrated by displays of boughs and garlands, and by the erection of maypoles; and all this was intimately associated with courtship and betrothal. Guy Fawkes' Day, November 5, was celebrated with fireworks and bonfires, especially in southern England; in Lewes in Sussex, for example, where the festivities were especially enthusiastic, blazing tar barrels were rolled through the streets. The Pope was often burned in effigy, and so were unpopular local figures. The celebrations had official backing, with a special church service to commemorate James I's deliverance from the Gunpowder Plot, but the open-air proceedings frequently became too rowdy for the comfort of the authorities, and attempts were already being made to control or limit them.

The most important holidays in most people's lives were the local wakes and fairs. Almost every village had an annual festival, ostensibly in commemoration of the patron saint of the parish church. The wake, tide, feast or revel, as it was variously known, brought dispersed families and old friends together in an atmosphere of friendship and conviviality, as householders brewed, cleaned and prepared special food in anticipation of the event. There was dancing and drinking and fairground amusements, and new clothes were on display if they could be afforded. Grafted on to this pattern were local and regional customs. Over much of north-west England, for example, rushes were ceremonially carried to the parish church at the wakes, accompanied by morris-dancers, to renew the covering of the church floor. This was the occasion of ritual conflict, and often real fighting, between the young men of different hamlets.

More generally, the wakes might be a time for settling grudges, and it would be misleading to overemphasise or romanticise their positive features. The same applies to the local fairs, which combined retailing and (often) the hiring of farm servants with booths, drinking, dancing and entertainment. Hiring fairs acquired a particularly awesome reputation for uninhibited revelry, as servants who spent the rest of the year under the discipline of a farmer's household were released from restraint with money in their pockets in a carnival atmosphere.

Wakes and fairs might draw in visitors from a wide area, disrupting work in the process. So might the more alluring of the local customary spectaculars, like the running of bulls through the streets of Stamford and Tutbury, in Staffordshire, and their subsequent baiting. On a smaller scale,

---

PREVIOUS PAGES *A formal assembly in progress at Bath in the early 1770s. The tyranny of fashion is well expressed in the serried ranks of near-identical costumes.*

conviviality marked the completion of the great tasks of the agricultural year, especially harvest, which generated and sustained a rich body of customary observances, while farmers feasted their workpeople. Trades had their own calendar customs. Most magnificent of all were the woolcombers' processions to commemorate Bishop Blaize, their patron saint. Parson Woodforde saw one in Norwich in 1783, which featured trumpeters, figures of Peace and Plenty, Hercules, the Golden Fleece, Jason and forty Argonauts, and the Bishop himself in a phaeton drawn by six horses. There were civic and patriotic emblems, a fife and drum band and a militia band. This was unusually elaborate, but it expresses the rich symbolism and sense of spectacle which was generally present in popular festivities. The communal holidays of the mid eighteenth century were numerous, lively and rumbustiously enjoyed.

These were the highlights. In between were the pleasures of the alehouse, the market and the fireside, of story-telling and singing. The sales of cheap story-books and almanacs were already increasing, and trinkets and cheap finery were becoming more widely available. Drink and conviviality invaded the workplace, where work was organised in terms of completing the task in hand rather than getting through a set number of hours per week. In most workshops little was accomplished on Monday or even Tuesday, as the dissipations of the weekend were continued; and long hours were worked at the other end of the week to make up for lost time and to salvage an acceptable income. The main beneficiaries of this system were the skilled men: their subordinates, women and children included, worked longer hours for lower pay, and had to cope with the erratic behaviour of their employers and supervisors. Indeed, many aspects of popular pleasures now seem brutal, violent and exploitative. These issues were highlighted by the campaigns to reform working practices and popular leisure which were beginning to develop in the later eighteenth century.

Employers and property-owners opposed the customary activities and behaviour for several reasons. They were held to threaten the industrious habits on which national prosperity depended. They were alleged to undermine thrift by encouraging irrational spending on drink and hospitality. Often they caused damage to property, or threatened property rights in other ways: owners of woodlands, for example, were becoming increasingly intolerant of villagers who claimed a customary right to take wood for maypoles and decorative boughs. They challenged notions of order and hierarchy, especially when mummers or morris-dancers demanded 'largesse' in a menacing way, or muscular women 'lifted' their employers on Easter Tuesday. The evangelical revival combined religious and moral objections with the concern for order and economic efficiency to create a potent array of pressures for reform. The old popular amusements promoted drunkenness, immorality, cruelty, desecration of the sanctity of Sunday, and a general forgetfulness of the duty to be thoughtful, sober, decorous and restrained. They were therefore to be suppressed if possible: if not, they were to be transformed into a more acceptable guise.

Economic changes also threatened the recreational calendar. Pressure to work longer hours, in workshops as well as factories, reduced free time, except when trade was depressed, and there was little money with which to enjoy it. Fields on which games had been played were enclosed and commandeered by farmers for more intensive agriculture. The growth of towns also ate up land which had been used for recreation. Large towns contained concentrations of property which seemed vulnerable to crowds of pleasure-seekers, and food riots and political disturbances made the urban middle classes increasingly suspicious of rowdy gatherings of the lower orders. The old pleasures required plenty of time as well as space, but the relaxed frame of mind which had sustained them was increasingly challenged by changes in attitudes and ways of life.

There was also pressure from above. The rich and powerful expressed their opposition to popular festivities by withdrawing moral and financial support. They might withhold drink, or donations, or access to their woods and fields. More important by the late eighteenth century was the use of coercion and the law to suppress activities that met with disapproval; and this trend developed in the new century. Customs could often be put down because they had no backing in written legal documents, and the oral testimony of the oldest inhabitant was becoming of less account. A campaign against unchartered fairs began in Essex as early as 1761–2, when 24 were put down by the

OVERLEAF *By the later eighteenth century London's milkmaids were celebrating May Day with increasingly elaborate garlands and displays, in the hope of securing more generous largesse from householders and passers-by.*

county magistrates. This was the beginning of a very long, piecemeal process which was still in train more than a century later. But for most of the old festivities the pressures really began to intensify in the 1830s and 1840s, when a restrictive evangelical seriousness was gaining ground in the churches to reinforce the objections of industrialists and a wide range of middle-class opinion. Most vulnerable of all were popular blood sports, and violent crowd activities like the mass football games.

Bull-baiting was finished almost everywhere by 1840, after a campaign by the Society for the Prevention of Cruelty to Animals (founded 1824) and legislation against cruel sports (which paid no attention to those of the wealthy) in 1835. Cock-fighting was more resilient: legislation against it was delayed until 1849, it was easier to conceal, and it kept the support of many gentry and magistrates. Football declined patchily over a long period: the

strength and tenacity of opposition varied from place to place. In some towns the army was called in to quell the footballers, and the new police forces were active against the sport in the 1830s and 1840s as well as helping to subdue other popular entertainments in public places.

But coercion was not enough. Counter-attractions were often provided, especially by religious bodies, to lure people away from morally 'dangerous' pleasures like fairs and races. Picnics, outings and field days for Sunday scholars attracted the support of the better-off, and trips to the countryside and seaside by canal and railway took participants further away from temptation. John Rule describes the successful alliance of Methodism and the temperance movement in Cornwall:

Miners were marched around behind banners and bands, their thirsts quenched with gallons of weak tea and their need for excitement and involvement met by meetings dominated by the passionate oral rendering of hard-won struggles with temptation.

A mixed gathering of gentlemen and roughs, engrossed in the action at a cock-fight in about 1800.

By the early Victorian years the old-style parish feasts, with their wrestling, donkey-racing, 'hurling' (the local mass football game) and drinking were pale shadows of their former selves.

But even here the victory of religion, restraint and respectability was neither complete nor permanent. Methodism failed to put down the Padstow Hobby Horse, and one reformer who offered a roast bullock in exchange for the abandonment of the custom was stoned out of town. In 1844 publicans, impressed by the crowds attracted to a teetotallers' meeting on Bodmin Moor in the previous year, came along with 'booths, stalls, donkey-riding and other amusements', more than trebling the attendance and completely changing the character of the proceedings. Elsewhere, in the Lancashire cotton towns for example, many people attended tea-meetings and found time to go to the fairs and races as well; and in the 1860s seaside resorts on the south coast were plagued by drunks arriving on excursions sponsored by the temperance movement.

This is a reminder that most people took whatever enjoyments were on offer, without necessarily subscribing to the values that were promoted by those who provided them. In the same way, the municipal parks which began to proliferate from the 1840s were enjoyed *in addition to* the pub and other unregenerate pursuits, rather than *instead of* them. So it is not surprising that most of the customary popular amusements survived tenaciously. So did the working week of domestic manufacture, with 'St Monday' devoted to drink and gaming, including low-key blood sports like ratting. The only serious dent in the eighteenth-century leisure calendar by 1850 was where factories became established; and even in cotton Lancashire the Wakes survived into the new environment, although they were briefer in duration and lost their more lurid and violent dimensions.

For the most part, indeed, survival was conditional on increased respectability. The reformers did not usually get everything they wanted; but their campaigns made a noticeable difference. The big events that were suppressed completely were those which failed to adapt to changing times, or even became more disreputable with the passing years. Dover's Cotswold Games, on Dover's Hill (NT) near Chipping Campden, provide a case in point. In their seventeenth-century origins, under the patronage of a local landowner, they had involved a variety of races, athletic contests and combat sports; but 200 years on they were

becoming an annual rendezvous for industrial workers on the spree. A later commentator gave a loaded but revealing version of the consequences:

To have the scum and refuse of the nearest great factory towns shot annually into Campden for a week's camping in tents on Dover's Hill, two or three thousand at a time, with unlimited beer from unlimited booths and hooligans of the type of Tantiatopee; to have Kingcomb Lane a whistling Pandemonium of roughs and the pleasant valleys of Saintbury and Weston tramped by armed bands of Birmingham yahoos was not a thing to be desired.

Instead of bringing the poor and the propertied together in order and harmony, the games had become a focus for all the fears and tensions of a changing society. In 1852 the fields surrounding their traditional site were enclosed, and it became possible to bring the event to an end.

Adaptation and survival were more usual. Thus the celebration of Whitsuntide was 'tamed' and rendered acceptable in nineteenth-century Oxfordshire. Drunkenness and animal-baiting declined, the festival became concentrated into a single day, and its central feature became the processions and dinners of the local Friendly Societies, complete with band, church service and dancing in the evening. Supervision by clergy and gentry became more pervasive, and celebrations terminated at a set time. But morris-dancing persisted strongly at mid century – its decline was more a feature of the 1870s and 1880s – and there remained a strong unofficial undercurrent of violence and sexuality. Limited changes of this sort, sometimes greater in appearance than in reality, were closer to the norm than outright victory for the forces of order and decorum.

The continuing vitality of the public house as a working-class institution reflected the limits of 'improvement'. The pub remained the main meeting-place for societies of all kinds, from singing clubs to trade unions. Its influence was, if anything, increased by the constraints on leisure activities in fields and streets which were being tightened by the pressure on space and by the intrusions of the new police forces. The pub offered sanctuary for gambling and cock-fighting. Pubs with large gardens even found room for competitive running, which was banished from the streets because it obstructed traffic and because the near-nudity of the participants offended respectable citizens. The number of drink outlets was enormously increased by legislation in 1830 which allowed any householder to sell beer on payment of a licence fee of 40 shillings a year. This was intended to promote temperance by weaning the working class away from spirits, but it resulted in a vast mushrooming of beerhouses which proved impossible to regulate. Nor did it check the growing numbers of sumptuously mirrored and decorated, gaslit urban 'gin palaces'. Instead, the effect of the legislation was to inaugurate a period of intense competition between drink outlets, which gave an immense stimulus to the growth of the pub-based entertainment industry.

In any case, the campaigns against popular amusements were not by any means universally supported by the propertied classes. The popularity of Dickens' *Hard Times*, with its support for the circus people and their spokesman's sentiment that 'The people mutht be amuthed', indicates a widespread acceptance of the legitimacy of harmless pleasures. Moreover, there was no shortage of raffish aristocrats to patronise prize-fighting and other forms of low life, and horse-racing, with its appeal across class boundaries, could not have survived and prospered without the active involvement of sporting aristocrats and gentry and their hangers-on. Derby Day, after all, was one of the great institutions of Victorian England. The sporting parson was not yet extinct in the 1830s: indeed, he never disappeared completely, though evangelical bishops might force him to keep a lower profile. And there were paternalistic industrialists, as well as squires, whose conservatism found expression in the patronage of 'traditional' enjoyments. Robert Poole's comments on the Tory manufacturers of early Victorian Bolton have a wider validity:

They tended to favour drinking, prize-fighting, blood sports and all sorts of revels as ways of stiffening the national fibre, keeping a disorderly people happy, and bringing the upper and lower classes together in common enjoyment – a sort of social safety valve.

On the other hand, there were plenty of articulate voices among the nonconformist, teetotal, often politically radical working class to urge that emancipation and advancement could only come through abstemiousness and self-improvement. Attitudes to leisure did not divide along class lines in any simple way.

The century after 1750 saw an accelerating trend towards the commercialisation of leisure for the better-off, which coincided with the evangelical revival but in many ways ran counter to it. The development of the theatre illustrates this theme well, as does the rise of the specialised pleasure resort.

As befitted the national centre of high society and high living, London's theatres both multiplied in number and increased in size and architectural pretensions. This trend reached a spectacular climax with Henry Holland's rebuilding of the Drury Lane theatre in the early 1790s to give it a capacity for over 3500 people. Meanwhile, purpose-built theatres were spreading through the provinces. Bath and Bristol, which had been among the pioneers in the early eighteenth century, saw investment in impressive new premises, while Norwich was also in the vanguard. More surprising is J. H. Plumb's finding that even rural Lincolnshire acquired fourteen theatres during the eighteenth century, in market towns as small and unpretentious as Brigg, Horncastle and Market Deeping. The county towns and regional centres of polite society drew large and opulent audiences during the fashionable season by the later eighteenth century; and it is in this context that the substantial investment in the surviving Theatre Royal (NT) at Bury St Edmunds makes sense. It was built in 1819, designed by William Wilkins, the architect of the National Gallery, and seated 660 people. By this time a national common culture of the polite and opulent had emerged, with tentacles which stretched into the remoter parts of East Anglia, and a good theatre had become an essential ingredient of urban civilisation. Some playgoers might be more concerned with gossip and display than with the actual content of the play, and the stage was to fall under a cloud of moral suspicion and disapproval in the next generation; but it never really lost this position of indispensability.

The development of a market in leisure facilities for the better-off posed problems for those who still thought in terms of a society based on inherited rank and breeding. Where pleasure was provided by speculators for profit, anyone who could afford the entrance fees might be admitted, and aristocrats might rub shoulders with their inferiors as if they were equals. The theatres largely solved this problem by having a scale of prices for different kinds of seating, or by putting on performances for different classes at different times. The resorts found this more difficult, especially when activities were concentrated into a few buildings where sociability was expected. Bath experienced this embarrassment early. As J. A. R. Pimlott pointed out, the novelist Smollett, in *Humphrey Clinker* (1771), mercilessly lampooned Bath's social mixture:

An eminent cowkeeper of Tottenham had arrived to

drink the waters for indigestion. A mulatto heiress, a broken-winded Wapping landlady, a brandy merchant, and a paralytic attorney from Shoe-lane mixed without distinction of rank or fortune with Ministers of State, Judges, Generals, and Bishops.

The Assembly Rooms, where the company met for dancing, tea-drinking and polite conversation, thus offered dangerous scope for social conflict. This was defused by the appointment of successive Masters of Ceremonies who laid down rules of behaviour for the company: Beau Nash was, of course, the most famous and effective of these. But in 1771 a new Assembly Rooms (NT) opened behind the King's Circus. It represented £20,000 of investment by 72 shareholders: a huge speculation for its time. And by defying the Master of Ceremonies and opening at times to suit the proprietors, the new establishment competed with the existing assemblies and threatened to divide the market and split the company. For a time, traditionalists tried to sustain a boycott, in the hope of returning to the old system of different assemblies opening at different times under the MC's control; but the new proprietors were adamant. The new rooms, designed by the Bath architect John Wood the younger, were novel, attractive and convenient enough to succeed. Commercial competition thus undermined the notion that the visitors were a 'company' or community.

Similar developments were soon apparent in the profusion of new resorts which were emerging and growing at this time. Assembly rooms, bazaars, circulating libraries, pleasure gardens and theatres competed for the attention of a rapidly widening visiting public. Such developments responded to, and were part of, the gradual spread of new fashions outwards from London and downwards through society. The growth of competitive consumption in this way affected the clothing trades, furniture, pottery and even shaving. Medicine, the ostensible reason for the early growth of the spas and seaside resorts, was not exempt, as a profusion of new treatments and quack remedies was assiduously peddled. But pleasure soon ousted health as the main motive for a visit to a resort; and the commercialisation of enjoyment became an important feature of a much wider set of trends. Here lay the roots of the growth of home demand which provided some of the essential markets for the spectacular developments in manufacturing industry and finance during these years.

By the 1830s the development of commercial entertainment was really beginning to make its mark at working-class level as well. Alehouses and fairground entertainers, among others, had long 'sold' entertainment in a low-key way. Even in the remotest countryside of northern England and southern Scotland, troupes of strolling players were taking the theatre to the labourers as well as the farmers and gentry. How else could the indefatigable Mrs Charlotte Deans have sustained a career which took her company to the tiniest hamlets of northern Cumbria and the Borders, in the difficult years of the early nineteenth century? And the commercial impulse was affecting the content and presentation of popular customs by the later eighteenth century. Thus London milkmaids and chimney sweeps displayed May Day garlands in increasingly elaborate and exotic forms, with the predominant intention of collecting as much money as possible from passers-by. Decorated pyramids of rushes on carts, at the Lancashire Wakes, were accompanied by processions of morris-dancers; and here again, the collection of money to divide among the participants became centrally important. As part of the process, the patronage of publicans became almost inescapable; and more generally, it was the publican who led the stronger and more sustained moves towards the development of catering for working-class leisure as a business, a trend which was gathering momentum at Victoria's accession.

The combination of rapidly rising urban populations and increasing drink consumption per head led to well-sited urban pubs becoming more elaborate in themselves. Bars became show-pieces of the carver's and gilder's art, with dark wood, stained glass and almost ecclesiastical arrangements of columns and shafts. The Crown Liquor Saloon (NT) in Belfast is a resplendent example of these themes at their climax, but it could have found emulators in London, Glasgow, Birmingham and many lesser places.

The pub also diversified into providing sport and entertainment on a more lavishly commercial scale than before. Informal singing-rooms and 'free-and-easies', where performers sang for no reward or were paid in beer, were replaced by staged events in larger rooms with formal seating, and ultimately such activities moved into separate premises. Acts became more sophisticated and the top artistes became household names, with incomes and life-styles to match.

One of the pioneers of these changes was Thomas Sharples of Bolton, who began his Star Concert Room in 1832 and moved to larger

Belfast's Crown Liquor Saloon, showing the elaborate carving, gilding, plaster, tile- and glass-work. On a Saturday afternoon, when there is horse-racing on the television and the bar is abuzz with jokes and conversation, the atmosphere is very unlike that of a conventional historic monument!

premises in 1840. His concert hall held up to 1500 people when crammed to the doors, and there was also a museum, and a promenade with roof-garden. Acrobats, clowns, freaks, jugglers and musical turns passed across the stage in rapid succession, and there were great set-pieces such as an 'illuminated tableau of the Great Fire of London'. Teenage cotton workers and working-class families flocked to these entertainments, especially on Saturday nights, while Monday afternoons were reserved for a rougher clientele of miners and other votaries of 'St Monday'. Bolton, and other provincial manufacturing towns, marched in step with the more famous developments in London in the early days of what became known as 'music-hall'.

As outlets multiplied and premises grew from the 1850s onwards, the sheer size of the potential audience in London pushed its music-hall tycoons to the forefront and made it the Mecca of the best-paid stars, whose songs celebrated the roistering of the 'swell' or charted the misfortunes of the aspiring clerk. The cheerful bawdiness of music-hall's early days was cleaned up under pressure from late Victorian licensing authorities, and from proprietors who did not want to upset the more 'particular' among their audiences; but much could still be done by innuendo and there remained large numbers of little back-street halls which were still attached to the pubs from which they sprang. Music-hall became perhaps the most popular form of mass commercial entertainment by the late nineteenth century, and the ditties it made popular even ousted folk-songs from the village pub in the remotest depths of rural England.

Professional sport was another great growth industry of Victorian Britain, and here again the publican played his part. The old mass football games, with their ritual violence and threats to property, had been suppressed almost everywhere by the 1860s; but their passing left a gap in working-class lives. Contemporaries remarked that working men were driven even more firmly into the beerhouse for their entertainment. The same decade saw the beginning of the rise of a new, formally organised kind of football, with limits to time, space and number of players, and codified rules. This was a product of the public schools, and it was transmitted to working-class players *via* the philanthropic evangelism of muscular Christianity, in the hope of encouraging healthy minds in healthy bodies. Churches and chapels often acted as seed-beds for the new football teams, which included such famous names as Aston Villa

and Bolton Wanderers. Paternalistic employers also played their part by sponsoring works teams: Thames Ironworks, for example, which later became West Ham United. The spread of the Saturday half-holiday after 1850 made it easier for large crowds of spectators to assemble, and commercial pressures and opportunities soon became apparent.

It was here, from the 1880s, that the publican could become involved, especially in the most popular form of football, the Association game. The most remarkable example was the assertive and avaricious John Houlding, a brewer and hotel owner who played a central part in the early years of Everton Football Club and then, after a dispute, went on to found Liverpool. Towards the turn of the century Association football at the highest levels became big business, and the pressures and temptations to introduce professionals became irresistible. As a result many of the apostles of moral and physical improvement began to disengage themselves from football as a spectator sport, unhappy about its developing aura of gambling and drink, and compromised ideals of sportsmanship. In this new world of commercial spectator sport, of Leagues and five-figure crowds and partisanship, the publican was one influence among many; but his presence was indicative.

Other sports were less relentlessly commercialised at the top; and Association football itself depended on a numerous substructure of amateur clubs and players. Cricket and horse-racing remained under the wing of aristocratic governing bodies, and the county cricket championship, which began in 1873, was altogether less intense and more genteel than the Football League. The development of professional Rugby League, which split off from the amateur code in 1895, ran more closely parallel to that of Association football, although it was largely confined to its regional stronghold in the textile and mining districts of Lancashire and Yorkshire. In general terms, the displacement of customary games by organised, codified sports, subject to the disciplines of time, space and rules, and in part to those of the market place, was a development of major importance.

Articulate observers at the time displayed mixed reponses to the rise of commercial entertainment. Some saw it as supplying degrading and trivial distractions from more important things, luring people away from church or chapel, trade-union activity or radical politics. Some, like the redoubtable Mrs Ormiston Chant, who campaigned against London's music-halls as haunts of prostitution and dens of vulgarity, saw it as more directly corrupting. But others argued that anything which reduced the primacy of the pub in the life of the lower classes was a step forward; and the decline in drink consumption, drunkenness convictions and (probably) public violence from the 1870s lends some substance to this argument. In Glasgow as well as London the tea-room began to rival the pub as a place for relaxation and refreshment. Towards the turn of the century it also seemed that some leisure activities were bringing the classes together in ways which might ultimately reduce social tensions and promote order. Working-class visitors to seaside resorts came as families and behaved more rarely in ways which scandalised their 'betters'. Music-halls in London's West End, and some in the centres of provincial towns, began to attract employers and 'well-to-do tradesmen' as well as dissolute young 'mashers' and clerks on the spree. Some sports, such as cricket, were already mixing the classes in the late eighteenth century, but rowing and amateur athletics froze out working-class participants.

But not too much should be made of this. Those seaside resorts which found room for large numbers of working-class people did so by encouraging their concentration into certain areas of the town and beach: only here and there, as in Blackpool's Tower Ballroom, did the classes mingle on the dance floor. Most music-halls were solidly working class, and in any case they were socially segregated by price, as were football grounds. And there was plenty of scope for those with sufficient money and time to escape beyond the reach of their social inferiors, whether on the golf course or the tennis court, in the grand hotel or at the remote and exclusive resort, in France or Italy as well as Devon or north Norfolk. It was easier for the rich to share the pleasures of the poor than for the working class to be able to afford or gain access to the range of options open to their 'betters'. The major change of the later nineteenth century for the middle classes in general, indeed, was that they became emancipated from the constraints of a narrow evangelical code of public respectability, and were able to enjoy activities which had hitherto been suspect: a frame of mind which also found expression in the widening range of acceptable Sunday pleasures.

Developments in the theatre illustrate these trends. The early Victorian years were difficult. Fears of immorality and frivolity drove away much of the mainstream middle-class audience, and an increasing dependence on the threepences and sixpences of gallery and pit drove programmes down-market and confirmed the worst fears of the respectable. The established theatres were undermined by competition from circus and music-hall, and from new rivals playing low comedy and melodrama; and their surroundings were often becoming seedy and threatening. The patronage of the comfortably-off was not lost altogether, especially in London, but the support of traditionalists and the raffish brought in only a small proportion of the potential market. Among those who made up the numbers were what Thomas Wright called 'the roughs':

. . . those who come to the theatre with unwashed faces and in ragged, dirty attire, who bring bottles of drink in with them, who *will* smoke despite of the notice . . . who favour the band with a stamping accompaniment, and take the most noisy part in applauding or giving 'the call' to the performers. The females of this class are generally accompanied by infants, who are sure to cry and make a disturbance at some interesting point in the performance.

It was difficult to present the theatre as 'improving' or even as suitable for those who valued their respectability under these conditions, as showers of nuts and orange peel descended from the 'gods', and subtleties were lost in the demand for blood and thunder. Even so, Shakespeare was sometimes enjoyed; but, significantly, the middle decades of the nineteenth century produced no plays or playwrights whose influence lived on. Only with the advent of Gilbert and Sullivan, and the reign of Henry Irving and Ellen Terry at the Lyceum, did the theatre begin to extend its appeal to the respectable classes: at mid century Queen Victoria's patronage of drama had attracted suspicion and censure rather than emulation. Intellectual interest came towards the turn of the century, with the controversial introduction of Ibsen and the emergence of Shaw as critic and author of 'social problem' plays. But society dramas, and the accessible sentimentality of J. M. Barrie, did more to bring the middle classes back to the West End. Such developments were far from universal: at Bristol's Theatre Royal, for example, the mid 1890s ushered in 'a routine of pantomime and melodrama', often featuring 'hairbreadth escapes from cremation, circular saw, Nasmyth hammer, flood or express train'. But among all this the status of theatre, and of the emergent acting profession, was rising, and even some branches of Nonconformity were losing their horror of the stage.

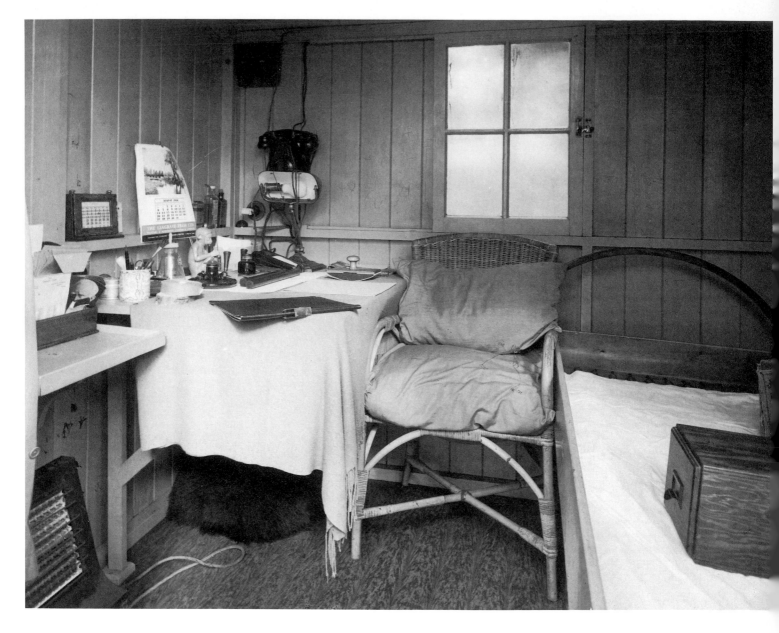

ABOVE *The garden hut at George Bernard Shaw's house at Ayot St Lawrence, Hertfordshire, in which he took refuge in pursuit of peace, creativity and uninterrupted working time.*

RIGHT *The actress Ellen Terry's country retreat, Smallhythe Place, near Tenterden in Kent: a complete contrast to her metropolitan world of theatre and business intrigue.*

The career of Ellen Terry, whose memento-packed house at Smallhythe in Kent belongs to the National Trust, pulls much of this together. Born in 1847 to an acting family, she began her stage career at nine. She was introduced early to the raffish and enjoyable literary and artistic world of Bohemian London, and made a disastrous teenage marriage to the artist G. F. Watts, who was much older than she. Her two children were illegitimate, born of a relationship with the architect and stage designer E. W. Godwin; and this put her beyond

the pale of polite society. Her second marriage, and her long partnership with Henry Irving at the Lyceum, brought social acceptance and the affectionate regard of an expanding middle-class theatre-going public. In 1906 her fiftieth year on the stage was celebrated with a Jubilee performance at the Theatre Royal, Drury Lane, sponsored (says Roger Manvell) by a committee 'made up of over a hundred names representing the nobility and men of distinction in every branch of public life'. The show featured everything from

Shakespeare and Molière to Gilbert and Sullivan's *Trial by Jury*, from Caruso to the musical comedy star Gertie Millar. In part, this astonishing occasion reflected the wide range of friendships enjoyed by Ellen Terry herself. But it also expressed not only the rehabilitation of the theatre in the fashionable and intellectual worlds, but also the ways in which its boundaries overlapped with other aspects of music and the performing arts. It had become popular across class boundaries, and had come to terms both with the working-class demand for melodrama and the middle-class pressure for respectability. In this it summed up the relaxation of attitudes to commercial leisure at the turn of the century.

Music was an essential ingredient of most Victorian and Edwardian entertainment, even accompanying professional football. At the fixture between Nottingham Forest and Bradford City in 1902:

A piccolo player came along and struck up a lively air. Immediately the 'boys' began a rhythmic accompaniment on handbells, bugles and tommy-talkers. The resulting effects have never been equalled by Strauss. Not far away another Yorkshire chorus was singing a hymn tune to the strain of concertinas.

This was one of many indicators of the universality of popular music-making and musical appreciation, which probably reached its peak at about this time. There was considerable enthusiasm for Handel and choral singing at working-class level by the 1840s. The spread of cheap sheet music and instruments in more prosperous times after mid century, together with improvements in musical education and the development of competitions, helped to build up a remarkably large constituency of active musical enthusiasts among the lower middle and upper working classes.

The brass band movement, especially, became immensely popular in parts of northern England. Working-class singers rubbed shoulders with the families of merchants and industrialists in the choral and philharmonic societies of the West Riding of Yorkshire. Handbell ringing societies and a rich variety of other organisations proliferated. The heartland of these activities was the West Riding textile district: at the turn of the century Slaithwaite, with fewer than 5000 inhabitants, supported a brass band, four choral societies and a famous amateur orchestra. Some of these societies grew out of religious bodies or were sponsored by enthusiastic employers, but most depended on the subscriptions of members and supporters: and they could make exacting demands on members' time as well as money. Their repertoires ranged from opera to music-hall, and they sent their quota of earnest working-class listeners to the cheaper seats of the concerts which were important events in the middle-class social calendar in most provincial towns. Eager listeners were far more numerous than serious performers, of course; and even the poorest had concerts in the parks or music of a sort from street buskers.

Music also had its private faces. The piano, especially, was an essential feature of middle-class Victorian domesticity, a symbol of conviviality and family life, and the centrepiece of courting rituals. It also became an emblem of working-class respectability, as cheap instruments and hire purchase encouraged its spread down the social scale in the later nineteenth century. In fact, a great deal of leisure activity was confined to the home and the family circle. It has been neglected by historians because it is less visible, less controversial and leaves less accessible sources than the great public commercial developments of the period. But for most married people, perhaps, and certainly for the vast majority of women, almost all leisure was domestic. This was also true of most children whose families were too careful of their respectability and safety to allow them to mix in the street. Even married working-class men were spending more of their free time at home towards the turn of the century, especially in London, where workplace-based conviviality was declining in the face of longer journeys to and from work and, in many cases, improved housing.

For a growing minority within the working class, the home was becoming more attractive, with smaller families occupying larger houses. The long rise in the popularity of gardening and home improvements was beginning. Better education and changes in printing technology helped to encourage a swelling flood of cheap literature, whose distribution (as with so many things) was eased by the ever-expanding railway network. Board games, card games and other amusements became more widely available. Although an aspect of the commercialisation of leisure, these activities were designed for enjoyment within the home, rather than in the public arena of the music-hall or football stadium. Home amusements also tied in neatly with leisure reformers' glorification of hearth and family, although they might have deplored some of the reading matter which was enjoyed by the fireside, as trivial scandal-sheets and 'penny dreadfuls' proliferated.

Even in the early twentieth century, however, much leisure activity remained beyond the reach of commercial providers, especially where women, children and the poor were concerned. Women's 'relaxation' often involved domestic activities which could be done sitting down: knitting, sewing and other contributions to the household economy. Gossiping and visiting relations and friends also loomed large in the use of 'free time', as many social investigators noticed. For men, of course, much of this kind of activity took place in the pub or, higher up the social ladder, in the club. Children's pleasures were often improvised, and many of their games were in some sense traditional: indeed, they were often the last perpetuators of customs which had been abandoned by adults. Markets provided

Robert Smail's printing works at Innerleithen, Borders. The printing press was originally driven by a water-wheel, and the whole enterprise illustrates the relative cheapness and ease of setting up and sustaining a printing business in a small Victorian town. This helps to account for the spectacular flowering of the remarkably high-quality local newspaper press of the period.

free entertainment for many working-class couples, who could enjoy the patter of cheap-jacks while buying essential supplies. And, of course, the clubs and societies associated with churches and chapels made their own vital contribution to sociability and enjoyment for millions. Even so, as this chapter should have made clear, they were increasingly being swamped by an overwhelming number of rivals in the rush to take advantage of opportunities in the growing leisure industry.

All these strands were pulled together by the rise of the open-air movement, with cycling and rambling becoming organised activities around the turn of the century. The appreciation of fresh air and countryside might be free, but for its full enjoyment equipment had to be bought and maintained, transport had to be paid for, and free time had to be available. Alongside the entrepreneurs in boot and bicycle manufacture, the churches and the socialist societies played their part in encouraging and helping to organise this most 'improving' kind of recreation. Changing attitudes to landscape and the countryside were at the heart of the growing popularity and acceptability of these pursuits, and also set the context for the emergence and early development of the National Trust.

CHAPTER ELEVEN

Countryside and People

As towns grew and industries spread to dominate the everyday horizons of ever-growing numbers in Britain, so attitudes to landscape and countryside changed. Barren and mountainous country was seen to be attractive in its own way, alongside the deeper-rooted appreciation of the cultivated, controlled and useful lowland patterns of field and farm. But finding beauty, and indeed awe and inspiration, in rugged uplands was not a natural or in-built reaction: it was the result of a series of changes in cultural values and aesthetic preferences which began in the early eighteenth century and gradually made a conquest of educated opinion. These values never became fully accepted by everyone, and a great deal of lip-service must have been paid to them by people who knew how they were *expected* to respond to a particular view or experience. But they came to dominate the language in which rural Britain was described, in everything from poetry to guidebooks; and indeed, their spread helped to stimulate the development of tourist industries in remote areas, thereby threatening to change their character and appearance. The emergence of new ways of seeing the landscape, and of deriving pleasure from it, is a theme of central importance. Changes in how people respond emotionally to their surroundings are every bit as significant as changes in the surroundings themselves. Without this revolution in values and perceptions, the rise of the outdoor movement, of conservation lobbies, and of the National Trust itself, would be literally unthinkable.

Daniel Defoe, that eager chronicler of industrial growth and commercial progress, provides telling illustrations of orthodox values and preferences in the first half of the eighteenth century. Here are his views on the 'frightful mountains' of the Pennines and Lakeland, with their 'terrible aspect':

Nor were these hills high and formidable only, but they had a kind of an unhospitable terror in them. Here were no rich pleasant valleys between them, as among the Alps; no lead mines and veins of rich oar, as in the Peak; no coal pits, as in the hills about Hallifax, much less gold, as in the Andes, but all barren and wild, of no use or advantage either to man or beast. . . . Here we entered Westmoreland, a country eminent only for being the wildest, most barren and frightful of any that I have passed over in England, or even in Wales it self. . . .

For Defoe and almost all his contemporaries, mountains were acceptable only if they produced useful articles. Even then, they were ugly and frightening to the urbane traveller from a society which valued regularity, symmetry and cultivation above all other visual considerations.

This attitude was beginning to change by the mid eighteenth century. A few intellectuals were beginning to confess to being thrilled by the sensations of awe and horror induced by the sublime vastness of mountain scenery. More widely, a vogue was developing among the wealthy and educated classes for the Italian landscape paintings of Claude, Poussin and Salvator Rosa, which pulled together crags, waterfalls, gnarled trees, temples and distant vistas into compositions whose popularity excited emulation amongst English artists. This helped to undermine the notion that beauty lay in straight lines and geometrical arrangements, the imposition of rationality and order on the threatening wildness of the natural world. Sinuous curves, scattered clumps of trees and contrived wildernesses became part of the vocabulary of the new landscape gardening; and mountains became part of the making of a desirable vista, although most followers of these fashions still preferred to keep them at a safe distance. It was in this climate of opinion that the indefatigable traveller Bishop Pococke could, in 1750, see a very different Lake District from that of Defoe. Ullswater was 'beautiful . . . there is a strip of fine land at the foot of the high mountains which appear very romantick'. As for Rydal, 'nothing can be imagin'd more beautiful', although, significantly, here again the mountains are appreciated as part of a more general view embracing 'hillocks, wood, houses, pasturage and corn': this is still a lived-in landscape, and its foreground is safely tamed and rendered productive.

Pococke's enthusiasm was a product of the changing sensibilities of his time. In the next generation came the full flowering of the 'picturesque', in which landscapes were assessed according to their potential qualities as artistic compositions, mixing rough and smooth, light and dark, woodland and water, in approved measure, and embracing elements of the quaint, the rustic and the ancient. By the 1770s this cultivated game was beginning to catch on in earnest, as travellers in

PREVIOUS PAGES *A Claude landscape of the kind that inspired the cult of the picturesque, with carefully-contrived contrasts of lighting, level and texture, and a carefully rationed and distributed supply of people, animals and points of historic interest.*

search of the picturesque began to invade the Wye Valley, the Derbyshire hills, the Welsh mountains and especially the Lake District. Guidebook writers rode the fashionable wave, with the industrious Revd. William Gilpin well to the fore, advising on what to see, how to see it, where to stand and how to respond aesthetically and emotionally. A whole new vocabulary of landscape appreciation developed, and was passed on from the pioneering intellectuals to the aspiring merchants and professionals of the provincial towns. Manchester manufacturers and Lancashire merchant families were soon touring the Lakes, keeping manuscript diaries of their experiences, and hoping to defray the cost of the trip by publishing their impressions. Almost inevitably, the whole business spawned cliché after cliché, and drew the fire of satirists; but by that time the new ways of seeing, or at least the new conventions of landscape appreciation, had been firmly established.

But the picturesque was not the whole story. Mountain mists and precipices, solitudes and remoteness were also becoming attractive for their own sake, not just as part of the search for ideal landscapes. The awe they inspired brought those who ventured on to the heights and fastnesses closer to Nature and to God. Solitary communion and contemplation, coupled with the spirit of adventure and discovery, drew travellers to the mountain tops and conveyed a sense that they were special places. These were new and powerful feelings, growing out of both the romantic celebration of untamed wilderness and the untrammelled self, and the evangelical search for closer communion with God.

Two other strands were also important in the development of new attitudes to landscape and countryside: a sensitivity to the past, and an awareness of nature. Ruined castles and abbeys, stone circles and other evidences of the distant human past enhanced the landscape, in themselves and for their associations with history, legend, and notions of the impermanence of human fame. Interest in the flora and fauna of rural England was well established among the educated by the early eighteenth century, and collectors, observers and book-buyers multiplied thereafter. Gilbert White of Selborne in Hampshire, where the National Trust owns the woods where he loved to wander, was only the most famous of a host of village naturalists, many of whom were also clergy. As White's occasional verse shows, his loving observation of nature and locality coexisted with

awareness of the conventions of the picturesque; but his letters present his delight in Selborne and its natural history without embellishment.

The journals of Sir Richard Colt Hoare of Stourhead, which describe his annual summer journeys in search of the picturesque between 1793 and 1810, illustrate the interests of an earnest and well-travelled landowner who had responded seriously to these new attitudes to landscape. Above all, he gave elaborate, effusive descriptions of the places he visited, sometimes with characteristic exaggeration of their scale and drama which echoes, for example, White's descriptions of the 'mountains' of Selborne. Thus Settle, in Yorkshire, is 'situated under a lofty perpendicular rock which overhangs it and bears an Alpine appearance'. But not only did he admire crags, woods and fields: he paid increasing attention to antiquities, and his picturesque interests extended to the contribution of modern industry and transport. Thus the new canal aqueduct at Chirk, in Wales, 'when time has given the stone a few mellow tints . . . will be a most picturesque object'. Or the industrial site at Aberdulais (NT) in South Wales in 1808: 'Turned off a few paces . . . to see a mill and another waterfall. A delightful scene and perfect composition for the pencil. The masses of fallen rock are particularly grand. . . .' Hoare's enthusiasms were widely shared among his class, though few chose to pursue these interests so assiduously.

Indeed, not everyone was quite so serious. The Lake District was beginning to attract more frivolous travellers, and residents. In the early 1780s Mr Pocklington built on his island in Derwentwater a sham church, a fanciful boathouse, and, says Norman Nicholson, 'a fort and a battery, fitted with cannon for echoes . . . and . . . a Druid Circle fifty-six feet in diameter, planned on the model of (nearby) Castlerigg' (NT). The same Mr Pocklington was a patron of regattas and firework displays on the lake, and from now on, here and elsewhere, amusements multiplied for the growing number of visitors who were sightseers rather than solemn admirers of the picturesque and sublime.

The pursuit of scenery, with its various cultural associations, was given a new boost in the early nineteenth century, as road improvements made the remoter areas of the north and west more accessible to people whose means and free time were limited. The key impulses were literary, and the central figures were Wordsworth and Sir Walter Scott. The growing celebrity of Wordsworth gave new resonances to the appreciation of

Lake District landscape, and Rydal Mount itself became a place of pilgrimage, until by the mid 1840s parties were queueing up in the summer to visit the house and garden and talk to the poet. The impact of Scott's novels on perceptions of their settings was much more sudden and dramatic. Tourists were already coming to admire the Falls of Clyde and the Highlands in the 1750s, and Scotland continued to attract its share of devotees of the picturesque; but much of the country seemed bare and empty of objects of interest to the demanding eyes of such as Gilpin. Scott peopled these landscapes with romantic figures and episodes from a vividly re-created past, and described their features in arresting ways which affected his readers' perceptions of them. Thus the Grey Mare's Tail (NTS) waterfall in Dumfriesshire had disappointed the opinion-forming travellers of the 1790s; but in 1808 Scott, in *Marmion*, found such evocative words to clothe it in magic that, as Holloway and Errington put it, 'Thereafter, those who saw the fall, saw it through Scott's description.' And he conjured up a similar aura for much of the Border country, while playing his part more generally in the invention and re-creation of Scottish traditions and the emergence of a distinctively Scottish idea of landscape.

By the 1850s and 1860s the countryside could never look the same again to the tutored sensibilities of the ever-expanding middle classes, with their pocket editions and their guidebooks. It was seen through a prism of picturesque aesthetics, paintings and prints, history, legend, folklore, theology, morality and poetry. Knowledge of plants and animals and their habits, and of geology, was being more widely diffused, and delight could be found in the contemplation, and collection, of mosses, ferns and specimens of all kinds, as well as in the grander panoramic spectacles. The diary of Revd. Francis Kilvert, with its unbounded delight in the beauties of the Wye Valley and the Black Mountains, and in the passage of a spider over a gravestone, shows how these strands could be twined together. Above all, Kilvert worshipped at the shrine of Wordsworth, and hungered for reminiscences of the poet's life; but his description of a March sunset on his beloved mountains shows the further range of influences which enriched his responses to his surroundings:

The last cloud and mist rolled away over the mountain tops and the mountains stood up in the clear blue heaven, a long rampart line of dazzling glittering snow so as no fuller on earth can white them . . . I never saw

anything to equal it I think, even among the high Alps. One's first involuntary thought . . . is to lift up the heart to God and humbly thank Him for having made the earth so beautiful. An intense glare of primrose light streamed from the west deepening into rose and crimson . . . I could have cried with the excitement of the overwhelming spectacle.

But as Kilvert immediately became aware, most people remained unmoved by such wonders:

I wanted someone to share the sight with me. A man came whistling along the road riding upon a cart horse. I would have stopped him and drawn his attention to the mountains but I thought he would probably consider me mad. He did not seem to be in the least struck by or to be taking the smallest notice of the great sight.

Kilvert was also regularly annoyed by the vulgarity and insensitivity of 'tourists', who invaded his favourite places and seemed more concerned with horseplay and jollification than with appreciating their surroundings in a way that he could approve. This reaction was snobbish and intolerant, but it is a reminder that only a small minority of the educated, with leisure for contemplation, could share Kilvert's capacity for appreciation to the full. Even so, and despite his strictures, something of the new framework of ideas and values had rubbed off on a very large number of people, including some serious-minded and self-improving members of the working class.

Nor was this appreciation of nature and countryside confined to the upland scenery of the north and west. Constable's Suffolk – and Hampstead Heath – together with the Norfolk landscapes of Crome and Cotman, Turner's coastal scenes and Linnell's views of the Home Counties are only a few illustrations of the creative explosion of English landscape painting over the century or so after 1750. There were many images of many countrysides, some of the most evocative being Wright of Derby's dramatic industrial landscapes depicting furnaces and factories in rural settings. The changes in perception and sensitivity were national in their coverage as well as in their impact.

As towns and cities coalesced and industry continued to spread, the British – and especially the English – attachment to countryside became more general and more deeply felt. It extended to

The Langdale Pikes, in the heart of the southern Lake District: a classic portrayal of the kind of landscape and ambience that the National Trust's founders sought to protect.

embrace vernacular architecture, folk-song, traditional crafts, local dialects and traditions, 'quaintness' and rusticity: everything that was felt to be under threat from the creeping uniformity encouraged by improved communications, metropolitan fashions and the stretching tentacles of commerce.

The identification of rural England with traditional virtues and national identity spanned the political divide which was becoming increasingly apparent at the turn of the century. It appealed to those who looked back with nostalgia to an idealised medieval society in which the rich did their duty and the poor knew their place, and sought to revive the pride in work that went with craftsmanship, and the mutual understanding between the classes which had been undermined by wage slavery and the single-minded pursuit of profit. It also attracted those who feared for the future of the race, as the sound stock of the countryside migrated to the cities to become degraded and enfeebled, creating a deepening spiral of inherited debility. How, it was asked, could England sustain her armies, her economy, her prestige and her power, under these conditions? The military failures of the Boer War, and the shortage of physically satisfactory recruits, reinforced these worries. And the positive attributes of countryside, building on the values which were already so clearly articulated in the 1860s and 1870s, were hymned in an ever-swelling flood of poems, articles, guidebooks and songs. Magazines and newspapers praised the manifold delights and virtues of contact with the land, from the socialist *Clarion*, with its associated rambling and cycling clubs, to *Country Life*. By 1914 the folk-song collector and propagandist Cecil Sharp had managed to get Board of Education endorsement for the sentiment that, 'The music learned by children in elementary schools should be drawn from our folk and traditional song'; but already, as Alun Howkins points out, visions of an ideal rural England were pervasive enough to sustain men as well as officers in the trenches, and to be widely accepted as potent images of 'what we are fighting for'.

Gradually and almost imperceptibly, idealised versions of the rural – and the past – changed over time, with an accompanying shift in the messages they enshrined. The search for order, security, beauty and fulfilment in medieval England and its survivals, which was a prominent mid Victorian theme, gave ground at the turn of the century, when the age of Elizabeth offered a more dynamic

and combative focus for nostalgia, giving the limelight to a strong monarch, intrepid seamen, entrepreneurial merchants and jingoistic patriotism. Wordsworth and Scott had been – or had become – strongly conservative influences; but John Ruskin, who took over the mantle of custodian of artistic and architectural values, remains much harder to categorise.

Ruskin followed the other towering Victorian sage and thundering controversialist, Thomas Carlyle, in endorsing strong, caring, paternal government in an idealised version of medieval society. But his work on architecture led him to place special emphasis on fulfilment through craftsmanship; and he came to contrast the workmanship of medieval cathedrals with the mechanical, uninspired tawdriness he associated with modern technology and the division of labour. He detested the chaos and ugliness, the smoke and filth of industrial towns, and feared that they would continue to expand and engulf the countryside he cherished. And these attitudes in turn led him to attack the dominant philosophy of *laissez-faire*, the idea that the good of humanity was best served by individuals buying in the cheapest market and selling in the dearest, and by wages and prices being allowed to find their own level without outside intervention. Ruskin believed that this produced scamped work by discontented labourers using inappropriate materials; and he argued that it was morally corrosive, leading people to value money and show above the true worth and utility of goods which really enhanced their lives. Thus he advocated wage regulation and a return to small-scale craft production; and it was here that his ideas fed back into the reinforcement of an ideal notion of English countryside.

This mixture of romantic feudalism and economic heresy attracted little support when it first began to crystallise in the early 1860s, when writings like *Unto This Last* were extremely unpopular with a general middle-class readership. The feudal nostalgia posed few problems: it had affinities with the fears of many famous contemporaries concerned with the lack of sympathy and understanding between the classes, and Carlyle, Disraeli and Dickens all wrote in similar vein. And such attitudes sustained their appeal well beyond the turn of the century. It was the attack on *laissez-faire* that provoked fierce dissent. The *Cornhill Magazine* was obliged to stop its serial publication of *Unto This Last*. It was not until late in the century, when Ruskin was a frail and silent recluse at his home on Coniston Water, that his

The house in Cheyne Row, London, where Thomas Carlyle lived, in a watercolour painted in 1881. Son of a master mason, he became 'the Sage of Ecclefechan', and one of the great controversialists of early Victorian Britain. But he failed to kindle the lasting influence of Ruskin.

economic ideas began to generate a following, as cheap editions became more readily available, and craft workshops were set up on Ruskinian lines. Working-class discussion groups analysed his books, and his writings became a formative moral and intellectual influence on many future leaders of the infant Labour Party. His ideas bore inspiring fruit in the career of William Morris as master craftsman, designer, poet and visionary, with his idyllic portrait in *News from Nowhere* of a post-revolutionary England of villages, sunlit hayfields and comradeship. Here, of course, Ruskin was one influence among several, and Morris's emergence as a socialist politician took him more on to the territory of Marx than Ruskin.

Ruskin was, indeed, in no sense a socialist. He saw himself as an old High Tory, and aimed to recall Britain's rulers to a higher and older morality than the pure and simple worship of money. In this he was at one with, among others, Dickens, Mrs Gaskell and Trollope. And he became a valued figurehead for campaigners against the untrammelled pursuit of profit when it threatened the beauty of existing landscapes, solitudes and buildings. The hard work, and hard cash, behind such campaigns came from a growing band of people who had decided that it was time to make a stand. Many of them, perhaps most, had come under the spell of Ruskin's ideas.

The specific issues on which campaigns developed involved the protection of access to countryside and places of interest against those who sought to block up footpaths; the preservation of common land against enclosure for private emparkment or development; the creation of urban open spaces for the pent-up city poor; and the prevention of damage to beautiful or remote places through the building of railway lines or other civil engineering works. Of related importance was William Morris's Society for the Protection of Ancient Buildings, founded in 1877 to oppose the kind of fashionable church 'restorations' which destroyed old work and ruined the texture and integrity of the medieval stone.

The rights-of-way protection movement had the longest pedigree. Local societies to oppose the blocking up of ancient footpaths by landlords who found them inconvenient were emerging in Manchester and York as early as the mid 1820s. Among the interests protected by such bodies were those of the large number of working-class people who enjoyed the woods and fields at every opportunity: a reminder that it was not necessary to have full access to the literary and artistic culture of

John Ruskin in old age, being visited by the Pre-Raphaelite painter Holman Hunt in the garden at Brantwood, Coniston.

the Lake Poets and the picturesque in order to take pleasure in attractive surroundings, although the taste for mountain solitudes and heathlands remained a minority interest. Defenders of rights of way were particularly busy in early Victorian Scotland. Here great landowners busily trying to exclude the public from their new deer parks were opposed from 1845 onwards by the Rights-of-Way Society.

By the 1880s footpath preservation groups were active over much of Britain, including Northern Ireland, where an access route to the Giant's Causeway (NT) was successfully protected. Frequent legal difficulties arose because some judges demanded an impossible burden of proof that a landowner had granted a right of way in the past, and customary usage might thus be held to be insufficient. But a very large number of paths was successfully defended, and the popularity of rambling was shown by a rapid late Victorian proliferation of rambling clubs, which added further weight – and respectability – to the footpath preservation lobby. So-called 'Gentlemen's Clubs' like the London Sunday Tramps, formed by Leslie Stephen in 1879, were soon augmented by organisations largely composed of clerks and skilled workers which developed in London and all over industrial northern England. A deeper and more general working-class attachment to grimy Lancashire moorland was revealed in 1896 when 12,000 people marched to defend their right to walk on Winter Hill, above Bolton, when the landowner tried to cut off their access to his grouse moors. There were other examples of mass demonstrations and direct action, although recourse to the law tended to produce better long-term results. Indeed, from 1884 onwards regular efforts were made by the emergent outdoor lobby to gain a legal entitlement to access to mountains and upland open spaces, although widespread parliamentary support did not bring success.

Working within the law was strongly urged by the Commons Preservation Society, which offered legal advice to rights-of-way campaigners and in 1899 took the National Footpaths Preservation Society under its wing. The CPS was formed in 1865 under the auspices of the radical Liberal MP G. J. Shaw-Lefevre, later Lord Eversley, to combat the threats to surviving common land in the London area by Lords of the Manor, who wanted to reap the profits of building development, and by railway companies who found that commons provided the cheapest lines of route. The old rights of local residents to graze animals, collect wood and so on were falling into disuse; and the right to use common land for fresh air and recreation, which was the main concern of the Society, was legally less secure. In any case, there were long-established legal traditions which favoured Lords of the Manor who wanted to enclose commons. The motives of Shaw-Lefevre and his colleagues were basically philanthropic: they wanted to retain suburban commons as breathing-spaces and amenities for town-dwellers of limited means. Some of their crucial support, admittedly, came from suburban residents who wanted to continue to enjoy the local commons themselves. But the Society attracted an impressive range of cross-party support, including even the active participation of the political economist John Stuart Mill. And they were remarkably successful, assisted by the legal expertise and tactical sense of Shaw-Lefevre and by his ministerial career in several of Gladstone's governments. His related achievements in this role included the Ancient Monuments Act of 1882, which began the process whereby historic sites could be maintained and protected by the State.

The Society's roll-call of preserved commons and ancient forests included Hampstead Heath, Wimbledon Common and Epping Forest; and as it extended its activities beyond the London area its influence was felt in the New Forest, the Forest of Dean and the Malvern Hills. Its most important propaganda coup came early. In February 1866 the trustees of Lord Brownlow enclosed 434 acres of Berkhamsted Common (NT), in Hertfordshire. The Society soon concluded that this was an illegal usurpation of the commoners' rights; and it found a wealthy and assertive local landowner, Augustus Smith, to champion its cause. A midnight special train with 120 navvies was sent from Euston on a March night, and when dawn broke all of Lord Brownlow's 2 miles of fencing had been demolished. This audacious stroke led to prolonged litigation, but it effectively saved the common. It also called forth unstinting praise in important sections of the press, including *Punch*. The episode gave encouragement not only to the Society itself, but also to isolated local groups opposing enclosure in other places. Indeed, one of the Society's most important contributions in the long run was to lend moral support to and provide legal advice for people whose protests would otherwise have been overwhelmed by those with local wealth and influence. The specialist expertise of Robert Hunter, its solicitor between 1868 and 1882, was especially important in the formative years.

In his unassuming way, Hunter was a key figure in many related concerns. He was involved, for example, in the Kyrle Society, founded in 1878 at the behest of Octavia Hill and her sister Miranda. Its aim was to encourage the 'beautification' of impoverished districts of London through the spread of flowers, gardens, wall decorations and mottoes, and the adaptation of small open spaces such as burial grounds to become 'open air sitting rooms for the poor'. In pursuing these goals, Octavia Hill was self-consciously acting as a disciple of Ruskin, who had been a direct formative influence on her ideas. She was also acting on the assumption that the lack of access to beauty and its appreciation was a worse deprivation than the more material aspects of poverty, which she was finding so much more difficult to cope with in her roles as manager of model housing and Charity Organisation Society activist. These efforts to bring natural beauty to the people, though not fruitless, drew less support and made less impact than the campaigns to preserve open spaces, natural beauty and historic monuments.

Octavia Hill, Robert Hunter and the Commons Preservation Society also contributed to campaigns against the disfiguring intrusion of railways, quarries, reservoirs and other large-scale invaders of rural solitude. Here the principal battleground was the Lake District rather than the Home Counties; and the territory had been marked out as early as 1844 by Wordsworth himself, in his pioneering opposition to the extension of the Kendal and Windermere Railway to the lake shore and onwards, perhaps, to Ambleside and even Keswick. Wordsworth feared that railways in the heart of Lakeland would not only damage the landscape, but also bring trippers on cheap tickets and their amusements to destroy the solitude, and villa-dwellers to further the suburbanisation of the lake shores, while corrupting the simple virtues of the local yeomanry. These objections were little heeded at the time, and the prevailing belief in progress through economic development was overwhelmingly triumphant. The railway stopped short of the lake shore, at its present terminus, but the reasons were to do with construction costs and traffic projections rather than aesthetic considerations.

By the mid 1870s, however, when railway plans resurfaced, there was wider support for Wordsworthian arguments. In 1876 Robert Somervell, a Kendal shoe manufacturer, led a pamphlet and newspaper war against a threat to extend the Windermere branch line; and Wordsworth's mantle descended upon Ruskin, who contributed a violent polemic against the proposal. Again, the railway company backed off; and again, the environmental arguments were not the decisive ones. But hereafter, no proposals for railway extension or large industrial-type development in Lakeland went unopposed. Manchester Corporation's proposals to take water from Thirlmere were fought tooth and nail in the late 1870s, on the grounds that they would spoil solitude and scenery; and Manchester's eventual triumph came in spite of opposition from Ruskin, the Bishop of Carlisle, and many other luminaries. And in 1883 a quarry syndicate's plan for a mineral railway from Braithwaite, near Keswick, to the Buttermere Fells (most of which are now owned by the National Trust) provoked an opposition which not only put the promoters to flight, but also led to the setting up of a permanent Lake District Defence Society. Its patrons included Tennyson, Browning, William Morris and the inevitable Ruskin, and its membership included forty professors and a cross-section of the British intellectual élite. But the central figure in organising the new society was Hardwicke Rawnsley, a clergyman who became vicar of Crosthwaite, near Keswick, in 1883.

Rawnsley had already come under the influence of Ruskin and Octavia Hill. As an Oxford undergraduate he had worked on a road-mending scheme set up by Ruskin when he was Professor of Fine Art, aiming to build bridges between privileged students and local labourers; and Ruskin remained his mentor, to the extent that he set up craft schools in Keswick on Ruskinian principles. He had also worked enthusiastically for one of Octavia Hill's London housing ventures, and met his first wife through her. For nearly forty years from 1883 he was the leading defender of Lakeland scenery against desecrations of all kinds, from dams and quarries to metalled roads, telephone cables, seaplanes on Windermere and the inevitable further railway plans. At times, too, his enthusiasm led him further afield, as when he campaigned unsuccessfully against the Snowdon Mountain Railway. Rawnsley was idiosyncratic and fiery-tempered, with a prodigious output of

Canon Hardwicke Rawnsley, fierce defender of the Lake District against commercial intrusions of all kinds, and one of the founders of the National Trust.

poetry of dubious quality; his contribution to the defence of Lakeland was sometimes disorganised but always energetic and heartfelt.

Some of these Lakeland campaigns had ambiguous implications. On the Thirlmere issue, it seemed to some that a few guardians of solitude and literary associations were putting their selfish concerns before the urgent need for an adequate water supply for the Manchester slums. Rawnsley himself was sensitive to such criticisms, and it is said that Robert Hunter withdrew his assistance when he found that some of Manchester's opponents were more interested in increased compensation for themselves as landowners than in protecting natural beauty. And the new railways would have made it easier for working-class visitors to share in the appreciation of the fastnesses of inner Lakeland. Ruskin, in 1876, had a short way with such objections: the kind of working people who would benefit from such places were the sort who would save enough from their beer money to get there anyway. For the rest, the railway would merely shovel 'stupid herds of modern tourists' from one place to another, and there was no virtue in seeing Helvellyn while drunk. It was generally accepted among the defenders of Lakeland that only a self-improving minority of the working class was really capable of responding to the Lakes. Such people could be welcomed, but most trippers were undesirable; and some campaigners, perhaps including Rawnsley himself, were less forward than they might have been in footpath preservation because they feared that hordes of trippers might destroy the beauty and atmosphere of the high fells without deriving benefits themselves.

But the Lake District defence campaigns made real and lasting gains. A sequence of parliamentary votes established the principle that damage to natural beauty and historic interest could be a legitimate ground for objecting to a scheme floated in pursuit of profit. 'Sentimental' notions based on aesthetic and moral criteria were given weight in decision-making alongside calculations of profit, loss and financial interest. These were important gains, achieved in the face of a strong presumption in general public opinion that technological advancement, 'progress' and profit were always to be favoured at the expense of less tangible considerations. But these developments were clearly not enough to protect vulnerable places against the pressure to develop, especially as there was no need to obtain parliamentary approval for the building of houses or quarries or the extension

of factories. And the introduction of planning controls of this kind was unthinkable to reformers of the stamp of Rawnsley or Octavia Hill. Even the Lake District, with its unique blend of scenic, literary and historical associations, could not be protected in this way, though there was no better candidate. As strict planning legislation, or land nationalisation, were completely out of the question, the only way forward was to form an organisation to take over or buy up threatened places, and to preserve them on behalf of the nation. This was the genesis of the National Trust.

The first ideas for something resembling the National Trust were being discussed between Robert Hunter and Octavia Hill in 1884; but it took ten years for the organisation to take shape. This was partly due to Shaw-Lefevre's fear that the new body would outflank the Commons Preservation Society; but as the threats of development in sensitive places became ever more pressing, it became clear that something with wider powers was necessary. At the founding meeting in 1894, Octavia Hill's resolution declared that the Trust was to be 'a corporate body, capable of holding land, and representative of national institutions and interests', 'to provide means by which landowners and others may be enabled to dedicate to the nation places of historic interest or natural beauty'. The relevant legal steps were taken early in 1895.

Over the next twenty years, the Trust steadily accumulated property. Most important were places like Barras Head near Tintagel, and Gowbarrow Park on Ullswater, which were saved from hotel and villa development. Gowbarrow Park was one of several places to be bought by public subscription. Many working-class donors contributed, as they did to the Brandlehow estate near the Ruskin memorial which the Trust erected on Friar's Crag above Derwentwater soon after his death in 1900. It was entirely fitting that Ruskin should be commemorated in this way. His practical contributions had been very limited, but his inspiration had been crucially important. The three prime movers in the foundation of the Trust were Octavia Hill, Robert Hunter and Hardwicke Rawnsley; and all had come directly and formatively under Ruskin's spell. Ruskin's influence and ideas, in turn, would be incomprehensible outside the context of the development of ideas about landscape and literature over a much longer period.

In spite of his own deepening pessimism, the rise of the National Trust was an astonishingly accurate expression of Ruskin's hopes for social improvement. He expected the initiative to come from above, as enlightened members of the ruling class shouldered their responsibilities and tried to raise the educational and cultural standards of the rest of society. The National Trust was cast in this mould. Its first president was the Duke of Westminster, one of Queen Victoria's wealthiest subjects, and an eminent Liberal politician. He was well calculated to guarantee the respectability of the Trust; and the extensive supporting cast of aristocrats, academics, eminent professional and artistic figures and representatives of established historical, scientific and amenity protection societies gave additional ballast. This was reform imposed from above, by well-educated philanthropists: there was no taint of the democracy which Ruskin had feared so much. Indeed, it is difficult to see how there could have been. The National Trust had, of necessity, to be led by the most respectable of reformers, working within the letter of the law and the spirit of prevailing orthodoxies about the relationship between the State and private property. It had to be able to work with the grain of propertied opinion, and it could not afford to take a strong line on issues like new rights of access to private land. Like so many other innovative organisations in modern British history, the National Trust moved forward slowly and cautiously, taking care not to antagonise the established order of which its leaders were part.

From this perspective, the rise and nature of the National Trust tells us a great deal, by analogy, about the stability of British society during the long period of potentially traumatic change which began in earnest in the mid eighteenth century. The revolutionary possibilities of these years of upheaval were neutralised by the ability of those in authority to make concessions and to adapt to new circumstances. Thus the aristocracy remained open to new blood, and conceded just enough of its power and privileges to enable its rule to continue

without serious challenge to its key institutions, at least until the end of the nineteenth century. The worst abuses were checked by legislation before they became politically dangerous, and what potentially divisive laws there were tended to be operated with less than their full rigour in practice. The wealthy lived comfortable and often luxurious lives, but enough of them gave enough time and money to charity and spectacle, and enough visible attention to reform and improvement, to seem to justify their position in society. Only in the early decades of the nineteenth century, when this sense of social responsibility was in abeyance, was there sustained social unrest and a real, though intermittent and localised, threat to property and established institutions.

In its own way, the National Trust fits into a well-established aristocratic and professional tradition of *noblesse oblige*, which also rubbed off on a lot of manufacturers. Its founders and activists sought to protect the places they loved; but they also sought to protect them for the benefit of others less fortunate than themselves. And they did so without challenging the existing framework of law, politics and property ownership. It is all very well to suggest, as an American historian has recently done, that Britain's economic decline can be blamed on too strong an attachment to rural preservationist values and on too obsessive an interest in the past, which diverts entrepreneurs away from profits and into an enervating rural idyll. It could equally be argued that without such values, and the sense of duty and obligation that went with them, Britain's nineteenth-century history would have been so conflict-ridden that economic growth would have been swallowed up in class war. Ultimately, the rise of the National Trust is as good a symbol as any of the continuities and values which helped to pull British society together, for better or worse, during a period of unparalleled transformation and strain.

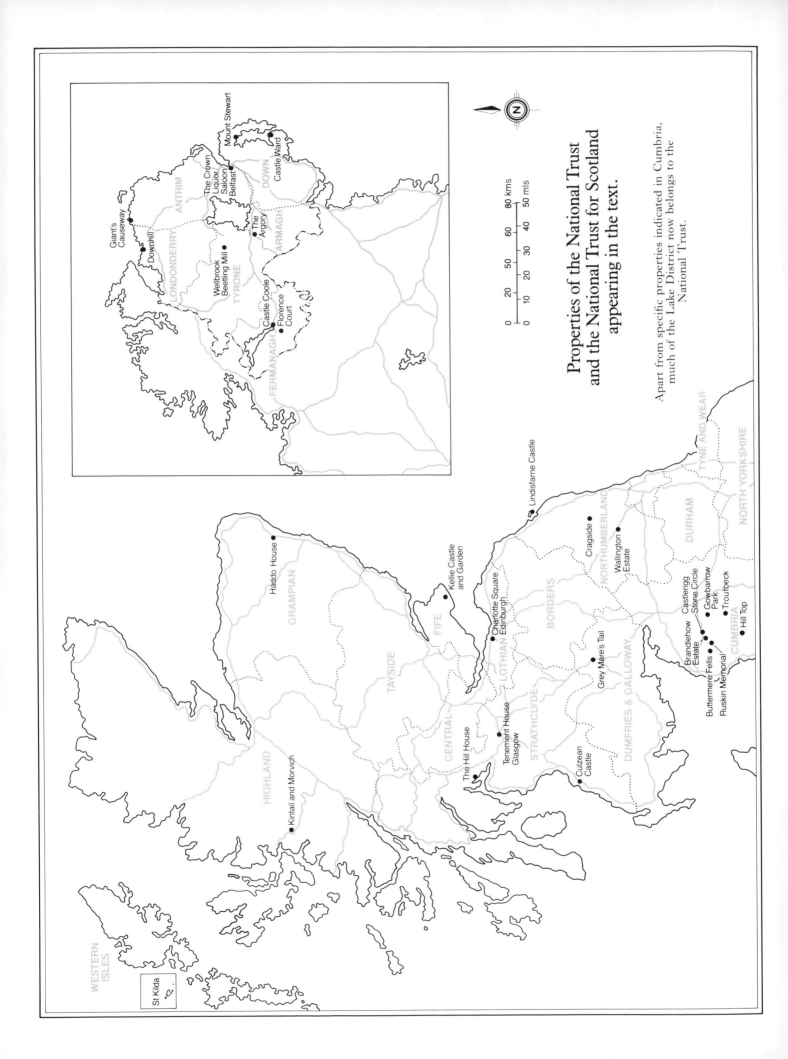

Properties of the National Trust
and the National Trust for Scotland
appearing in the text.

Apart from specific properties indicated in Cumbria,
much of the Lake District now belongs to the
National Trust.

Mount Stewart
Castle Ward
DOWN
The Crown
Liquor
Saloon
Belfast
ANTRIM
The
Argory
ARMAGH
Giants
Causeway
Downhill
LONDONDERRY
Wellbrook
Beetling Mill
TYRONE
Castle Coole
Florence
Court
FERMANAGH

80 kms
50 mls
70
40
60
50
30
40
20
30
10 20
0 10
0

Haddo House
GRAMPIAN

WESTERN
ISLES

St Kilda

HIGHLAND

Kintail and Morvich

TAYSIDE

CENTRAL

The Hill House

Tenement House
Glasgow

STRATHCLYDE

Culzean
Castle

DUMFRIES & GALLOWAY

Kellie Castle
and Garden
FIFE

Charlotte Square
Edinburgh
LOTHIAN

BORDERS

Grey Mare's Tail

Lindisfarne Castle

Cragside
NORTHUMBERLAND
Wallington
Estate

DURHAM

TYNE AND WEAR

NORTH YORKSHIRE

Castlerigg
Stone Circle
Gowbarrow
Park
Troutbeck
Brandlehow
Estate
Hill Top
CUMBRIA
Buttermere Fells
Ruskin Memorial

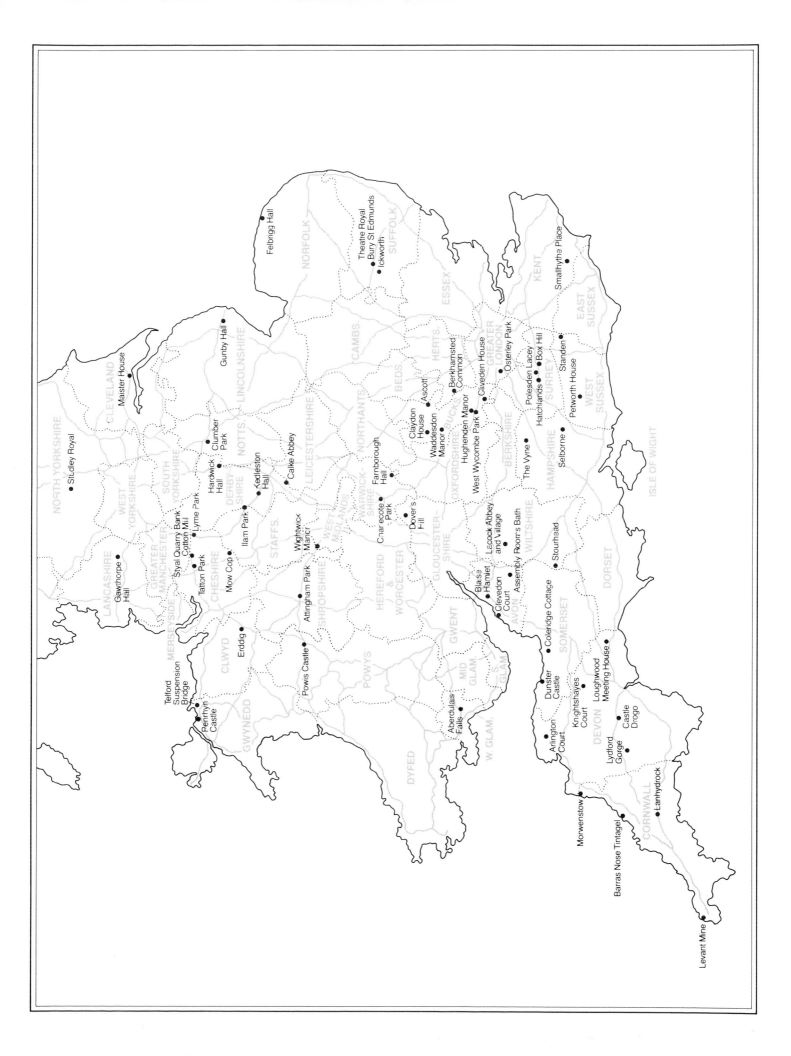

Further Reading

1 Britain 1750–1914

The best general introduction to British social history in this period is E. Royle, *Modern Britain: a Social History 1760–1985* (Edward Arnold, 1987). F. M. L. Thompson, *The Rise of Respectable Society 1830–1900* (Fontana, 1988) combines scholarship with wit and readability. For Britain in wider context, E. J. Hobsbawm, *Industry and Empire* and *The Age of Capital* (various edns.). For Wales, Gwyn A. Williams, *When Was Wales?* (Penguin, 1985). For Scotland, T. C. Smout, *A History of the Scottish People 1560–1830*, and *A Century of the Scottish People 1830–1950* (both Fontana). *People and Society in Scotland 1760–1830*, ed. T. Devine and R. Mitchison (John Donald, Edinburgh), is the first of a three-volume series. For Northern Ireland, the excellent L. Kennedy and P. Ollerenshaw (eds.), *An economic and social history of Ulster 1820–1940* (Manchester Univ. Press, 1985).

2 Prestige and Property

J. V. Beckett, *The Aristocracy in Britain 1660–1914* (Oxford, 1986), is lucid and massively thorough. G. Mingay, *The Gentry* (Longman, 1976) is less daunting; and his *English Landed Society in the Eighteenth Century* (Routledge, 1963), together with the companion volume on the nineteenth century by F. M. L. Thompson, should be read. W. D. Rubinstein, *Men of Property* (Croom Helm, 1981), gives interesting new ideas about the very rich. D. Cannadine, *Lords and Landlords* (Leicester, 1980), and *Patricians, Power and Politics* (Leicester, 1982), looks at landlords as industrialists and town builders. Two controversial books to finish with: H. J. Perkin, *The Origins of Modern English Society* (Routledge, various edns.), and M. J. Wiener, *English Culture and the Decline of the Industrial Spirit* (Cambridge, 1981).

3 Country Houses and Country Living

The essential starting point is Mark Girouard's brilliant, and beautifully illustrated, *The Victorian Country House* (Yale Univ. Press, 1979). His *Life in the English Country House* (Yale Univ. Press, 1978), is also full of fascinating ideas and evidence. Clive Aslet, *The Last Country Houses* (Yale Univ. Press, 1982), has similar virtues. Lawrence and Jeanne C. F. Stone, *An Open Elite?* (Oxford, 1984), is characteristically combative and stimulating. Jill Franklin, *The Gentleman's Country House and its Plan 1835–1914* (Routledge, 1981), is lively and informative. P. Horn, *The Rise and Fall of the Victorian Domestic Servant* (1975 and 1986) ranges widely. M. Waterson, *The Servants' Hall* (Routledge, 1980), is entertaining to good effect about Erddig, and H. Colvin, *Calke Abbey* (George Philip, 1985), is full of revealing anecdotes. Charles E. Hardy, *John Bowes and the Bowes Museum* (three edns., 1970–82), is a readable biography of a remarkable man.

4 The Farm and the Village

G. Mingay (ed.), *The Victorian Countryside* (2 vols., Routledge, 1981), has short chapters on an immense range of topics. His *Rural Life in Victorian England* (Futura, 1979) is a short, lively introduction. K. D. M. Snell, *Annals of the Labouring Poor* (Cambridge, 1985) is a superb reinterpretation of the fate of the rural labourer. It counterbalances J. D. Chambers and G. Mingay, *The Agricultural Revolution 1750–1880* (various edns.), which concentrates more on technical improvements in farming. For other aspects of rural labouring life, E. J. Hobsbawm and G. Rudé, *Captain Swing* (Penguin, 1973: the 1830 riots); J. Obelkevich, *Religion and Rural Society* (Oxford, 1975); A. Howkins, *Poor Labouring Men* (Routledge, 1985); P. Munsche, *Gentlemen and Poachers*

(Cambridge, 1981). For Scotland see especially J. Hunter, *The Making of the Crofting Community* (John Donald, 1976), and Ian Carter, *Farm Life in North-East Scotland 1840–1914* (John Donald, 1979), both excellent pieces of compelling social history. For Magilligan see the chapter by G. Kirkham in P. Roebuck (ed.), *Plantation to Partition* (Belfast, 1981).

5 Factories and Industries

For a recent reinterpretation of the Industrial Revolution, N. F. R. Crafts, *British Economic Growth during the Industrial Revolution* (Oxford, 1985); and also R. Floud and D. McCloskey (eds.), *The Economic History of Britain since 1700* (2 vols., Cambridge, 1981). For the visual impact, B. Trinder, *The Making of the Industrial Landscape* (Dent, 1982). Studies of key areas discussed in this chapter include B. Trinder, *The Industrial Revolution in Shropshire* (Chichester, 1973); J. K. Walton, *Lancashire: a Social History 1558–1939* (Manchester Univ. Press, 1987); and John Rowe, *Cornwall in the Age of the Industrial Revolution* (Liverpool Univ. Press, 1953). For factories and their impact in general, P. Joyce, *Work, Society and Politics* (Harvester, 1980); and in particular, Mary B. Rose, *The Gregs of Quarry Bank Mill* (Cambridge, 1986). See also S. Walby, *Patriarchy at Work* (Polity Press, Oxford, 1986). For London's East End, G. Stedman Jones, *Outcast London* (various edns.), and E. P. Thompson and E. Yeo (eds.), *The Unknown Mayhew* (various edns.). A pungent flavour of what it was like to live through the early industrial years comes from Samuel Bamford's autobiographies, *Early Days* and *Passages in the Life of a Radical* (several modern edns.).

6 Transport, Travel and Trade

Two recent books edited by D. Aldcroft and M. Freeman, *Transport in the Industrial Revolution* (Manchester Univ. Press, 1983), and *Transport in the Railway Age* (Manchester Univ. Press, 1988), present new research with clarity and economy. J. Simmons, *The Railway in Town and Country* (David and Charles, 1986) combines a lifetime's scholarship with compulsive readability. H. J. Perkin, *The Age of the Railway* (Granada, 1971) is a brief, accessible introduction to the main themes. James McGurn, *On Your Bicycle* (John Murray, 1987) combines instruction with enjoyment very successfully. A. R. B. Haldane, *New Roads through the Glens*, (David and Charles, 1962) is vividly informative about the Scottish Highlands. But

perhaps the most readily available general book on transport history is P. S. Bagwell, *The Transport Revolution from 1770* (Batsford, new edn. 1988).

7 Towns and Cities

Excellent introductions to this topic are P. Corfield, *The Impact of English Towns 1700–1800* (Oxford, 1982) and P. J. Waller, *Town, City and Nation: England, 1850–1914* (Oxford, 1983). R. Dennis, *English Industrial Cities of the Nineteenth Century* (Cambridge, pbk. ed. 1986) is sharp and lively, and has an excellent bibliography. James Walvin, *English Urban Life 1776–1851* (Hutchinson, 1984), is less penetrating but a good read. For resorts, J. K. Walton, *The English Seaside Resort* (Leicester Univ. Press, 1983), and R. S. Neale, *Bath 1680–1850* (Routledge, 1981). For urban housing, M. J. Daunton, *House and Home in the Victorian City* (Edward Arnold, 1983), and S. Muthesius, *The English Terraced House* (Yale Univ. Press, 1982). For suburbia, L. Davidoff and C. Hall, *Family Fortunes* (Hutchinson, 1987); H. J. Dyos, *Victorian Suburb* (various edns.; a classic study of Camberwell); and K. Chorley, *Manchester Made Them* (Faber, 1950: deserves a new edn.). On individual towns examined in the text: D. Fraser (ed.), *A History of Modern Leeds* (Manchester Univ. Press, 1980); J. Foster, *Class Struggle and the Industrial Revolution* (Weidenfeld, 1974: Oldham); Gwyn A. Williams, *The Merthyr Rising* (Croom Helm, 1978); G. Malmgreen, *Silk Town: Macclesfield 1750–1835* (Hull Univ. Press, 1985); A. Youngson, *The Making of Classical Edinburgh* (Edinburgh Univ. Press, 1966); and A. Gibb, *Glasgow: the Making of a City* (Croom Helm, 1983).

8 The Urban Working Class

The essential starting point is still E. P. Thompson's magnificent *The Making of the English Working Class* (several edns. since 1963). For Scotland, James D. Young, *The Rousing of the Scottish Working Class* (Croom Helm, 1980). A more conventional text is E. H. Hunt, *British Labour History 1815–1914* (Weidenfeld, 1981). J. Benson, *The Penny Capitalists* (Gill and Macmillan, 1983), and (ed.) *The Working Class in England 1875–1914* (Croom Helm, 1985), give interesting perspectives. So does J. H. Treble, *Urban Poverty in Britain 1830–1914* (1979). K. Burgess, *The Origins of British Industrial Relations* (Croom Helm, 1975) is a thorough introduction to trade unions. Paul Johnson, *Saving and Spending* (Oxford, 1985) is full of new interpretations. David

Vincent, *Bread, Knowledge and Freedom* (Europa, 1981) uses working-class autobiographies very effectively. Among the readily available contemporary writings used in the chapter are Lady Bell, *At The Works* (1907; reprinted Virago, 1985); Robert Tressell, *The Ragged-Trousered Philanthropists* (classic Socialist novel, many editions); Maud Pember Reeves, *Round About a Pound a Week* (1913; reprinted Virago, 1979); Thomas Wright, *Some Habits and Customs of the Working Classes* (1867; reprinted Cass, 1967); Allen Clarke, *The Effects of the Factory System* (1899; reprinted George Kelsall, Littleborough, 1985). Oral history now provides new windows: see especially Paul Thompson, *The Voice of the Past* (Oxford, 1978), and Elizabeth Roberts, *A Woman's Place* (Blackwell, 1984).

9 Church, Chapel and People

Hugh McLeod, *Religion and the Working Class in Nineteenth-Century Britain* (Macmillan, 1984), is an excellent starting point. For Scotland specifically, Callum Brown, *The Social History of Religion in Scotland since 1730* (Methuen, 1987). For the Church of England, B. I. Coleman, *The Church of England in the mid-nineteenth century* (Historical Association, 1980), and Owen Chadwick, *The Victorian Church* (Black, 2 vols., 1966 and 1970). For the Methodists, David Hempton, *Methodism and Politics in British Society 1750–1850* (Hutchinson, 1984). For a cross-section through English Nonconformity, C. Binfield, *So Down to Prayers* (Dent, 1977). For Roman Catholicism, J. Bossy, *The English Catholic Community 1570–1850* (Darton, Longman and Todd, 1975). For popular religious beliefs, J. Obelkevich, *Religion and Rural Society* (Oxford, 1975), and especially Ruth Richardson, *Death, Dissection and the Destitute* (1987). Tom Steel, *The Death and Life of St Kilda* (Fontana, 1975), covers a very special case. On popular schooling, two books by J. S. Hurt, *Education in Evolution* (Paladin, 1972), and *Elementary Schooling and the Working Classes* (Routledge, 1979), cover the period well; and see T. Laqueur, *Religion and Respectability* (Yale Univ. Press, 1976), for Sunday schools. Finally, a word of enthusiasm for the delightful diary of Revd. Francis Kilvert, edited by William Plomer and available in several editions.

10 Leisure and Enjoyment

The best general interpretations of this theme are Hugh Cunningham, *Leisure in the Industrial Revolution* (Croom Helm, 1980); Peter Bailey, *Leisure and Class in Victorian England* (Routledge, 1978; new pbk. edn., 1987); and Cunningham's chapter in J. Benson (ed.), *The Working Class in England 1875–1914* (Croom Helm, 1985). J. Clarke and C. Critcher, *The Devil Makes Work* (Hutchinson, 1987) offer some readable sociology. Interesting general material can be found in R. Malcolmson, *Popular Recreations in English Society 1700–1850* (Cambridge, 1973); Bob Bushaway, *By Rite* (Junction Books, 1982); R. Storch (ed.), *Popular Culture and Custom in Nineteenth-Century England* (Croom Helm, 1982); and J. K. Walton and J. Walvin (eds.), *Leisure in Britain 1780–1939* (Manchester Univ. Press, pbk. edn., 1986). On specific topics, see Tony Mason, *Association Football and English Society 1863–1915* (Harvester, 1980); Dave Russell, *Popular Music in England 1840–1914* (Manchester Univ. Press, 1987); D. Itzkowitz, *Peculiar Privilege: a Social History of English Foxhunting* (Harvester, 1977); W. Vamplew, *The Turf* (Penguin, 1976); P. Bailey (ed.), *Music Hall: the Business of Pleasure* (Milton Keynes, 1986); J. S. Bratton, *Music Hall: Performance and Style* (Milton Keynes, 1986).

11 Countryside and People

Keith Thomas, *Man and the Natural World* (Penguin, 1984), provides fascinating and essential introductory reading. F. Klingender, *Art and the Industrial Revolution* (Paladin pbk. edn., 1972) remains a very accessible way in to important themes. John Ruskin, *Unto This Last*, is available in many editions, and easily found in second-hand bookshops. P. D. Anthony, *Mr Ruskin's Labour* (Cambridge, 1983) is a recent interpretation. For William Morris, E. P. Thompson, *William Morris* (Pantheon pbk. edn., 1976), is still indispensable. Lord Eversley, *Commons, Forests and Footpaths* (Cassell, rev. edn. 1910), is still very useful. For general ideas about countryside, Raymond Williams, *The Country and the City* (a classic: many editions), and R. Colls and P. Dodd (eds.), *Englishness: Politics and Culture 1880–1920* (Croom Helm, 1986), which contains some chapters which deserve to become classics. For Lake District background and the origins of the National Trust, J. D. Marshall and J. K. Walton, *The Lake Counties from 1830 to the Mid-Twentieth Century* (Manchester Univ. Press, 1981); Graham Murphy, *Founders of the National Trust* (Helm, 1987); G. Berry and G. Beard, *The Lake District: a Century of Conservation* (Bartholomew, Edinburgh, 1980). The works of Gilbert White are readily available in various editions, and M. W. Thompson has edited *The Journeys of Sir Richard Colt Hoare* (Alan Sutton, 1983).

It remains to apologise to the many authors whose work has had to be omitted due to shortage of space, and to urge the interested reader to follow up her or his chosen themes through the bibliographies and footnotes of the books cited here. There is plenty of scope for further work on all the themes of this book, and I hope that some of my readers will be encouraged to have a go themselves!

Index